Journey Through the Bible: Lesson Plans to Teach and Study the Bible

Chapter by Chapter

New Testament

Thomas E. Young, Sr., D. Min.

Acknowledgments

I would like to thank my granddaughter, Audrey LeeAnn Young Johnson, for taking on the complex task of organizing, coordinating, and researching the best approach for getting these 135 plus bonus Bible lessons on the New Testament into the hands of God's children.

Also, I want to acknowledge the great value of the following resources that were available to me during over 21 years of teaching:

- Liberty University's Dr. Harold Willmington's outstanding two-year Bible Course.

- The "Word of Life Study Bible" ©1993 by Thomas Nelson, Inc. Used by permission.

- Prophecy Study Bible, NKJV, John C. Hagee, General Editor, Thomas Nelson Publishers, Nashville ©1997.

- Scripture taken from the New King James, ©1979, 1980, 1982, by Thomas Nelson, Inc. Used by permission. All rights reserved.

- Perry Stones teachings and studies on the Rapture and on the Book of Revelation and on his many trips to the Holy Land.

- And to all who have not been mentioned but have contributed to my understanding of the Scriptures, our Good Lord will acknowledge you and bless you when we all get home.

In addition, Mary Alice Padgett, and all the ladies who served as substitutes, who provided the Friday Bible Study refreshments over a 21-year period which made our studies a family setting.

Thank you all.

Table of Contents

PREFACE

I believe it was in September 1997 when I went to a local Bible Study in my community. The Bible teaching minister did not show up because of low class attendance. This particular Friday, only I and a young lady (Mary Alice Padgett) were present. No teacher or leader.

I said to her, "What do we do?"

She said, "Let's read the Bible."

And that is what we did. I prepared future lessons and Mary Alice supplied the refreshments for the Bible Study for the next twenty plus years. During the twenty plus years, if Mary Alice or I were not present due to an illness or travel, volunteer Bible class members filled the gap providing lessons and goodies.

The Bible Study grew, and attendees gravitated to an environment that allowed all of us to read and interpret the Scriptures weekly. After two decades (21 years and being 88 years old), I stopped teaching the class, but it was recognized that what was created was a valuable tool that should be shared. The Bible Study continues today and is now taught by a younger Man of God with approximately 30 attendees each week. Thank God.

INTRODUCTION

I desire to see the Word of God accessible to all and inexpensive for all. Why should those who desire to study the Bible have to pay $12.00 to $20.00 for a book to study the scripture of each book of the Bible? Why not just read the scripture itself and discuss it? Hence the creation of *Journey Through the Bible: Lesson Plans to Teach and Study the Bible Chapter by Chapter.*

This resource provides a framework for pastors, ministers, or individuals desiring to facilitate a Bible class or small group. Each book of the New Testament is organized with a formatted Lesson Plan allowing the facilitator and student to read the scripture directly and be inspired by the Word of God.

Each Book of the Bible begins with an overview of the main components organized by chapter. After the general overview, each chapter is organized into individual lessons with a Lesson Plan providing the format to study that particular section. I recommend that the facilitator provide a copy of each Lesson Plan to the students so that everyone can actively participate, take notes, and have the lesson available after the class.

How to Use this Resource to Facilitate Bible Study Groups/Classes:

1. Open in Prayer (thanksgiving for our health, family, our Country, our leaders, for those that we know may be sick or in need of prayer, and for a deeper understanding of God's Word).

2. Welcome each student by asking them to introduce themselves (just sharing their names).

3. Read through the lesson's Lesson Plan aloud so that everyone is aware of how, where, and what will be discussed.

4. After walking through the Lesson Plan, read each of the scriptures noted (encourage participants to volunteer to read a scripture aloud to the group). After each scripture, ask for comments and or questions.

5. Close in prayer.

Each class should last about an hour. Ideally, 1–1.5 hours is great for morning or evening Bible studies in homes or churches. If possible, allow time for fellowship.

The Lesson Plans end with the same two scriptures for specific reasons.

II Chronicles 7:14:

About 2900+ years ago (2952 years), God appeared to Solomon just after he had completed the Temple and offered him the promise of Conditional Covenant for His people. God knew there would be wars, pestilence, famines, persecutions, and lack of rain (see 2 Chronicles 7:13) and therefore was giving us (you and me and His chosen people) an opportunity to have our land healed. He had covenants with Abraham, Noah, David, etc., and here He was offering us a conditional promise or covenant.

There are approximately 37,000 Catholic Priests, about 109,000 pastors/clergy, and countless Bible teachers who should be leading the sheep/flock in taking advantage of God's conditional promise to heal our land. We are suffering because we are not taking advantage of God's promise in II Chronicles 7:14.

Psalm 122:6:

This psalm is not a suggestion. It is a command from God. Thus, we should heed His command. His Son will reign from Jerusalem for a thousand years during the millennium so we should be praying for its tranquility.

The Book of Matthew

Scripture Focus Chapters 1 - 28

Objective: To gain an understanding that Matthew presents Jesus as Israel's promised messianic king and that Jesus also fulfills the qualifications for their Messiah.

Objective Breakdown:

1. Genealogy of Christ	Chapter 1:1-17
2. Birth of Christ	Chapter 1:18-25
3. Visit of the Wise Men	Chapter 2:1-12
4. Flight into Egypt	Chapter 2:13-15
5. Herod Kills the Children	Chapter 2:16-23
6. The Person of John the Baptist	Chapter 3:1-6
7. The Preaching of John the Baptist	Chapter 3:7-12
8. Baptism of Jesus	Chapter 3:13-17
9. First Temptation of Jesus	Chapter 4:1-4
10. The Second Temptation of Jesus	Chapter 4:5-7
11. The Third Temptation of Jesus	Chapter 4:8-11
12. Jesus Begins His Ministry	Chapter 4:12-17
13. Jesus Calls His First Disciples	Chapter 4:18-22
14. Jesus Ministers in Galilee	Chapter 4:4:23-25
15. The Beatitudes	Chapter 5:1-12
16. The Similitudes	Chapter 5:13-16
17. Jesus Fulfills the Law	Chapter 5:17-19
18. Murder	Chapter 5:20-26

Lesson Plan 1

The Book of Matthew

Chapters 1 & 2

Objective: To acquaint us with the first Book of the New Testament and how Matthew records Jesus's teachings which Jesus gave to His followers and eventually to the world.

Objective Breakdown:

1. Introduction

2. Background of Christ   Matthew 1:1-17

3. The Birth of Christ   Matthew 1:18-25

4. Wise Men Visit   Matthew 2:1-12

5. The Family Flees to Egypt   Matthew 2:13-15

6. Herod Slaughters Infants   Matthew 2:16-18

7. The Family Returns to Nazareth   Matthew 2:19-23

Introduction: After a prophetic silence of about four hundred years, Matthew's Gospel is a bridge between the Old Testament and the New Testament. It was written by a Jew to Jews about a Jew. Thus, Matthew is the writer, his countrymen are the readers, and Jesus Christ is the subject.

Matthew's design is to present Jesus as the King of the Jews, the long-awaited Messiah. Through a carefully selected series of Old Testament quotations, Matthew documents Jesus Christ's claim to be the Messiah. His genealogy, baptism, messages, miracles all point to the same inescapable conclusion: Christ is King. Even in Jesus Christ's death, seeming defeat is turned to victory by the Resurrection, and the message again echoes forth: The King of the Jews lives.

To show that Jesus fulfills the qualification for the Messiah, Matthew used more Old Testament quotations and allusions than any other book (almost 130). Often used in this Gospel is the revealing phrase "that (which) was spoken through the prophet might be fulfilled," it appears nine times in Matthew and not once in the other Gospels.

Of some interest is the phrase "The Kingdom of Heaven" which appears thirty-two times in Matthew but nowhere else in the New Testament. The likely timeframe of Matthew authoring this Book is A.D. 58–68 and it may have been written in Palestine or Syrian Antioch. It covers the period of 4 B.C. to 33 A.D.

Words to Live By:

Ephesians 4:29: Let not any filthy word go out of your mouth, but what is good for necessary edification, that it may impart grace to the hearers.

Ephesians 4:30: And do not grieve the Holy Spirit of God, by whom you are sealed until *the* day of redemption.

Ephesians 4:31: Let all bitterness and wrath and anger and tumult and evil speaking be put away from you, with all malice.

Ephesians 4:32: And be kind to one another, tenderhearted, forgiving one another, even as God for Christ's sake has forgiven you.

Matthew 12:25: And Jesus knew their thoughts and said to them, Every kingdom divided against itself is brought to desolation. And every city or house divided against itself shall not stand.

Mark 3:24: And if a kingdom is divided against itself, that kingdom cannot stand.

Romans 13:1: Let every soul be subject unto the higher powers. For there is no power but of God: the powers that be are ordained of God.

Author's Commentary: God is the ultimate authority. The government as an institution has been established by God. God raises up and does away with leaders.

Romans 13:2: Whosoever therefore resisteth the power, resisteth the ordinance of God: and they that resist shall receive to themselves damnation.

Author's Commentary: Government as an institution has been established by God to serve His purposes. Both followers and leaders are ultimately accountable to God. Submission to human authority as it aligns with God's Word reflects our submission to God's authority. We must serve the highest of all authorities, God Himself.

II Chronicles 7:14

If my people who are called by my name will humble themselves and pray, and seek my face, and turn from their wicked ways, then I will hear from heaven and will forgive their sin and heal their land.

Psalm 122:6

Pray for the peace of Jerusalem; they shall prosper who love thee.

Note: If we do not speak out in support of Christian matters, we will forfeit our authority given to us by God! We as the "Church" and "Ambassadors" should not hide. We should "Shine" because there can be beautiful miracles in our mouth. Amen!

If we are not part of the solution, then we are part of the problem.

Homework: Read Psalm 119 and 2 Peter Chapters 1 & 2.

Time is of the essence to be Born Again!

Lesson Plan 2

The Book of Matthew

Chapters 3, 4, & 5

Objective: To acquaint us with the first Book of the New Testament and how Matthew records Jesus's teachings which Jesus gave to His followers and eventually to the world.

Objective Breakdown:

1. Introduction

2. The Ministry of John the Baptist   Chapter 3:1-12

3. John Baptizes Jesus   Chapter 3:13-17

4. The Temptation of Jesus   Chapter 4:1-11

5. Jesus Begins His Ministry   Chapter 4:12-17

6. Jesus Calls Disciples   Chapter 4:18-22

7. Galilean Ministry   Chapter 4:23-25

8. The Sermon on the Mount   Chapter 5:1-2

9. The Beatitudes   Chapter 5:3-12

10. You are Salt and Light   Chapter 5:13-16

11. The Morality of Christ   Chapter 5:17-48

Introduction: "Repent for the kingdom of heaven is at hand," Jesus warned as He began His public ministry in Galilee (Matthew 4:17). His message quickly spread, and huge crowds came to hear Him from Galilee, from nearby Syria, and Decapolis, and from as far away as Jerusalem, Judea, and east of the Jordan River (Matthew 4:24-15).

Jesus initiated His public life with a simple but stiff challenge to repentance (Matthew 4:17). It was a familiar message–identical, in fact to the message of John the Baptist, Jesus's forerunner (Matthew 3:2). Both urged their listeners to repent, to change their minds and hearts, not merely for the sake of change, but in light of what they called "the kingdom."

What is the Kingdom? Is there any simple way to understand this puzzling doctrine of the kingdom? Probably not. Jesus's followers have not ceased to puzzle over His statement about it since the moment they were made. But most would generally agree that Christ's kingdom began in some way with His first coming. It continues to advance as His people live the Gospel message throughout the world. However, it will not realize its ultimate completion until He returns.

Where is the Kingdom? For a few brief decades, Israel had enjoyed a relatively prosperous, peaceful monarchy under David and His Son Solomon. Some Old Testament passages prophesied that the Messiah would reestablish that sort of kingdom. Was now the time? Would Jesus overthrow the iron rule of the Romans and set up a political state?

He did not. In fact, He told the Roman governor Pilate that His kingdom was not of this world, that He did not have an army fighting on His behalf (John 18:36). And He told the Pharisees that the kingdom was not something tangible and observable but was "within" them (Luke 17:20–21). Then is Christ's kingdom simply a spiritual concept, a powerful but abstract ideal? No, because He made a definite promise to His disciples that they would rule the tribes of Israel in His kingdom (Matthew 19:23, 28). They apparently took Him literally (Acts 1:6).

When is the Kingdom? No less puzzling is the question of when the kingdom has or will come. As they began their ministries, John the Baptist and Jesus declared that the kingdom was "at hand." But a few years later, when Jesus's followers asked whether He was ready to restore Israel's Kingdom, He put them off; that was something that only His Father could know, He told them (Acts 1:6–7). Sometimes the kingdom seemed to be a present reality (Matthew 12:28; 13:18-23; 21:43). At other times, it seemed to be a hope for the future (Matthew 16:28; 20:20 –23; 26:29).

II Chronicles 7:14

If my people who are called by my name will humble themselves and pray, and seek my face, and turn from their wicked ways, then I will hear from heaven and will forgive their sin and heal their land.

Psalm 122:6

Pray for the peace of Jerusalem; they shall prosper who love thee.

Lesson Plan 3

The Book of Matthew

Chapters 6 & 7

Objective: To acquaint us with the first Book of the New Testament and how Matthew records Jesus's teachings which Jesus gave to His followers and eventually to the world.

Objective Breakdown:

1. Introduction

2. Spiritual Disciplines   Chapter 6:1-18

3. Treasures on Earth   Chapter 6:19-34

4. Judge Not   Chapter 7:1-6

5. Asking and Receiving   Chapter 7:7-12

6. A Challenge to Obedience   Chapter 7:13-29

Synopsis: Chapter 6

Against Hypocrisy in Alms Giving (Verses 1-4)

Against Hypocrisy in Prayer (Verses 5-8)

How to Pray (Verses 9-15)

Respecting Fasting (Verses 16-18)

Evil of Being Worldly-minded (Verses 19-24)

Trust in God Commended (Verses 25-34)

Verses 1-4: Our Lord next warned against hypocrisy and outward show in religious duties. What we do, must be done from an inward principle, that we may be approved of God, not that we may be praised of men. When we take least notice of our good deeds ourselves, God takes most notice of them.

Verses 5-8: The Scribes and Pharisees were guilty of two great faults in prayer, vain-glory and vain repetitions. If He does not give his people what they ask, it is because He knows they do not need it, and that it is not for their good.

Verses 9-15: Christ saw it needful to show His disciples what must commonly be the matter and method of their prayer. The petitions are six; the first three relate more expressly to God and His honor, the last three to our own concerns, both temporal and spiritual. This prayer teaches us to seek first the kingdom of God and His righteousness, and that all other things shall be added. Here is a promise, if you forgive, your heavenly Father will also forgive. We must forgive, as we hope to be forgiven. Those who desire to find mercy with God, must show mercy to their brethren. Christ came into the world as the great Peacemaker, not only to reconcile us to God, but one to another.

Verses 16-18: Religious fasting is a duty required of the disciples of Christ, but it is not so much a duty itself, as a means to dispose us for other duties. Fasting is the humbling of the soul, Psalm 35:13; that is the inside of the duty; let that, therefore, be thy principal care, and as to the outside of it, covet not to let it be seen. God sees in secret and will reward openly.

Verses 19-24: God requires the whole heart and will not share it with the world. When two masters oppose each other, no man can serve both. He who holds to the world and loves it, must despise God; he who loves God, must give up the friendship of the world.

Verses 25-34: Take no thought for your life. Not about the length of it; but refer it to God to lengthen or shorten it as he pleases; our times are in his hand, and they are in a good hand. Leave it to God to make it bitter or sweet as He pleases. Food and raiment God has promised, therefore we may expect them. Take no thought for the morrow, for the time to come. Be not anxious for the future, how you shall live next year, or when you are old, or what you shall leave behind you. As we must not boast of tomorrow, so we must not care for tomorrow or the events of it. If we take care about our souls and for eternity, which is more than the body and its life, we may leave it to God to provide for us food and raiment, which are less.

Synopsis: Chapter 7

Christ Reproves Rash Judgment (Verses 1-6)

Encouragements to Prayer (Verses 7-12)

Broad and Narrow Way (Verses 13-14)

Against False Prophets (Verses 15-20)

To Be Doers of the Word, Not Hearers Only (Verses 21-29)

Verses 1-6: We must judge ourselves, and judge of our own acts, but not make our word a law to everybody. We must not judge rashly, nor pass judgment upon our brother without any ground. We must not make the worst of people. Some sins are as motes, while others are as beams; some as a gnat, others as a camel. Not that there is any sin little; if it be a mote, or splinter, it is in the eye; if a gnat, it is in the throat; both are painful and dangerous, and we cannot be easy or well till they are got out.

Verses 7-12: Prayer is the appointed means for obtaining what we need. Pray often; make a business of prayer and be serious and earnest in it. Ask, as a beggar asks alms. Whatever you pray for, according to the promise, shall be given you, if God see it fit for you, and what would you have more?

Verses 13-14: Enter by the narrow gate, for wide is the gate and broad is the way that leads to destruction, and there are many who go in by it. Because narrow is the gate and difficult is the way that leads to life, and there are few who find it.

Verses 15-20: Nothing so much prevents men from entering the strait gate, and becoming true followers of Christ, as the carnal, soothing, flattering doctrines of those who oppose the truth. They may be known by the drift and effects of their doctrines.

Verses 21-29: Not everyone who says to Me, Lord, Lord shall enter the kingdom of Heaven, but he who does the will of My Father in Heaven. Many will say to Me in that day, Lord, Lord have we not prophesied in Your name, cast out demons in Your name and done many wonders in Your name? And I will declare to them, "I never knew you; depart from Me, you who practice lawlessness!" Therefore whoever hears these sayings of Mine, and does them, I will liken him to a wise man who built his house on the rock: and the rains descended, the floods came, and the winds blew and beat on that house; and it did not fall, for it was founded on the rock. "Now everyone who hears these sayings and does not do them will be like a foolish man who built his house on sand: and the rain descended, the floods came, and the winds blew and beat on that house; and it fell. And great was the fall. And so it was, when Jesus had ended these sayings, that the people were astonished at His teachings. For He taught them as one having authority, and not as the Scribes.

II Chronicles 7:14

If my people, which are called by my name, shall humble themselves, and pray, and seek my face, and turn from their wicked ways; then will I hear from heaven, and will forgive their sin, and will heal their land.

Psalm 122: 6

Pray for the peace of Jerusalem; they shall prosper who love thee.

Lesson Plan 4

The Book of Matthew

Chapters 8 & 9

Objective: To acquaint us with the first Book of the New Testament and how Matthew records Jesus's teachings which Jesus gave to His followers and eventually to the world.

Objective Breakdown:

1. Introduction

2. Jesus Heals a Leper   Chapter 8:1-4

3. Jesus Heals a Centurions' Servant   Chapter 8:5-13

4. Peter's Mother-in-Law   Chapter 8:14-17

5. Following Jesus Has Its Costs   Chapter 8:18-22

6. Jesus Calm the Storm   Chapter 8:23-27

7. Two Demon-Possessed Men Are Healed   Chapter 8:28-34

8. Jesus Heals the Paralytic   Chapter 9:1-8

9. Matthew Follows Jesus   Chapter 9:9-13

10. The Old and the New   Chapter 9:14-17

11. Four Dramatic Healings   Chapter 9:18-34

12. Jesus Feels Compassion for the Crowds   Chapter 9:35-38

Introduction: Jesus often encountered demons like those that possessed the man at Gadara (Matthew 8:28-34). The mention of demons affirms the reality of powerful spiritual forces in the universe. Scripture has much to say about angels and demons. Jesus often encountered demons like those that possessed the man at Gadara (Matthew 8:28-34).

Angels are members of an order of heavenly beings who are superior to humans in power and intelligence (Hebrews 2:7; 2 Peter 2:11). However, unlike God, they are not all-powerful or all-knowing (Psalm 103:20; 2 Thessalonians 1:7). God often sends them to announce good news, such as the birth of Jesus (Luke 1:30-31), or warn of coming dangers, such as the destruction of Sodom (Genesis18:16–19:29).

Angels played a particularly active role in the events surrounding Jesus's birth, resurrection, and ascension. They:

- Counseled Joseph to wed Mary (Matthew 1:20);

- Warned Joseph to flee to Egypt with Mary and the Christ child (Matthew 2:13);

- Instructed Joseph to return the family to Palestine (Matthew 2:19);

- Foretold to Zacharias the birth of John the Baptist (Luke 21:11–38);

- Announced to the shepherds the birth of Christ (Matthew 2:8–15);

- Appeared to Jesus in Garden of Gethsemane to strengthen Him (Matthew 22:43);

- Rolled back the stone from Jesus's empty tomb (Matthew 28:2);

- Appeared to women at the empty tomb to announce Jesus's resurrection (Luke 24:4–7, 23; John 20:12);

- Promised Jesus's return after His ascension (Acts 1:9–11)

Since Pentecost, the frequency of angelic activity in human affairs appears to have diminished, perhaps because of the larger role played by the Holy Spirit in our lives.

Demons are fallen angels that have been cast out of heaven. They seek to undermine the cause of righteousness in the world (1 Peter 3:19–20; 2 Peter 2:4; Jude 6). Scripture presents demons not as mythological creatures, but as real beings involved in historical events.

What was Jesus calling for when He ordered His followers to "Judge not" (Matthew 7:1)? Did He want us to close our eyes to error and evil? Did He intend that managers forego critical performance reviews of their employees? Should we decline any assessment of others since none of us are perfect?

No, those would all be misapplications of Jesus's teaching. In the first place, He was not commanding blind acceptance, but grace toward others. Since all of us are sinners, we need to stop bothering with the failings of others and start attending to serious issues of our own

(Matthew 7:3-5). His words here extend His earlier expose of hypocrisy (Matthew 6:1-18). Jesus was saying don't blame or put down others while excusing or exalting yourself.

Is there room, then, to assess others, especially when we know we are not perfect? Yes, but only in Jesus's way: with empathy and fairness (Matthew 7:12), and with a readiness to forgive freely and fully (Matthew 6:12, 14). When we are called upon to correct others, we should act like a good doctor whose purpose is to bring healing–not like an enemy who attacks. Scripture gives clear guidance to believers in cases where judgments need to be rendered. See Matthew 18:15–17; 1 Corinthians 6:1–8; and Galatians 6:1–5.

<u>Guidance for Our Spirit</u>

Ephesians 4:29: Let no corrupt communication proceed out of your mouth, but that which is good to the use of edifying, that it may minister grace unto the hearers.

Ephesians 4:30: And grieve not the holy Spirit of God, whereby ye are sealed unto the day of redemption.

Ephesians 4:31: Let all bitterness, and wrath, and anger, and clamor, and evil speaking, be put away from you, with all malice:

Ephesians 4:32: And be ye kind one to another, tenderhearted, forgiving one another, even as God for Christ's sake hath forgiven you.

In Happy moments, PRAISE GOD.

In Difficult moments, SEEK GOD.

In Quiet moments, WORSHIP GOD.

In Painful moments, TRUST GOD.

Every moment, THANK GOD.

In A Hundred Years' Time

In a hundred years' time it won't matter

if the house you've lived in wasn't done,

the garden and outside wasn't finished,

or the chores not even begun.

In a hundred years' time it won't matter

if the paint still sat in the tin,

that was meant for the wall in the study.

Would it really be such a sin?

In a hundred years' time it won't matter

if that shiny new car was not yours.

or that fancy new watch you'd admired

still sat in the case at the store.

In a hundred years' time it won't matter

if you were never on TV,

you'd never reached Hollywood stardom

or even been in a movie.

At sunset a graveyard is quiet

You'll see life summed up on each headstone.

What kind of treasures are these?

Store up your treasures in heaven

where thieves and moths cannot find.

Love God, love your neighbor as yourself.

Be patient, gentle, and kind.

Live today and enjoy it.

Grasp every moment you can.

For life is the eternal race-

No winners, it's just that you ran.

-Unknown

Angels are members of an order of heavenly beings who are superior to humans in power and intelligence (Hebrews 2:7; 2 Peter 2:11). However, unlike God, they are not all-powerful or all-knowing (Psalm 103:20; 2 Thessalonians 1:7). God often sends them to announce good news, such as the birth of Jesus (Luke 1:30-31), or warn of coming dangers, such as the destruction of Sodom (Genesis18:16–19:29).

Angels played a particularly active role in the events surrounding Jesus's birth, resurrection and ascension. They:

- Counseled Joseph to wed Mary (Matthew 1:20);

- Warned Joseph to flee to Egypt with Mary and the Christ child (Matthew 2:13);

- Instructed Joseph to return the family to Palestine (Matthew 2:19);

- Foretold to Zacharias the birth of John the Baptist (Luke 21:11–38);

- Announced to the shepherds the birth of Christ (Matthew 2:8–15);

- Appeared to Jesus in Garden of Gethsemane to strengthen Him (Matthew 22:43);

- Rolled back the stone from Jesus's empty tomb (Matthew 28:2);

- Appeared to women at the empty tomb to announce Jesus's resurrection (Luke 24: 4–7, 23; John 20:12);

- Promised Jesus's return after His ascension (Acts 1:9–11)

Since Pentecost, the frequency of angelic activity in human affairs appears to have diminished, perhaps because of the larger role played by the Holy Spirit in our lives.

Demons are fallen angels that have been cast out of heaven. They seek to undermine the cause of righteousness in the world (1Peter 3:19–20; 2 Peter 2:4; Jude 6). Scripture presents demons not as mythological creatures, but as real beings involved in historical events.

II Chronicles 7:14

If my people who are called by my name will humble themselves and pray, and seek my face, and turn from their wicked ways, then I will hear from heaven and will forgive their sin and heal their land.

Psalm 122:6

Pray for the peace of Jerusalem; they shall prosper who love thee.

Lesson Plan 5

The Book of Matthew

Chapters 10 & 11

Objective: To acquaint us with the first Book of the New Testament. How Matthew records Jesus's teachings, which had been given to Jesus's followers and eventually to the world.

Objective Breakdown:

1. Introduction

2. The Twelve   Chapter 10:1-4

3. Jesus Sends and Warns the Twelve   Chapter 10:5-42

4. Jesus Speaks About John the Baptist   Chapter 11:1-19

5. Unbelievable Cities are Condemned   Chapter 11:20-24

6. An Invitation   Chapter 11:25-30

Introduction: What it means to be like Jesus. Jesus invested Himself in the development of other people, particularly the Twelve. He gave them responsibility and authority, resisting the temptation to get the job done "right" by doing it Himself. In doing so, He accepted the risk that they might fail. Of course, He gave them adequate preparation before sending them out, and on their return. He affirmed them on their successful completion of the mission. Jesus calls us to help others grow. If we want to be like Him, we will share the joys and risks of working together with our brothers and sisters.

What does it mean to "be like Jesus," especially for Christians in today's marketplace? Eight portraits in Matthews's eyewitness account gives us some clues:

1. To be like Jesus means to accept our roots (Matthew 1:1-17)

2. To be like Jesus means to engage the world's pain and struggle (Matthew 1:18-2:23).

3. To be like Jesus means to commit ourselves to other believers, no matter how "weird" they appear to be (Matthew 3:1-17).

4. To be like Jesus means to admit our vulnerability to temptation (Matthew 4:1-11).

5. To be like Jesus means to openly proclaim the message of Christ (Matthew 4:12-25).

6. 6. To be like Jesus means to commit ourselves to changed thinking and behavior (Matthew 5: 1-7:27).

7. To be like Jesus means to serve others, especially those who are oppressed or without Christ (Matthew 8:1-9:38).

8. To be like Jesus means to affirm others in leadership (Matthew 10:1-42).

The moral of this story is, do not let any mortal have absolute control over your mind. The only thing that should have absolute control over your mind and soul is the "Word of God."

II Chronicles 7:14

If my people, which are called by my name, shall humble themselves, and pray, and seek my face, and turn from their wicked ways; then will I hear from heaven, and will forgive their sin, and will heal their land.

Psalm 122:6

Pray for the Peace of Jerusalem; they shall Prosper That Love thee.

Lesson Plan 6

The Book of Matthew

Chapters 12 & 13

Objective: To acquaint us with the first Book of the New Testament. How Matthew records Jesus's teachings, which had been given to Jesus's followers and eventually to the world.

Objective Breakdown:

1. Introduction

2. Sabbath Controversies   Chapter 12:1-14

3. Jesus Seeks a Low Profile   Chapter 12:15-21

4. Allegations of Satanism   Chapter 12:22-45

5. Family Loyalty   Chapter 12:46-50

6. Parables by the Sea   Chapter 13:1-23

7. Wheat and the Tares   Chapter 13:24-30

8. A Mustard Seed   Chapter 13:31-32

9. Leaven   Chapter 13:33

10. The Use of Parables   Chapter 13:34-35

11. Wheat and Tares Explained   Chapter 13:36-43

12. Hidden Treasure   Chapter 13:44

13. A Pearl of Great Price   Chapter 13:45

14. A Dragnet   Chapter 13:47-50

15. A Householder   Chapter 13:51-52

16. Jesus is Dishonored in His Own Country   Chapter 13:53-58

Introduction: Using parables–brief tales illustrating moral principles–He frequently spoke about the nature of His Kingdom. Matthew's gospel discusses eight of these parables:

The parable of the soils (Matthew 13:1-23) addresses those who hear about the kingdom.

The parable of the wheat and the Tares (Matthew 13:24-30) warns the people who pretend to be part of the kingdom may be able to fool others, but they can't fool God.

The parable of the mustard seed (Matthew 13:31-32) warns the kingdom would be a force to be reckoned with. Do not despise small beginnings.

The parable of the leaven (Matthew 13:33) describes the influence of the kingdom: it quietly and effectively spreads among people and accomplishes significant results.

The parable of the hidden treasure (Matthew 13:44) puts a value on the kingdom: it is the most important thing one can possess.

The parable of the pearl of great price (Matthew 13:45-46) also describes the kingdom's value: it is worth sacrificing everything to possess it.

The parable of the dragnet (Matthew 13:47-50) warns that a day of reckoning is coming, when those who accept the kingdom will be separated from those who reject it.

The parable of the householder (Matthew 13:51-52) places a responsibility on those who understand about the kingdom to share their insight with others.

Jesus's stories connected with the real world: agriculture (sowing, growing, and harvesting), the food industry (baking, fishing) real estate (land purchasing, homeownership, and retailing (the sale of pearls, etc.)).

II Chronicles 7:14

If my people, which are called by my name, shall humble themselves, and pray, and seek my face, and turn from their wicked ways; then will I hear from heaven, and will forgive their sin, and will heal their land.

Psalm 122:6

Pray for the Peace of Jerusalem; they will prosper that love thee.

<u>Guidance for Our Spirit</u>

Ephesians 4:29: Let no corrupt communication proceed out of your mouth, but that which is good to the use of edifying, that it may minister grace unto the hearers.

Ephesians 4:30: And grieve not the holy Spirit of God, whereby ye are sealed unto the day of redemption.

Ephesians 4:31: Let all bitterness, and wrath, and anger, and clamor, and evil speaking, be put away from you, with all malice.

Ephesians 4:32: And be ye kind one to another, tenderhearted, forgiving one another, even as God for Christ's sake hath forgiven you.

In Happy moments, PRAISE GOD.

In Difficult moments, SEEK GOD.

In Quiet moments, WORSHIP GOD.

In Painful moments, TRUST GOD.

Every moment, THANK GOD.

Homework: Psalms 126 & 127 & 1 John Chapter 5

Lesson Plan 7

The Book of Matthew

Chapters 14 & 15

Objective: To acquaint us with the first Book of the New Testament. How Matthew records Jesus's teachings, which had been given to Jesus's followers and eventually to the world.

Objective Breakdown:

1. Introduction

2. Herod Executes John the Baptist   Chapter 14:1-12

3. Jesus Feeds Five Thousand   Chapter 14:13-21

4. Jesus Walks on Water   Chapter 14:22-33

5. Many Are Healed in Gennesaret   Chapter 14:34-36

6. Debates Over Tradition   Chapter 15:1-9

7. Jesus Denounces the Pharisees   Chapter 15:10-20

8. A Canaanite Woman's Plea   Chapter 15:21-28

9. Jesus Heals on a Mountain   Chapter 15:29-31

10. Jesus Feeds Four Thousand   Chapter 15:32-39

Introduction: Herodias (Matthew 14:3) was a powerful woman. The wife of Palestine's appointed ruler, she enjoyed privilege and position. But one thing she had no control over was the outspoken tongue of John the Baptist.

John had publicly condemned Herodias' marriage to Herod Antipas. A granddaughter of Herod the Great. Herodias had first married her father's brother, Herod Philip I. But she left Philip to marry his half-brother, Herod Antipas, who divorced his wife to marry Herodias.

John denounced their immorality, and Herodias was determined to silence the troublesome prophet. So, she persuaded Herod to have John arrested and imprisoned. However, she could not convince her husband to execute the man.

Eventually, however, an opportunity presented itself when Herod's lust led him foolishly promise Herodias' daughter Salome anything (Matthew 14:7). The extent of Herodias's evil and cunning is evident from the unusual request. Imagine the control Herodias must have had over her daughter's mind.

Again, the moral of this story is do not let any mortal have absolute control over your mind. The only thing that should have absolute control over your mind and soul is the "Word of God."

II Chronicles 7:14

If my people, which are called by my name, shall humble themselves, and pray, and seek my face, and turn from their wicked ways; then will I hear from heaven, and will forgive their sin, and will heal their land.

Psalm 122:6

Pray for the Peace of Jerusalem; they shall Prosper That Love thee.

Lesson Plan 8

The Book of Matthew

Chapters 16 & 17

Objective: To acquaint us with the first Book of the New Testament. How Matthew records Jesus's teachings, which had been given to Jesus's followers and eventually to the world.

Objective Breakdown:

1. Introduction

2. Leaders Ask for a Sign   Chapter 16:1-4

3. Beware of the Leaven of the Pharisees   Chapter 16:5-12

4. You Are the Christ   Chapter 16:13-20

5. Following Christ Means Sacrifice   Chapter 16:21-28

6. The Transfiguration   Chapter 17:1-13

7. Jesus Heals an Epileptic   Chapter 17:14-21

8. Jesus Predicts His Betrayal`   Chapter 17:22-23

9. Jesus and Taxation   Chapter 17:24-27

Introduction: We know that there were at least five major political parties among the Hebrews of Jesus's day. The Herodians —Loyal Defenders of the Status Quo. They took their name from Herod the Great (37–4B.C) and his supporters (Acts12:1–2). They supported the adoption of Greco-Roman culture and policies in Palestine. Like the Pharisees, they favored local political autonomy. Fearing military intervention by Rome, they stridently resisted challengers to the status quo, such as the zealots; John the Baptist, Jesus, and the apostles. They joined other forces with other parties in the plot to eliminate Jesus (Matthew 22:16; Mark 3:6; 12:13).

The Pharisees –Religious Legalists. Probably derived from a group of the faithful called the Hasidim. The name means to separate. Shared similar vies with the Essene's but chose to stay within the larger society. Nevertheless, many chose to study the Law on their own, having lost respect for the priesthood as a result of its corruption. Many served on the council (Acts 6:12).

They were considered doctors of the Law; scribes were considered laymen. They collected and preserved the Talmud and the Mishnah, voluminous products of oral tradition and Old Testament commentary. By reputation, legalistic and fanatically devoted to rabbinic tradition. Some even refused to eat with non-Pharisees for fear of being contaminated by food not rendered ritually clean. They differed with the Sadducees over the doctrine of resurrection. They believed in angels and that they intervened in human affairs.

The Sadducees –The Urban Elite. May have come from Zadok, the high priest under King David. They tended to represent the aristocrats, priests, merchants, and urban elite in Jerusalem and other cities in Judea. Hostile to Jesus and His followers. Many served on the council. Most of the high priests in the days of Jesus and the apostles were Sadducees. Denied the resurrection or life after death, along with the doctrines of everlasting punishment and a literal kingdom. Denied that God controls history, insisting on free will and responsibility of humans to make wise choices according to the Law. Denied the existence of angels and held only to the Law of Moses or the first five books of the Old Testament.

The Zealots –Firebrands of Revolution. Ardent nationalist who awaited an opportunity to revolt against Rome. Resisted paying taxes to Rome or the temple. One particular tax revolt against Rome led by Judas the Galilean (6 B.C.), secured the Galilee's reputation as a seedbed of revolutionaries. They were blamed by some for the collapse of Judea to Rome in the war of A.D. 66–70. Josephus, a Jewish historian, claimed that they degenerated into mere assassins or Sicarii ("dagger men"). Sided with the Pharisees in supporting Jewish Law. Opposed the Herodians and Sadducees, who tried to maintain the political status quo. Intolerant of the Essenes and later the Christians for their tendencies toward nonviolence.

The Essenes –Detached Purist. A sect of ascetics that thrived between the middle of second century B.C. until the Jewish-Roman war in A.D. 66-70. Once members of the Hasidim, but, unlike the Pharisees, separated from society, withdrawing into monastic communities lie Qumran where the Dead Seas Scrolls were found. They lived in societies that held properties in common. Believed in immortality of the soul, angels, and an elaborate scheme of end-times prophecies. Some were looking for as many as three Messiahs. Known for celibacy, pacifism, opposition to slavery, caring for their own sick and elderly, trading with their own sect, simplicity in meals and dress, and rejection of all ostentatious display. Paid more attention to ceremonial purity than the Pharisees and carefully guarded the Sabbath. Practice ritual baptism and communal dinner called the messianic banquet. Their practices may have influenced early Christian practices and rituals.

II Chronicles 7:14

If my people, who are called by my name, shall humble themselves, and pray, and seek my face, and turn from their wicked ways; then I will hear from heaven, and forgive their sin, and heal their land.

Psalm 122:6

Pray for the Peace of Jerusalem; they shall prosper who love thee.

<u>Guidance for Our Spirit</u>

Ephesians 4:29 Let no corrupt communication proceed out of your mouth, but that which is good to the use of edifying, that it may minister grace unto the hearers.

Ephesians 4:30 And grieve not the holy Spirit of God, whereby ye are sealed unto the day of redemption.

Ephesians 4:31 Let all bitterness, and wrath, and anger, and clamor, and evil speaking, be put away from you, with all malice:

Ephesians 4:32 And be ye kind one to another, tenderhearted, forgiving one another, even as God for Christ's sake hath forgiven you.

Lesson Plan 9

The Book of Matthew

Chapters 18 & 19

Objective: To acquaint us with the first Book of the New Testament. How Matthew recordsJesus's teachings, which had been given to Jesus's followers and eventually to the world.

Objective Breakdown:

1. Introduction

2. Who is the Greatest in the Kingdom   Matthew 18:1-19

3. About Forgiveness   Matthew 18:20-35

4. Marriage and Divorce   Matthew 19:1-12

5. Jesus Blesses Children   Matthew 19:13-15

6. A Rich Man's Question   Matthew 19:16-26

7. Reward for the Twelve   Matthew 19:27-30

Introduction: The Challenge of Commitment. Commitment is in jeopardy these days. Some even call it the "C" word, as is to shame it as something we won't acknowledge. After all, the demands and costs are too great. Today, convenience usually wins out over the sacrifice involved in being committed to someone or something.

The situation was no less confused in Jesus's day. As He began to unveil a new way of life for His followers, critics appeared and challenged Him on the difficulties of keeping the marriage commitment (Matthew 19:3,7). Even His disciples quivered as they perceived the cost of maintaining one's marriage vows (Matthew 19:10). Later, they wanted to send away some bothersome children in order to deal with more "important things" (Matthew 19:13). It seems that Jesus was surrounded by men who were a little unsure about domestic matters.

The discussion of divorce followed appropriately on the heels of Jesus's remarks about the merits of boundless forgiveness (Matthew 18:21-35). Followers of Christ need to be known for their commitment—to marriage, family, community, work, and above all to Christ. Such loyalty often means messy obedience, but it is the way of Christ. How desperately that is needed in a day when people make vows of convenience rather than commitment. Commitment is one of the hallmarks of a godly "work style."

II Chronicles 7:14

If my people, who are called by my name, shall humble themselves, and pray, and seek my face, and turn from their wicked ways; then I will hear from heaven, and forgive their sin, and heal their land.

Psalm 122:6

Pray for the Peace of Jerusalem; they shall prosper who love thee.

Guidance for Our Spirit

Ephesians 4:29: Let no corrupt communication proceed out of your mouth, but that which is good to the use of edifying, that it may minister grace unto the hearers.

Ephesians 4:30: And grieve not the holy Spirit of God, whereby ye are sealed unto the day of redemption.

Ephesians 4:31: Let all bitterness, and wrath, and anger, and clamor, and evil speaking, be put away from you, with all malice:

Ephesians 4:32: And be ye kind one to another, tenderhearted, forgiving one another, even as God for Christ's sake hath forgiven you.

Lesson Plan 10

The Book of Matthew

Chapters 20 & 21

Objective: To acquaint us with the first Book of the New Testament. How Matthew records Jesus's teachings, which had been given to Jesus's followers and eventually to the world.

Objective Breakdown:

1. Introduction

2. A Parable About Wages   Matthew 20:1-16

3. Jesus Predicts His Death   Matthew 20:17-19

4. A Mother's Big Request   Matthew 20:20-28

5. Two Blind Men Are Healed at Jerico   Matthew 20:29-34

6. Jesus Enters Jerusalem   Matthew 21:1-11

7. Jesus Purges the Temple   Matthew 21:12-17

8. Jesus Curses a Fig Tree   Matthew 21:18-22

9. Pharisees Challenge Jesus's Authority   Matthew 21:23-27

10. A Parable About Two Sons   Matthew 21:28-32

11. A Parable About a Vineyard Owner   Matthew 21:33-46

Introduction: Anyone who feels that they are not paid what they are worth can appreciate the reaction of the workers in the parable Jesus told (Matthew 20: 1-16). He spoke of an employer who hired workers for a full day, others for two-thirds of a day. Others for half a day, and others for even less. Yet he paid them all the same (Matthew 20: 9-11)! Naturally, those who had worked longer demanded, "What is going on here?" (Matthew 20:11-12). Good question!

The first thing to notice is that none of the workers were employed before the landowner hired them (Matthew 20:3, 6, 7). The fact that they got a job in the first place was due to the employer's goodwill, not anything they brought to the situation. Furthermore, the employer promised the first group fair wages of a day's pay (a denarius, Matthew 20:2); and the rest an undetermined amount ("whatever is right"). As it turned out, he paid everyone an entire day's wage.

Jesus was trying to help His followers grasp something about grace in the kingdom of God. They had been asking about the kingdom's makeup and benefits earlier (Matthew 19:16, 25, 27). Jesus was not encouraging an unjust pay scale and discrimination. He was merely illustrating the nature of God's grace in terms that His followers could understand.

In the kingdom of God, grace is given because of the nature of the Giver, not the worthiness of the recipient. Receiving God's grace is a privilege for sinners—who after all, really deserve nothing but condemnation.

II Chronicles 7:14

If my people, who are called by my name, shall humble themselves, and pray, and seek my face, and turn from their wicked ways; then I will hear from heaven, and forgive their sin, and heal their land.

Psalm 122:6

Pray for the Peace of Jerusalem; they shall prosper who love thee.

<u>Guidance for Our Spirit</u>

Ephesians 4:29: Let no corrupt communication proceed out of your mouth, but that which is good to the use of edifying, that it may minister grace unto the hearers.

Ephesians 4:30: And grieve not the holy Spirit of God, whereby ye are sealed unto the day of redemption.

Ephesians 4:31: Let all bitterness, and wrath, and anger, and clamor, and evil speaking, be put away from you, with all malice:

Ephesians 4:32: And be ye kind one to another, tenderhearted, forgiving one another, even as God for Christ's sake hath forgiven you.

Lesson Plan 11

The Book of Matthew

Chapters 22 & 23

Objective: To acquaint us with the first Book of the New Testament. How Matthew recordsJesus's teachings, which had been given to Jesus's followers and eventually to the world.

Objective Breakdown:

1. Introduction

2. A Parable about a Rejected Invitation   Matthew 22:1-14

3. Jesus Confounds His Challengers   Matthew 22:15-33

4. The Greatest of the Commandments   Matthew 22:34-45

5. Jesus Denounces the Scribes and Pharisees   Matthew 23:1-12

6. Woe to the Scribes   Matthew 23:13-36

7. Jerusalem's Refusal   Matthew 23:37-39

Introduction: "Love" is a very confusing concept these days. People use the word "love" to describe very different relationships: people "love" their dog...a certain type of car...a brand of pizza...another person for whom they have deep feelings.

What can "love" possibly mean if it applies to dogs, machines, food, or close companions?

The Bible is not confused or vague about the powerful concept it calls "love." Greek, the international language of Jesus's day and the language in which the New Testament was written, had four distinct words for love, each with its own shade of meaning:

1. *Eros* denoted the relationship between male and female, including physical desire. craving, and longing. This word is not used in the New Testament.

2. *Stergos* described affection and was applied especially to the mutual love between family

members. It is not used in the New Testament either.

3. *Philos* reflected the care and concern that friends have for each other, what we would call brotherly love. Peter spoke of this kind of love when he and Jesus discussed his future task of serving others (John 21:15-17).

4. *Agape* describes a unique type of supreme love involving a conscious and deliberate choice to do good for another, a commitment based on the willful choice of the lover, not the qualities of the person receiving the love. Agape love is perhaps best seen in God's love for the world (John 3:16) and in the love that God calls believers to display (1 Corinthians 13:1-13).

When Jesus recalled the greatest of the commandments, both of which had to do with love (Mathew 22:34-40), He was calling for agape love, a sustained and conscious choice to graciously serve God, neighbor, and self, expecting nothing in return. Followers of Christ learn this kind of love as God loves them first. He then commands us to live in the same way toward others (John 3:11-24). God's love empowers us to love by choice rather than just emotions or senses, and to sustain our love even in the face of hostility or rejection.

God wants to deliver a new kind of love—agape love--to families, workplaces, and communities through His people. Who around you needs that kind of intentional touch of compassion and grace?

II Chronicles 7:14

If my people who are called by my name will humble themselves and pray, and seek my face, and turn from their wicked ways, then I will hear from heaven and will forgive their sin and heal their land.

Psalm 122:6

Pray for the peace of Jerusalem; they shall prosper who love thee.

Lesson Plan 12

The Book of Matthew

Chapter 24

Objective: To acquaint us with the first Book of the New Testament. How Matthew recordsJesus's teachings, which had been given to Jesus's followers and eventually to the World.

Objective Breakdown:

1. Introduction/Background

2. Jesus Predicts the Temple's Destruction   Chapter 24:1-2

3. The Disciples' Three Questions   Chapter 24:3

4. The Tribulation   Chapter 24:4–27

5. The Second Coming   Chapter 24:27–31

6. Parable of the Fig Tree   Chapter 24:32–35

7. Illustration of the Days of Noah   Chapter 24:36–44

8. Illustration of the Two Servants   Chapter 24:45–51

Introduction/Background: The Holy City. For centuries before and after Christ, Jerusalem has been viewed as more than just a city. It stands as a great symbol of the Bible and the Near East. As the center of Judaism and Hebrew culture, it bore the brunt of Jesus' dramatic cry of anguish over its rejection of Him (Matthew 23:37-38). Jesus knew all too well that in a matter of years, Jerusalem would indeed be left desolate by a myriad of Roman siege troops.

Main city of Palestine in Biblical Times. It is well situated for defense on two triangular ridges that converge to the south, bordered by the Kidron Valley on the east and the valley of Hinnom on the west. Although, the city appears in the Bible as early as Abraham (Genesis 14:18), the site had probably been inhabited for centuries before.

The city was captured by David and made the capital of Israel. It is the site of Solomon's temple and, in the first century, Herod's temple. The estimated population in Jesus' day was about 60,000 to 70,000, though estimates range from 40,000 to 12 million. Jerusalem was besieged and destroyed by Rome in A.D. 70. Although, relatively small geographically, it was a sizable metropolitan area with numerous suburban towns.

Jesus visited Jerusalem several times. Yet its population as a whole never did respond to the Son of God. Nor did it accept Christ's followers later when they tried to penetrate it with His message. Known as the Holy City (Matthew 4:5), Jerusalem nevertheless rejected the Holy One of Israel, the Messiah.

Jesus Predicts the Temple to be Destroyed: Matthew 24:1-2 also See Mark 13:1–2;

   Luke 21:5–6

Matthew 24

1. And Jesus went out, and departed from the temple: and his disciples came to him for to shew him the buildings of the temple.

2. And Jesus said unto them, See ye not all these things? verily I say unto you, There shall not be left here one stone upon another, that shall not be thrown down.

Mark 13

1. And as he went out of the temple, one of his disciples saith unto him, Master, see what manner of stones and what buildings are here!

2. And Jesus answering said unto him, Seest thou these great buildings? there shall not be left one stone upon another, that shall not be thrown down.

Luke 21

3. And as some spake of the temple, how it was adorned with goodly stones and gifts, he said,

4. As for these things which ye behold, the days will come, in the which there shall not be left one stone upon another, that shall not be thrown down.

The Disciples' Three Questions: Matthew 24:3 also see Mark 13:3-4; Luke 21:7

Matthew 24:3

3. And as he sat upon the mount of Olives, the disciples came unto him privately, saying, Tell us, **when shall these things be? and what shall be the sign of thy coming, and of the end of the world?**

Mark 13:3–4

3. And as he sat upon the mount of Olives over against the temple, Peter and James and John and Andrew asked him privately,

4. Tell us, when shall these things be? and what shall be the sign when all these things shall be fulfilled?

Luke 21:7

7. And they asked him, saying, Master, but when shall these things be? and what sign will there be when these things shall come to pas

The Tribulation—Matthew 24:4-27; See Mark 13:5–23; Luke 21:5–24.

Matthew 24:4–27

4. And Jesus answered and said unto them, Take heed that no man deceive you.

5. For many shall come in my name, saying, I am Christ; and shall deceive many.

6. And ye shall hear of wars and rumours of wars: see that ye be not troubled: for all these things must come to pass, but the end is not yet.

7. For nation shall rise against nation, and kingdom against kingdom: and there shall be famines, and pestilences, and earthquakes, in divers places.

8. All these are the beginning of sorrows.

9. Then shall they deliver you up to be afflicted, and shall kill you: and ye shall be hated of all nations for my name's sake.

10. And then shall many be offended, and shall betray one another, and shall hate one another.

11. And many false prophets shall rise, and shall deceive many.

12. And because iniquity shall abound, the love of many shall wax cold.

13. But he that shall endure unto the end, the same shall be saved.

14. And this gospel of the kingdom shall be preached in all the world for a witness unto all nations; and then shall the end come.

15. When ye therefore shall see the abomination of desolation, spoken of by Daniel the prophet, stand in the holy place, (whoso readeth, let him understand:)

16. Then let them which be in Judaea flee into the mountains:

17. Let him which is on the housetop not come down to take any thing out of his house:

18. Neither let him which is in the field return back to take his clothes.

19. And woe unto them that are with child, and to them that give suck in those days!

20. But pray ye that your flight be not in the winter, neither on the sabbath day:

21. For then shall be great tribulation, such as was not since the beginning of the world to this time, no, nor ever shall be.

22. And except those days should be shortened, there should no flesh be saved: but for the elect's sake those days shall be shortened.

23. Then if any man shall say unto you, Lo, here is Christ, or there; believe it not.

24. For there shall arise false Christs, and false prophets, and shall shew great signs and wonders; insomuch that, if it were possible, they shall deceive the very elect.

25. Behold, I have told you before.

26. Wherefore if they shall say unto you, Behold, he is in the desert; go not forth: behold, he is in the secret chambers; believe it not.

27. For as the lightning cometh out of the east, and shineth even unto the west; so shall also the coming of the Son of man be.

Mark 13: 5–23

5. And Jesus answering them began to say, Take heed lest any man deceive you:

6. For many shall come in my name, saying, I am Christ; and shall deceive many.

7. And when ye shall hear of wars and rumours of wars, be ye not troubled: for such things must needs be; but the end shall not be yet.

8. For nation shall rise against nation, and kingdom against kingdom: and there shall be earthquakes in divers places, and there shall be famines and troubles: these are the beginnings of sorrows.

9. But take heed to yourselves: for they shall deliver you up to councils; and in the synagogues ye shall be beaten: and ye shall be brought before rulers and kings for my sake, for a testimony against them.

10. And the gospel must first be published among all nations.

11. But when they shall lead you, and deliver you up, take no thought beforehand what ye shall speak, neither do ye premeditate: but whatsoever shall be given you in that hour, that speak ye: for it is not ye that speak, but the Holy Ghost.

12. Now the brother shall betray the brother to death, and the father the son; and children shall rise up against their parents, and shall cause them to be put to death.

13. And ye shall be hated of all men for my name's sake: but he that shall endure unto the end, the same shall be saved.

14. But when ye shall see the abomination of desolation, spoken of by Daniel the prophet, standing where it ought not, (let him that readeth understand,) then let them that be in Judaea flee to the mountains:

15. And let him that is on the housetop not go down into the house, neither enter therein, to take any thing out of his house:

16. And let him that is in the field not turn back again for to take up his garment.

17. But woe to them that are with child, and to them that give suck in those days!

18. And pray ye that your flight be not in the winter.

19. For in those days shall be affliction, such as was not from the beginning of the creation which God created unto this time, neither shall be.

20. And except that the Lord had shortened those days, no flesh should be saved: but for the elect's sake, whom he hath chosen, he hath shortened the days.

21. And then if any man shall say to you, Lo, here is Christ; or, lo, he is there; believe him not:

22. For false Christs and false prophets shall rise, and shall shew signs and wonders, to seduce,

if it were possible, even the elect.

23. But take ye heed: behold, I have foretold you all things.

Luke 21:5–24

5. And as some spake of the temple, how it was adorned with goodly stones and gifts, he said,

6. As for these things which ye behold, the days will come, in the which there shall not be left one stone upon another, that shall not be thrown down.

7. And they asked him, saying, Master, but when shall these things be? and what sign will there be when these things shall come to pass?

8. And he said, Take heed that ye be not deceived: for many shall come in my name, saying, I am Christ; and the time draweth near: go ye not therefore after them.

9. But when ye shall hear of wars and commotions, be not terrified: for these things must first come to pass; but the end is not by and by.

10. Then said he unto them, Nation shall rise against nation, and kingdom against kingdom:

11. And great earthquakes shall be in divers places, and famines, and pestilences; and fearful sights and great signs shall there be from heaven.

12. But before all these, they shall lay their hands on you, and persecute you, delivering you up to the synagogues, and into prisons, being brought before kings and rulers for my name's sake.

13. And it shall turn to you for a testimony.

14. Settle it therefore in your hearts, not to meditate before what ye shall answer:

15. For I will give you a mouth and wisdom, which all your adversaries shall not be able to gainsay nor resist.

16. And ye shall be betrayed both by parents, and brethren, and kinsfolks, and friends; and some of you shall they cause to be put to death.

17. And ye shall be hated of all men for my name's sake.

18. But there shall not an hair of your head perish.

19. In your patience possess ye your souls.

20. And when ye shall see Jerusalem compassed with armies, then know that the desolation thereof is nigh.

21. Then let them which are in Judaea flee to the mountains; and let them which are in the midst of it depart out; and let not them that are in the countries enter thereinto.

22. For these be the days of vengeance, that all things which are written may be fulfilled.

23. But woe unto them that are with child, and to them that give suck, in those days! for there shall be great distress in the land, and wrath upon this people.

24. And they shall fall by the edge of the sword, and shall be led away captive into all nations:and Jerusalem shall be trodden down of the Gentiles, until the times of the Gentiles be fulfilled.

The Second Coming: Matthew 24:24–31;   See Luke 21:25–28.

Matthew 24:24-31

24. For there shall arise false Christs, and false prophets, and shall shew great signs and wonders; insomuch that, if it were possible, they shall deceive the very elect.

25. Behold, I have told you before.

26. Wherefore if they shall say unto you, Behold, he is in the desert; go not forth: behold, he is in the secret chambers; believe it not.

27. For as the lightning cometh out of the east, and shineth even unto the west; so shall also the coming of the Son of man be.

28. For wheresoever the carcase is, there will the eagles be gathered together.

29. Immediately after the tribulation of those days shall the sun be darkened, and the moon shall not give her light, and the stars shall fall from heaven, and the powers of the heavens shall be shaken:

30. And then shall appear the sign of the Son of man in heaven: and then shall all the tribes of the earth mourn, and they shall see the Son of man coming in the clouds of heaven with power and great glory.

31. And he shall send his angels with a great sound of a trumpet, and they shall gather together his elect from the four winds, from one end of heaven to the other.

Mark 13:24–27

24. But in those days, after that tribulation, the sun shall be darkened, and the moon shall not give her light,

25. And the stars of heaven shall fall, and the powers that are in heaven shall be shaken.

26. And then shall they see the Son of man coming in the clouds with great power and glory.

27. And then shall he send his angels, and shall gather together his elect from the four winds, from the uttermost part of the earth to the uttermost part of heaven.

Luke 21:25–28

25. And there shall be signs in the sun, and in the moon, and in the stars; and upon the earth distress of nations, with perplexity; the sea and the waves roaring;

26. Men's hearts failing them for fear, and for looking after those things which are coming on the earth: for the powers of heaven shall be shaken.

27. And then shall they see the Son of man coming in a cloud with power and great glory.

28. And when these things begin to come to pass, then look up, and lift up your heads; for your redemption draweth nigh.

Parable of the Fig Tree: Matthew 24:32–35; See Mark 13:28–31; Luke 21:29–33.

Matthew 24:32-35

32. Now learn a parable of the fig tree; When his branch is yet tender, and putteth forth leaves, ye know that summer is nigh:

33. So likewise ye, when ye shall see all these things, know that it is near, even at the doors.

34. Verily I say unto you, This generation shall not pass, till all these things be fulfilled.

35. Heaven and earth shall pass away, but my words shall not pass away.

Mark 13:28–31

28. Now learn a parable of the fig tree; When her branch is yet tender, and putteth forth leaves,

ye know that summer is near:

29. So ye in like manner, when ye shall see these things come to pass, know that it is nigh, even at the doors.

30. Verily I say unto you, that this generation shall not pass, till all these things be done.

31. Heaven and earth shall pass away: but my words shall not pass away.

Luke 21:29–33

29. And he spake to them a parable; Behold the fig tree, and all the trees;

30. When they now shoot forth, ye see and know of your own selves that summer is now nigh at hand.

31. So likewise ye, when ye see these things come to pass, know ye that the kingdom of God is nigh at hand.

32. Verily I say unto you, This generation shall not pass away, till all be fulfilled.

33. Heaven and earth shall pass away: but my words shall not pass away.

Illustration of the Days of Noah: Matthew 24:36–44; See Mark 13:32–37; Luke 21:34–36.

Matthew 24:36–44

36. But of that day and hour knoweth no man, no, not the angels of heaven, but my Father only.

37. But as the days of Noe were, so shall also the coming of the Son of man be.

38. For as in the days that were before the flood they were eating and drinking, marrying and giving in marriage, until the day that Noe entered into the ark,

39. And knew not until the flood came, and took them all away; so shall also the coming of the Son of man be.

40. Then shall two be in the field; the one shall be taken, and the other left.

41. Two women shall be grinding at the mill; the one shall be taken, and the other left.

42. Watch therefore: for ye know not what hour your Lord doth come.

43. But know this, that if the good man of the house had known in what watch the thief would

come, he would have watched, and would not have suffered his house to be broken up.

44. Therefore be ye also ready: for in such an hour as ye think not the Son of man cometh.

Mark 13:32–37

32. But of that day and that hour knoweth no man, no, not the angels which are in heaven, neither the Son, but the Father.

33. Take ye heed, watch and pray: for ye know not when the time is.

34. For the Son of man is as a man taking a far journey, who left his house, and gave authority to his servants, and to every man his work, and commanded the porter to watch.

35. Watch ye therefore: for ye know not when the master of the house cometh, at even, or at midnight, or at the cock crowing, or in the morning:

36. Lest coming suddenly he find you sleeping.

37. And what I say unto you I say unto all, Watch.

Luke 21:34–36

34. And take heed to yourselves, lest at any time your hearts be overcharged with surfeiting, and drunkenness, and cares of this life, and so that day come upon you unawares.

35. For as a snare shall it come on all them that dwell on the face of the whole earth.

36. Watch ye therefore, and pray always, that ye may be accounted worthy to escape all these things that shall come to pass, and to stand before the Son of man.

Illustration of the Two Servants: Matthew 24:45–51; See Luke 12:41–28.

Matthew 24:45–51

45. Who then is a faithful and wise servant, whom his lord hath made ruler over his household, to give them meat in due season?

46. Blessed is that servant, whom his lord when he cometh shall find so doing.

47. Verily I say unto you, That he shall make him ruler over all his goods.

48. But and if that evil servant shall say in his heart, My lord delayeth his coming;

49. And shall begin to smite his fellow servants, and to eat and drink with the drunken;

50. The lord of that servant shall come in a day when he looketh not for him, and in an hour that he is not aware of,

51. And shall cut him asunder, and appoint him his portion with the hypocrites: there shall be weeping and gnashing of teeth.

Luke 21:41–48

41. Then Peter said unto him, Lord, speakest thou this parable unto us, or even to all?

42. And the Lord said, Who then is that faithful and wise steward, whom his lord shall make ruler over his household, to give them their portion of meat in due season?

43. Blessed is that servant, whom his lord when he cometh shall find so doing.

44. Of a truth I say unto you, that he will make him ruler over all that he hath.

45. But and if that servant say in his heart, My lord delayeth his coming; and shall begin to beat the menservants and maidens, and to eat and drink, and to be drunken;

46. The lord of that servant will come in a day when he looketh not for him, and at an hour when he is not aware, and will cut him in sunder, and will appoint him his portion with the unbelievers.

47. And that servant, which knew his lord's will, and prepared not himself, neither did according to his will, shall be beaten with many stripes.

48. But he that knew not, and did commit things worthy of stripes, shall be beaten with few stripes. For unto whomsoever much is given, of him shall be much required: and to whom men have committed much, of him they will ask the more.

II Chronicles 7:14

If my people who are called by my name will humble themselves and pray, and seek my face, and turn from their wicked ways, then I will hear from heaven and will forgive their sin and heal their land.

Psalm 122:6

Pray for the peace of Jerusalem; they shall prosper who love thee.

Lesson Plan 13

The Book of Matthew

Chapter 25

Objective: To acquaint us with the first Book of the New Testament. How Matthew records Jesus's teachings, which had been given to Jesus's followers and eventually to the world.

Objective Breakdown:

1. Introduction/Background

2. Parables About Ten Virgins   Chapter 25:1-13

3. A Parable About Investments   Chapter 25:14-30

4. Judgments of the Nations   Chapter 25:31-46

Introduction: True Success Means Faithfulness. The story of the Talents (Matthew 25:14-30) is about the Kingdom of Heaven (Matthew 25:14), but it offers an important lesson about success. God measures our success not what we have, but by what we do with what we have–for all that we have is a gift from Him. We are only managers to whom He has entrusted resources and responsibilities.

The key thing He looks for is faithfulness (Matthew 25:21,23), doing what we can to obey and honor Him with whatever He has given us. We may or may not be successful as our culture measures success, in terms of wealth, prestige, power, or fame. In the long run that hardly matters. What counts is whether we have faithfully served God with what He has entrusted to us. By all means, we must avoid wasting our lives in the way the third servant wasted his talents, by failing to carry out the Master's business.

Have you ever wondered whether God is going to give you a final exam when you stand before Him? If you pass you go to heaven, but if you fail...? Fortunately, Jesus has taken care of the exam for us–and passed (Ephesians 2:4-10). Nevertheless, Matthew 25:31–46 reveals a final exam for the nations at Christ's return with a five-part question below.

Were you a friend of Jesus when He was hungry?   Yes   No

50

Were you a friend of Jesus when He was thirsty?	Yes	No
Were you a friend of Jesus when He was a stranger?	Yes	No
Were you a friend of Jesus when He was sick?	Yes	No
Were you a friend of Jesus when He was in prison?	Yes	No

II Chronicles 7:14

If my people who are called by my name will humble themselves and pray, and seek my face, and turn from their wicked ways, then I will hear from heaven and will forgive their sin and heal their land.

Psalm 122:6

Pray for the peace of Jerusalem; they shall prosper who love thee.

Lesson Plan 14

The Book of Matthew

Chapter 26 & 27

Objective: To acquaint us with the first Book of the New Testament. How Matthew records Jesus's teachings, which had been given to Jesus's followers and eventually to the world.

Objective Breakdown:

1. Introduction

2. Leaders Plot to Kill Jesus   Chapter 26:1-5

3. A Woman Anoints Jesus For Burial   Chapter 26:6-13

4. Judas Sells Out   Chapter 26:14-16

5. A Final Passover Meal   Chapter 26:17-35

6. Jesus Prays in the Garden of Gethsemane   Chapter 26:36-46

7. Jesus is Betrayed   Chapter 26:47-56

8. Jesus is Brought Before the High Priest   Chapter 26:57-68

9. Peter Denies Knowing Jesus   Chapter 26:69-75

10. Jesus is Taken to Pilate   Chapter 27:1-2

11. Judas Hangs Himself   Chapter 27:3-10

12. Jesus Before Pilate   Chapter 27:11-26

13. Soldiers Mock Jesus   Chapter 27:27-31

14. The Crucifixion   Chapter 27:32-37

15. This is Jesus King of the Jews   Chapter 27:38-56

16. Jesus is Buried in a Borrowed Tomb   Chapter 27:57-66

Introduction: Have you ever been trapped in a situation where there is no good alternative? Jesus faced that as He stood trial before Caiaphas and the Jewish elders (Matthew 26:59-62). The situation was so distorted and malicious that there was no good response. So, Jesus remained silent (Matthew 26:63).

As their anger intensified, the high priest placed Jesus "under oath by the living God" (Matthew 26:63). This meant that Jesus was bound to answer and answer truthfully. In effect, Caiaphas was coercing a response. Jesus rewarded him by giving him the response he expected and wanted–a claim to be "the Christ, the Son of God." This sent His accusers into a frenzy as it allowed them to impose their prearranged verdict (Matthew 26:65-68).

Now looking at tainted money. The chief priests knew that the coins tossed back at them by Judas were unacceptable to God (Matthew 27:6). It was blood money, money they had paid to apprehend their enemy Jesus (Matthew 26:14-16). Yet they turned around and used it to buy a cemetery for the poor—a good deed, yet hypocritical all the same. Thus, we need to be sure that our gifts to the Lord are from our first and best of what we have accumulated, and not giving just from our leftovers.

The Lord knows whether our gifts cost us little or nothing (see 2 Samuel 24:21–24).

II Chronicles 7:14

If my people who are called by my name will humble themselves, and pray and seek my face, and turn from their wicked ways, then I will hear from heaven, and will forgive their sin and heal their land.

Psalm 122:6

Pray for the Peace of Jerusalem: may they prosper who love you.

Lesson Plan 15

The Book of Matthew

Chapter 28

Objective: To acquaint us with the first Book of the New Testament. How Matthew records Jesus's teachings, which had been given to Jesus's followers and eventually to the world.

Objective Breakdown:

1. Introduction

2. The Empty Tomb   Chapter 28:1-8

3. The Appearance of Jesus to the Woman   Chapter 28:9-10

4. The Bribery of the Soldiers   Chapter 28:11-15

5. The Appearance of Jesus to the Disciples   Chapter 28:16-17

6. The Great Commission   Chapter 28:18-20

Introduction: Jesus sent His followers to make disciples of all the nations. That mandate (Matthew 28:19-20) may seem obvious to us today. After all, we live at the end of 2000 years of Christian outreach based on this and similar passages. Christianity now is an overwhelmingly Gentile religion subscribed to by roughly one-third of the world's population. And with modern technology, it appears to be a relatively simple task to expand that outreach even further.

In Matthew's discourse in chapter 24, the apostles had asked three questions: The first question, "When will these things be?" The second question, "What will be the sign of Your coming?" The third question. "What will be the sign of the end of the age?" Jesus answered, "Take heed that no one deceives you. For many will come in My name saying I am the Christ, and will deceive many." Jesus continues confirming that deception would be the foremost problem in the terminal generation. There are nine types of Deception:

Religious Deception. Paul teaches "Therefore let no one judge you in food or in drink, or regarding a festival or new moon or Sabbaths" (Colossians 2:16). Fasting without godliness is an illustration of religious deception. Forbidding people to marry is religious deception. Declaring people holy for keeping manmade rules of righteousness is deception. (1 Timothy 4:1-5).

Doctrinal Deception. Doctrinal deception occurs when people leave the simple meaning of the Word of God. An illustration of doctrinal deception is those who say, "we have no need of water baptism because the thief on the cross wasn't baptized."

Ethical Deception. This is when Christians profess the lordship of Jesus Christ, but cheat and lie in their business dealings.

Moral Deception. Secular humanism is the cornerstone of moral deception. It says, "If it feels good do it!" But scripture says, "It is written. Man shall not live by bread alone, but by every word that proceeds from the mouth of God." (Matthew 4:4). You don't break God's law; God's law breaks you!

Intellectual Deception. Intellectual deception is when an individual believes that his opinions, formed by his intellect, are equal or superior to the teachings of the Word of God.

Fanatical Deception. Jesus taught, "the time is coming that whoever kills you will think he offers God service" (John 16:2). The crusaders and leaders of the Spanish Inquisition are historical illustrations of fanatical deception.

Mystical Deception. Experiencing dreams, visions, voices, angels, or "a bright light" does not mean you have had a visitation from an angel or Jesus Christ. Paul says that "Satan himself transforms himself into an angel of light" (2 Corinthians 11:14). Anything that inspires you to do anything contrary to the Word of God is demonic.

Sexual Deception. Sexual deception is the belief or philosophy that rejects the God-ordained monogamous sexual relationship between man and his wife as the only acceptable sexual relationship.

Spiritual Deception. When Christians become bored with the discipline of the Word of God and begin practices that are contrary to New Testament orthodoxy, this represents the genesis of spiritual deception.

Prophecies of the Old Testament were included here. Taken from John Hagee's Bible, pages 1146 & 1147.

II Chronicles 7:14

If my people who are called by my name will humble themselves, and pray and seek my face, and turn from their wicked ways, then I will hear from heaven, and will forgive their sin and heal their land.

Psalm 122:6

Pray for the Peace of Jerusalem: May they prosper who love you.

The Book of Mark

Scripture Focus Chapters 1 - 16

Objective: Mark presents Jesus as an active, compassionate, and obedient servant who constantly ministers to the physical and spiritual needs of others.

Objective Breakdown:

1. The Forerunner of the Servant	Chapter 1:1-8
2. The Baptism of the Servant	Chapter 1:9-11
3. The Temptation of the Servant	Chapter 1:12-13
4. The Work of the Servant	Chapter 1:14-15
5. The First Disciples Are Called	Chapter 1:16-20
6. Demons Are Cast Out	Chapter 1:21-28
7. Peter's Mother-in-Law Is Healed	Chapter 1:29-31
8. Many Healings	Chapter 1:32-39
9. The Leper Is Healed	Chapter 1:40-45
10. A Paralytic Is healed	Chapter 2:1-12
11. Call of Matthew	Chapter 2:13-17
12. Parable of the Cloth and Wineskins	Chapter 2:18-22
13. Controversy over Sabbath-Work	Chapter 2:23-28
14. Controversy over Sabbath-Healing	Chapter 3:1-5
15. Pharisees Counsel to Destroy Jesus	Chapter 3:6-12
16. Selection of the Twelve	Chapter 3:13-19
17. Opposition of His Friends	Chapter 3:20-21
18. Scribes Commit the Unpardonable Sin	Chapter 3:22-30

Lesson Plan 16

The Book of Mark

Chapter 1

Objective: To obtain an understanding of the contribution to the overall gospel story of Jesus Christ the Creator of the Universe.

Objective Breakdown:

1. Introduction

2. John the Baptist Prepares the Way   Chapter 1:1-8

3. John Baptizes Jesus   Chapter 1:9-11

4. Jesus Faces Temptation in the Wilderness   Chapter 1:12-13

5. Jesus Launches His Ministry   Chapter 1:14-15

6. Jesus Calls Fisherman to Follow Him   Chapter 1:16-20

7. Demons Are Cast Out at Capernaum   Chapter 1:21-28

8. Jesus Heals Simon's Mother-in-Law   Chapter 1:29-31

9. Many Are Healed in Galilee   Chapter 1:32-45

Introduction: The Book of Mark is the shortest (16 chapters) of the four Gospels. Matthew has 28 chapters, Luke has 24, and John has 21 chapters. The Book of Mark was largely neglected by scholars from the 4th until the 19th century because it was commonly regarded as an abridgment of Matthew. But by the 19th century, the theory that Mark was the first Gospel written gained widespread acceptance. Since then, Mark has been the subject of intense interest and study.

Jesus began His ministry in Galilee (Mark 1:9) after John the Baptist was arrested by Herod Antipas "For Herod himself had sent forth and laid hold upon John, and bound him in prison for Herodias' sake, his brother Philip's wife: for he had married her. For John had said unto Herod, "It is not lawful for thee to have thy brother's wife" (Mark 6:17-18).

Before entering Galilee, Jesus ministered in Judea for about a year (John 1:19-4:45), which Mark did not mention. This shows that Mark's purpose was not to give a complete chronological account of Jesus's life.

In New Testament times there were two Galilees, upper and lower. Jesus of Nazareth grew up in densely populated lower Galilee. Among its urban centers, He carried out most of His ministry (Mark 1:14). As many as eleven of His twelve disciples may have come from that region, the exception being Judas Iscariot (who was from Kerioth-Judea).

Galilee represented the periphery of traditional Jewish life, a cultural frontier between the Hebraic and Graeco-Roman worlds. As a result, Galileans were scorned by their neighbors in Judea. Judeans used the term "Galilean" as a synonym for fool, heathen, sinner, or worse. Most significantly for Jesus, they were certain that no prophet could come from Galilee (John 7:52).

Yet a prophet did come from Galilee. It was there that Jesus announced the character of His message (Luke 4:14-19) and demonstrated its power. He performed at least 33 known miracles there, and 32 recorded parables, 19 were spoken in Galilee. See Matthew 11:20–24:

20 Then began he to upbraid the cities wherein most of his mighty works were done, because they repented not:

21 Woe unto thee, Chorazin! woe unto thee, Bethsaida! for if the mighty works, which were done in you, had been done in Tyre and Sidon, they would have repented long ago in sackcloth and ashes.

22 But I say unto you, It shall be more tolerable for Tyre and Sidon at the day of judgment, than for you.

23 And thou, Capernaum, which art exalted unto heaven, shalt be brought down to hell: for if the mighty works, which have been done in thee, had been done in Sodom, it would have remained until this day.

24 But I say unto you, That it shall be more tolerable for the land of Sodom in the day of judgment, than for thee."

II Chronicles 7:14

If my people who are called by my name will humble themselves, and pray and seek my face, and turn from their wicked ways, then I will hear from heaven, and will forgive their sin and heal their land.

Psalm 122:6

Pray for the Peace of Jerusalem: May they prosper who love you.

Lesson Plan 17

The Book of Mark

Chapters 2 & 3

Objective: To obtain an understanding of the contribution to the overall gospel story of Jesus Christ the Creator of the Universe.

Objective Breakdown:

1. Introduction

2. Persistence Brings Healing and Forgiveness   Chapter 2:1-12

3. Levi (Matthew) is Called   Chapter 2:13-14

4. Jesus Dines with Levi and His Friends   Chapter 2:15-17

5. Cloth and Wine skin   Chapter 2:18-22

6. Sabbath Controversies   Chapter 2:23-28

7. Sabbath Healings   Chapter 3:1-6

8. Massive Crowds Follow Jesus   Chapter 3:7-12

9. Jesus Calls the Twelve   Chapter 3:13-19

10. Jesus's Family Tries to Slow Him down   Chapter 3:20-21

11. Scribes Call Jesus Satanic   Chapter 3:22-30

12. Who Are My Mother and Brothers   Chapter 3:31-35

Introduction: The Book of Mark is the shortest and simplest of the four Gospels It gives a crisp fast-moving look at the life of Christ. With a few comments, Mark lets the narrative speak for itself as it tells the story of the Servant who constantly ministers to others through preaching, healing, teaching, and ultimately His own death. Mark traces the steady building of hostility and opposition to Jesus as he resolutely moves toward the fulfillment of His earthly mission. Almost forty percent of this gospel is devoted to a detailed account of the last eight days of Jesus's life, climaxing in His resurrection. The Lord is vividly portrayed in this book in two parts: to serve (chapters 1-10) to sacrifice (chapters 11-16).

II Chronicles 7:14

If my people, which are called by my name, shall humble themselves, and pray, and seek my face, and turn from their wicked ways; then will I hear from heaven, and will forgive their sin, and will heal their land.

Psalm 122:6

Pray for the peace of Jerusalem; they will prosper that love thee.

Lesson Plan 18

The Book of Mark

Chapters 4 & 5

Objective: To obtain an understanding of the contribution to the overall gospel story of Jesus Christ the Creator of the Universe.

Objective Breakdown:

1. Introduction

2. Jesus Teaches by the Sea   Chapter 4:1-2

3. A Parable about Soils   Chapter 4:3-20

4. Warnings   Chapter 4:21-25

5. A Growing Seed   Chapter 4:26-29

6. A Mustard Seed   Chapter 4:30-32

7. The Use of Parables   Chapter 4:33-34

8. Jesus Stills the Storm   Chapter 4:35-41

9. A Demon Possessed Man finds Help   Chapter 5:1-20

10. Jairus Pleads for His Daughter   Chapter 5:21-24

11. A Desperate Woman Reaches out to Jesus   Chapter 5:25-34

12. Jesus Heals Jairus's Daughter   Chapter 5:35-43

Introduction: Jesus frequently taught using parables (Mark 4:2), short simple stories designed to communicate spiritual truths and principles. Sometimes these were extended tales with character and plot development; sometimes they were little more than figures of speech that illustrated truth through comparison or examples drawn from everyday life.

Jesus sometimes spoke in parables to reveal truth to His followers but to conceal it from those who had rejected Him (Matthew 13:10–17, Mark 4:10):

Matthew 13:10-17

1. And the disciples came, and said unto him, Why speakest thou unto them in parables?

2. He answered and said unto them, Because it is given unto you to know the mysteries of the kingdom of heaven, but to them it is not given.

3. For whosoever hath, to him shall be given, and he shall have more abundance: but whosoever hath not, from him shall be taken away even that he hath.

4. Therefore speak I to them in parables: because they seeing see not; and hearing they hear not, neither do they understand.

5. And in them is fulfilled the prophecy of Esaias, which saith, By hearing ye shall hear, and shall not understand; and seeing ye shall see, and shall not perceive:

6. For this people's heart is waxed gross, and their ears are dull of hearing, and their eyes they have closed; lest at any time they should see with their eyes, and hear with their ears, and should understand with their heart, and should be converted, and I should heal them.

7. But blessed are your eyes, for they see: and your ears, for they hear.

8. For verily I say unto you, That many prophets and righteous men have desired to see those things which ye see, and have not seen them; and to hear those things which ye hear, and have not heard them."

Mark 4:10–12

1. And when he was alone, they that were about him with the twelve asked of him the parable.

2. And he said unto them, Unto you it is given to know the mystery of the kingdom of God: but unto them that are without, all these things are done in parables:

3. That seeing they may see, and not perceive; and hearing they may hear, and not understand; lest at any time they should be converted, and their sins should be forgiven them." Thus He fulfilled the prophecy of Isaiah 6:9–10. Like a double-edged sword, His words cut two ways – enlightening those who sought the truth but blinding the disobedient.

II Chronicles 7:14

If my people, which are called by my name, shall humble themselves, and pray, and seek my face, and turn from their wicked ways; then will I hear from heaven, and will forgive their sin, and will heal their land.

Psalm 122:6

Pray for the peace of Jerusalem; they shall prosper who love thee.

Lesson Plan 19

The Book of Mark

Chapters 6 & 7

Objective: To obtain an understanding of the contribution to the overall gospel story of Jesus Christ the Creator of the Universe.

Objective Breakdown:

1. Introduction

2. Unbelief in Jesus's Own Country (Nazareth)   Chapter 6:1-6

3. The Twelve Are Sent Out   Chapter 6:7-13

4. Herod Hears and Fears   Chapter 6:14-20

5. The Murder of John the Baptist   Chapter 6:21-29

6. Jesus Feeds Five Thousand   Chapter 6:30-44

7. Jesus Walks on Water   Chapter 6:45-52

8. Many Healed in Gennesaret   Chapter 6:53-56

9. Jesus Answers the Pharisees   Chapter 7:1-23

10. Jesus Heals a Gentile Woman's Daughter   Chapter 7:24-30

11. A Deaf and Mute Man is Healed   Chapter 7:31-37

Introduction: Jesus and Ethnicity. Jesus's encounters with the Syro-Phoenician woman (Mark 7:24-30; Matthew 15:21-28) could raise some troubling and ethnic attitudes. His treatment of the woman seems to a contradiction of His image as the international Christ, the Savior of the whole world. Because of her persistent faith, Jesus praised her and healed her daughter (Mark 7:29; Matthew 15:28).

But what are we to make of His treatment of her? The woman came in utter sincerity and with great respect, yet Jesus rebuffed her with hard words. Why would He do that? Perhaps the words were intended less for the woman's ears than for His disciples'. Maybe it was to them, not the woman, that He said, "I was not sent except to the lost sheep of the house of Israel" (Matthew 15:24). They wanted Him to heal her and send her away, but He refused–by appealing to their own national pride and exclusivism.

In other words, Jesus may have turned this incident into a living parable to show His disciples how hardened they were in their attitude toward Gentiles. Tyre, the setting for this story, was only 50 miles from the Galilee region where most of the Twelve had grown up. But it was an entirely different culture, dominated by Greek influences and populated almost exclusively by Gentiles. Many of them had already come South to learn more about Jesus (Mark 3:8). Now Jesus was taking His followers North on a Crash course in cross-cultural awareness.

So, encountering the woman, it could be that Jesus treated her the way His disciples would have treated her. Perhaps He wanted to illustrate in a way they would never forget that despite the rejection, Gentiles hungered for God's grace and power. In the end, Jesus's high praise for the woman's faith and the healing of her daughter repudiated the notion that God was concerned only with Israel.

II Chronicles 7:14

If my people, which are called by my name, shall humble themselves, and pray, and seek my face, and turn from their wicked ways; then will I hear from heaven, and will forgive their sin, and will heal their land.

Psalm 122:6

Pray for the peace of Jerusalem; they shall prosper who love thee.

Lesson Plan 20

The Book of Mark

Chapters 8 & 9

Objective: To obtain an understanding of the contribution to the overall gospel story of Jesus Christ the Creator of the Universe.

Objective Breakdown:

1.	Jesus Feeds Four Thousand	Chapter 8:1-10
2.	The Pharisees Demand a Sign	Chapter 8:11-12
3.	Jesus Warns His Disciples	Chapter 8:13-21
4.	A Blind Man is Healed at Bethsaida	Chapter 8:22-26
5.	Peter Calls Jesus "the Christ"	Chapter 8:27-30
6.	Jesus Rebukes Peter	Chapter 8:31-33
7.	Discipleship is Costly	Chapter 8:34-38
8.	Jesus is Transfigured	Chapter 9:1-13
9.	A Young Demon-Possessed Man is Healed	Chapter 9:14-29
10.	Jesus Predicts His Death	Chapter 9:30-32
11.	A Discussion About Rank	Chapter 9:33-37
12.	Taking Sides	Chapter 9:38-50

Introduction: Peter's memorable declaration, "You are the Christ" (Mark 8:29) was made near Caesarea Philippi (Mark 8:27), a town named in honor of Caesar Augustus. In Old Testament times, the city was a center of the Canaanites' Baal worship. Later the Greeks substituted their god Pan for Baal, and eventually the Romans used it to develop worship of their emperors.

Significantly, Jesus took His followers outside of Palestine to a center of pagan, Gentile deities, where He asked them two vital questions:

- Who do men say that I am? (Mark 8:27)

- Who do you say that I am? (Mark 8:29)

The answer to the first question was easy enough. People believed that He was more or less a powerful religious leader such as John the Baptist, Elijah, or one of the Old Testament prophets. Even King Herod's counselors saw Him that way (Mark 6:14-16).

But Peter had finally settled in his own mind who Jesus was, so he immediately stepped forward to answer the second question: "You are the Christ, the Son of the living God" (Mark 8:29; Matthew 16:16). "And I say to you that you are Peter, and on this rock I will build My church" (Matthew 16:17-18). Some have understood "rock" to mean the bedrock of faith, like the faith Peter was demonstrating here. Others believe that Peter himself was the rock, the key figure on whom the church was to stand, and his successors have continued that foundational role. Jesus made a wordplay on Peter's name to indicate Himself (Jesus) as the rock on which His church is to be built.

II Chronicles 7:14

If my people, which are called by my name, shall humble themselves, and pray, and seek my face, and turn from their wicked ways; then will I hear from heaven, and will forgive their sin, and will heal their land.

Psalm 122:6

Pray for the peace of Jerusalem; they shall prosper who love thee.

Lesson Plan 21

The Book of Mark

Chapters 10, 11, & 12

Objective: To obtain an understanding of the contribution to the overall gospel story of Jesus Christ, the Creator of the Universe.

Objective Breakdown:

1. Jesus Teaches About Divorce   Chapter 10:1-12

2. Jesus Lets Children Come to Him   Chapter 10:13-16

3. A Rich Man Asks About Eternal Life   Chapter 10:17-22

4. Jesus Speaks About Riches   Chapter 10:23-27

5. Rewards for the Twelve   Chapter 10:28-31

6. Jesus Again Predicts His Death   Chapter 10:32-34

7. James & John's Request   Chapter 10:35-45

8. Blind Bartimaeus Sees   Chapter 10:46-52

9. The Triumphal Entry into Jerusalem   Chapter 11:1-11

10. Jesus Curses a Fig Tree   Chapter 11:12-14

11. Jesus Drives Merchants from the Temple   Chapter 11:15-19

12. Lessons from the Cursed Fig Tree   Chapter 11:20-26

13. Leaders Question Jesus's Authority   Chapter 11:27-33

14. A Parable About a Vineyard Owner   Chapter 12:1-12

15. A Test Regarding Taxes   Chapter 12:13-17

16. Jesus's Confounds the Sadducees   Chapter 12:18-27

Introduction: In the first century, Jewish men were allowed to divorce their wives for many different reasons (Mark 10:12). Depending on which interpretation of the Torah one followed, a man could even send his wife away if she burned a meal. By contrast, women were far more restricted in their grounds for divorce. One of them had to do with the husband's occupation. If he were a copper smelter, tanner, or dung collector, she could get a divorce, even if she knew before she married what his trade was, because she couldn't have known how awful the smell would be. (See Deuteronomy 24:1-4).

On the final trip to Jerusalem, something of a power struggle began to emerge among Jesus's disciples. James and John were the first to try to obtain positions of power in the coming kingdom (Mark 10:35-37). Jesus rebuked them in an interesting way. He compared them to the leaders of the Gentiles that they so despised (Mark 10:42), people like Pilate and Augustus and all their governors, tax collectors, soldiers, and centurions. The disciples detested those people as living only for themselves. Yet Jesus implied that this was the way His disciples were acting when they jockeyed for positions of power. The comparison must have challenged them to the core. Jesus was telling them, "You are no different than Gentiles!"

Why did Jesus destroy an innocent fig tree and then promise mountain-moving powers (Mark 11:12-14, 20-24)? The context of these events and statements is important. Jesus and His disciples were entering Jerusalem, where He was about to be killed (Mark 15). When He came upon the fig tree, He used it as an illustration and a warning of what ultimately awaits those who oppose the kingdom of God–like the Jewish leaders of that day. Rather than bearing fruit, the nation was misusing its privilege as God's people (Mark 11:12-18).

Cursing the fig tree was not a wanton act of environmental destruction, but a teaching method for Jesus's disciples. They would soon be very confused and frightened by events. Perhaps the memory of this graphic illustration would help.

As for moving mountains into the sea by prayer, Jesus was talking about the power of forgiveness. (Mark 11:25). He was not holding out false hopes of the free use of power to one's personal advantage. He was showing the significance of moving heaven and earth with another power–forgiving one's enemies.

II Chronicles 7:14

If my people, which are called by my name, shall humble themselves, and pray, and seek my face, and turn from their wicked ways; then will I hear from heaven, and will forgive their sin, and will heal their land.

Psalm 122:6

Pray for the peace of Jerusalem; they shall prosper who love thee.

Lesson Plan 22

The Book of Mark

Chapters 13 & 14

Objective: To obtain an understanding of the contribution to the overall gospel story of Jesus Christ, the Creator of the Universe.

Objective Breakdown:

1. Introduction

2. Questions from the Disciples   Chapter 13:1-4

3. The Tribulation   Chapter 13:5-23

4. The Second Coming   Chapter 13:24-27

5. The Parable of the Fig Tree   Chapter 13:28-31

6. Exhortation to Watch   Chapter 13:32-37

7. Leaders Plot to Do Away with Jesus   Chapter 14:1-2

8. A Woman Anoints Jesus with Costly Oil   Chapter 14:3-9

9. Judas Betrays Jesus   Chapter 14:10-11

10. The Upper Room   Chapter 14:12-31

11. Jesus Prays in the Garden of Gethsemane   Chapter 14:32-42

12. Judas Brings About Jesus's Arrest   Chapter 14:43-52

13. Jesus is Taken to the High Priest   Chapter 14:53-65

Introduction: Jesus knew that His disciples would be anxious about the time of His return. Even on the day of His ascension to Heaven, they asked Him about the timing of things to come (Acts 1:6). Jesus replied that God had not given them the timetable of His future works. In Mark 13:32, Jesus expresses this idea in a way that some found puzzling, because of the way He refers to Himself. Doesn't the Son know everything that the Father knows?

When Jesus was born into mankind, He set aside His Deity and made Himself of no reputation, taking the form of a servant and coming into this world as the likeness of a man emptied of His privileges.

On earth, Jesus did everything the Father told him to do even to the point of death (Philippians 2:7-8). In the Book of John 8:28-29, Jesus says He does nothing of Himself, but as the Father has taught Him. Also, in the Book of John, Chapter 5:30 Jesus said, "I can of myself do nothing. As I hear, I judge; and My judgment is righteous, because I do not seek my own will but the will of the Father who sent me."

Jesus is saying that the Father has not published His timing to human beings, to angels, or even to the Son in His capacity as Savior and Mediator. As the second Person of the Godhead, Jesus has always known the appointed time, but His knowledge of this is not intended for men or angels, and it is not accessible to them. The Father did not intend for Him to reveal this knowledge to His disciples.

A Parting Gift: What the disciples saw as waste (Mark14:4-9) the Lord saw as worship. The woman's gift of costly oil was worth a years' average wages, yet she poured it out, apparently sensing that her days with Jesus were drawing to a close.

This incident raises the issue of how one's material wealth enters into worship. While Jesus was still physically present and available to her, the woman did "what she could" (Mark 14:8). She took one of her most valuable possessions and gave it to Jesus in an unusual act of devotion. A waste? Not to the one she honored by it.

Today Jesus is not physically among us. Yet while we are alive, we control a certain measure of the world's resources. We might ask: What act of worship might we give while we have the opportunity? How might we honor the Lord materially?

There are no easy answers. But did Jesus give us a clue when He told His disciples that just as the woman had done Him "a good work," so they could do good to the poor at any time (Mark 14:6)?

II Chronicles 7:14

If my people, which are called by my name, shall humble themselves, and pray, and seek my face, and turn from their wicked ways; then will I hear from heaven, and will forgive their sin, and will heal their land.

Psalm 122:6

Pray for the peace of Jerusalem; they shall prosper who love thee.

Lesson Plan 23

The Book of Mark

Chapters 15 & 16

Objective: To obtain an understanding of the contribution to the overall gospel story of Jesus Christ, the Creator of the Universe.

Objective Breakdown:

1. Introduction

2. Jesus Is Brought Before Pilate   Chapter 15:1-20

3. The Crucifixion   Chapter 15:21-26

4. The King of the Jews   Chapter 15:27-41

5. Jesus Is Buried   Chapter 15:42-47

6. An Angel Announces the Resurrection   Chapter 16:1-8

7. Jesus Appears to Many Witnesses   Chapter 16:9-13

8. Final Instructions   Chapter 16:14-18

9. The Ascension and its Effect   Chapter 16:19-20

Introduction: A Burial Fit for a King. How much should you spend on a funeral? A fortune or only enough to pay for the barest essentials? The four gospel writers recorded that Jesus's body was treated as a rich man's corpse might be. Which is not surprising since rich people buried Him.

Joseph of Arimathea bought fine linen to wrap the body in before laying it in his own very expensive tomb (Mark 15:43-46; Matthew 27:60).

Nicodemus helped with the arrangements and brought 100 pounds of myrrh and aloes, costly substances used to perfume and wrap the body (John 19:39).

Women who had supported Jesus in His Ministry, including Mary Magdalene, Mary the mother of James, and Salome, prepared spices and fragrance oils to place on the body as soon as the Sabbath was over (Mark 16:1; Luke 23:56)

Those who took charge of Jesus's burial did so out of love, not guilt. And under the circumstances, they were not trying to make a prideful show of their wealth. Rather they honestly expressed their grief, devotion, respect, adoration, and desire to protect the Lord's body from His enemies. They did what they could according to their desires and financial resources, and in keeping with the laws, customs, and traditions of their day.

II Chronicles 7:14

If my people, who are called by my name, shall humble themselves, and pray, and seek my face, and turn from their wicked ways; then will I hear from heaven, and will forgive their sin, and will heal their land.

Psalm 122:6

Pray for the peace of Jerusalem; they shall prosper who love thee.

The Book of Luke

Scripture Focus Chapters 1 - 24

Objective: To gain the understanding that Luke presented. Luke emphasizes Jesus' ancestry, birth, and early life before moving carefully and chronically through His earthly ministry.

Objective Breakdown:

1. The Purpose and Method of Luke's Gospel	Chapter 1:1-4
2. Zacharias Ministers in the Temple	Chapter 1:5-10
3. An Angel Announces the Birth of John the Baptist	Chapter 1:11-17
4. Zacharias Is Unable to Speak	Chapter 1:18-25
5. Gabriel Announces Christ's Birth	Chapter 1:26-33
6. Mary Miraculously Conceives	Chapter 1:34-38
7. Mary Visits Elizabeth	Chapter 1:39-56
8. Elizabeth Gives Birth to John	Chapter 1:57-66
9. Zacharias Prophesies of John's Ministry	Chapter 1:67-80
10. Christ Is Born	Chapter 2:1-7
11. The Angels Announce Jesus to the Shepherds	Chapter 2:8-14
12. The Shepherds Visit Jesus	Chapter 2:15-20
13. Christ Is Circumcised	Chapter 2:21-24
14. Simeon's Prophecy	Chapter 2:25-35
15. Anna's Testimony	Chapter 2:36-38
16. Jesus Returns to Nazareth	Chapter 2:39-40
17. Jesus Celebrates the Passover	Chapter 2:41-50
18. Jesus Grows in Wisdom	Chapter 2:51-52

Lesson Plan 24

The Book of Luke

Chapter 1

Objective: To acquaint us with the detailed account of Luke's Gospel and how it portrays a message that compliments the other two synoptic gospels (Matthew and Mark).

Objective Breakdown:

1. Introduction

2. The Purpose and Method of Luke's Gospel   Chapter 1:1-4

3. Zacharias Ministers in the Temple   Chapter 1:5-10

4. An Angel Announces the Birth of John the Baptist   Chapter 1:11-17

5. Zacharias Is Unable to Speak   Chapter 1:18-25

6. Gabriel Announces Christ's Birth   Chapter 1:26-33

7. Mary Miraculously Conceives   Chapter 1:34-38

8. Mary Visits Elizabeth   Chapter 1:39-56

9. Elizabeth Gives Birth to John   Chapter 1:57-66

10. Zacharias Prophesies of John's Ministry   Chapter 1:67-80

Introduction: Luke a physician, writes with the compassion and warmth of a family doctor as he carefully documents with the perfect humanity of the Son of Man, Jesus Christ. He emphasizes Jesus's ancestry, birth, and early life before moving carefully and chronologically through His earthly ministry.

Luke may have been a Hellenistic Jew, but it more likely that he was a Gentile (this would make him the only Gentile contributor to the New Testament). In Colossians 4:10-14, Paul lists three fellow workers who are "of circumcision" (verses 10-11) and then includes Luke's name with two Gentiles (verses 12-14). Luke's obvious skill with Greek language and his phrase "their own language" in Acts 1:19 also imply that he was not Jewish.

Although Luke was not an eyewitness of the events in his gospel, he relied on the testimony of eyewitnesses and written sources (Luke 1:1-4). He carefully investigated and arranged his material and presented it to Theophilus ("Friend of God") the title "most excellent or most noble indicates that Theophilus was a man of high social standing.

Luke clearly stated his purpose in the prologue of his gospel: to give an orderly account that you may know the certainty of those things you instructed (Luke 1:3-4). Luke wanted to create an accurate and chronological account of the life of Jesus Christ. To strengthen the belief and faith of Gentile believers and stimulate saving faith among unbelievers.

II Chronicles 7:14

If my people, which are called by my name, shall humble themselves, and pray, and seek my face, and turn from their wicked ways; then will I hear from heaven, and will forgive their sin, and will heal their land.

Psalm 122:6

Pray for the peace of Jerusalem; they will prosper who love thee.

Lesson Plan 25

The Book of Luke

Chapter 2

Objective: To acquaint us with the detailed account of Luke's Gospel and how it portrays a message that compliments the other two synoptic gospels (Matthew and Mark).

Objective Breakdown:

Introduction: When Gabriel appeared to Mary of Nazareth (Luke:1-26-38), she was perhaps no more than 15 years old. His startling announcement—that she would soon bear the very Son of the Highest—meant the end of a normal life. Mary's name would forever be on the lips of gossipers and rumor mongers. Joseph, her husband-to-be could decide to end their betrothal through a public, humiliating divorce. Even if he "put her away secretly" (Matthew 1:19), she would still have to return in shame to her father's house or else survive on her own by whatever means she could.

Faced with these ruinous prospects that she had neither caused nor sought, Mary would have had plenty of reason to balk at Gabriel's message. Instead, she accepted her assignment: "let it be unto according to your word" (Luke 1:38). Her response was submissive obedience to the revealed will of God. It was her duty as one of God's people.

Luke was careful to record the family's obedience to Jewish law in having Jesus circumcised (Luke 2:21), regarding Mary's purification (Luke 2: 22), and the presentation of Jesus and a sacrifice at the Tempe (Luke:22-24). Assuming that such observance carried over into the home, Mary would probably provide Jesus's earliest instruction in the ways and values of the Hebrews.

II Chronicles 7:14

If my people, which are called by my name, shall humble themselves, and pray, and seek my face, and turn from their wicked ways; then will I hear from heaven, and will forgive their sin, and will heal their land.

Psalm 122:6

Pray for the peace of Jerusalem; they will prosper who love thee.

Lesson Plan 26

The Book of Luke

Chapter 3

Objective: To acquaint us with the detailed account of Luke's Gospel and how it portrays a message that compliments the other two synoptic gospels (Matthew and Mark).

Objective Breakdown:

1. Introduction

2. The Ministry of John the Baptist   Chapter 3:1-20

3. The Baptism of Christ   Chapter 3:21-22

4. The Genealogy of Christ Through Mary   Chapter 3:23-38

Introduction: Luke paints a picture of Jesus a model student. The rabbis He encountered at Jerusalem were preeminent experts in Judaism who researched, developed, and applied the body of Old Testament Law and rabbinical tradition to the issues of the day. Some were members of the council, the governing tribunal of Judea. These teachers were fond of waxing eloquent on religious and legal questions in the temple courtyard for the benefit of any who would listen (Matthew 6.5; 7:28-29; 23:1-7).

Nevertheless, Jesus made strategic use of these authorities during His visit to the big city for Passover. Now age 12, He was considered a man. So, He went to the temple to learn all He could about the Law of God. He proved to be an avid student listening carefully and asking questions about His "Father's Business" (Luke 2:49). Rather than embarrass His parents and offend His teachers by spouting off what He knew, He humbly subjected Himself to the discipline of education (Luke 2:51). His turn to teach would come later. For now, He accepted the role of learner.

It is a good example for all of us who must go through school and learn on the job. Like Jesus, we need to learn all we can from the best teachers we can find, showing ourselves to be teachable, with an attitude of humility.

II Chronicles 7:14

If my people, which are called by my name, shall humble themselves, and pray, and seek my face, and turn from their wicked ways; then will I hear from heaven, and will forgive their sin, and will heal their land.

Psalm 122:6

Pray for the peace of Jerusalem; they will prosper who love thee.

Lesson Plan 27

The Book of Luke

Chapter 4

Objective: To acquaint us with the detailed account of Luke's Gospel and how it portrays a message that compliments the other two synoptic gospels (Matthew and Mark).

Objective Breakdown:

1. Introduction

2. The Temptation of Christ   Chapter 4:1-13

3. Acceptance through Galilee   Chapter 4:14-15

4. Rejection at Nazareth   Chapter 4:16-30

5. Demons Are Cast Out   Chapter 4:31-37

6. Peter's Mother-in-law Is Healed   Chapter 4:38-39

7. Jesus Ministers Throughout Galilee   Chapter 4:40-44

Introduction: In addition to the substance of what was happening when Satan tempted Jesus, we see an environmental aspect in this passage as well. Jesus was tempted in three very different settings: (1) In a barren desert (Luke 4:1-4). In the ancient world, deserts were believed to be inhabited by spirits that engaged in never-ending warfare.

(2) On a mountain (Luke 4: 5-8). A mountain setting may seem an unlikely environment for temptation. But in the ancient world, many religious shrines were carved or carried into the mountains where they became sources of idolatry and superstition.

(3) In Jerusalem, a city (Luke 4: 9-13). Like us, Jesus was tempted to take command of a city. Any city—especially "the holy city" – can tempt a person with power. Power itself is normally neutral, but like fire, it has grave potential to destroy people when mishandled. One has only to review the political history of cities like New York, Chicago, Hong Kong, Portland, or Seattle to appreciate that grim reality.

Satan promised to give Jesus authority over all the kingdoms of the world. "The Father of Lies" spoke the truth when he declared, "this has been delivered to me, and I will give it to whomever I wish" (Luke 4:6). He neglected, of course, to mention who had delivered the world powers to him—God the Son Himself, who possessed authority over the entire created universe (Colossians 1:15-17).

II Chronicles 7:14

If my people, which are called by my name, shall humble themselves, and pray, and seek my face, and turn from their wicked ways; then will I hear from heaven, and will forgive their sin, and will heal their land.

Psalm 122:6

Pray for the peace of Jerusalem; they will prosper who love thee.

Lesson Plan 28

The Book of Luke

Chapter 5

Objective: To acquaint us with the detailed account of Luke's Gospel and how it portrays a message that compliments the other two synoptic gospels (Matthew and Mark).

Objective Breakdown:

1. Introduction

2. The First Disciples Are Called   Chapter 5:1-11

3. The Leper Is Cleansed   Chapter 5:12-15

4. The Paralytic Is Healed   Chapter 5:16-26

5. Matthew Is Called   Chapter 5:27-28

6. Jesus Eats with Sinners   Chapter 5:29-32

7. Jesus Teaches About Fasting   Chapter 5:33-35

8. Parable of the Cloth and the Wine Skins   Chapter 5:36-39

Introduction: Jesus launched His public ministry with a dramatic first sermon in a synagogue at Nazareth. Using Isaiah 61:1-2 as His text, He announced that He was the One anointed by the spirit to preach the gospel (Luke 4:18), the Good News.

Jesus also said that the acceptable year of the Lord had come (Luke 4:19), a reference to the Old Testament concept of the Jubilee Year (Leviticus 25:8-19). Every fifty years, the Israelites were to set their slaves free, cancel each other's debts, and restore lands to their original owners. Jesus intended to make a difference in the lives of people, not only spiritually, but also socially and economically as well.

Jesus, claim startled the hometown crowd for at least two reasons, First, He reminded His listeners of whom the Good News was for: the poor, the brokenhearted, the captives (or prisoners), the blind, and the oppressed. At first, the people welcomed these words (Luke

4:22). But soon they began to question His right to make such claims. "We know this fellow, don't we?" isn't He Joseph's boy? Isn't He one of us? Can He be the One to fulfill Isaiah's prophecy?" They doubted His credentials.

Jesus backed up His claim of being the Messiah by healing the sick (Luke 4:40). Later, His followers used similar miracles to verify their message. Not only did healing demonstrate Christ's divine power over disease and infirmity, but it also revealed God's heart of compassion. The Great Physician and the apostles treated people with disabilities or conditions from birth, diseases of a permanent or semi-permanent nature, spiritual and psychological conditions, sickness, and even death.

II Chronicles 7:14

If my people, which are called by my name, shall humble themselves, and pray, and seek my face, and turn from their wicked ways; then will I hear from heaven, and will forgive their sin, and will heal their land.

Psalm 122:6

Pray for the peace of Jerusalem; they will prosper who love thee.

Lesson Plan 29

The Book of Luke

Chapter 6

Objective: To acquaint us with the detailed account of Luke's Gospel and how it portrays a message that compliments the other two synoptic gospels (Matthew and Mark).

Objective Breakdown:

1. Introduction

2. Jesus Works on the Sabbath   Chapter 6:1-5

3. Jesus Heals on the Sabbath   Chapter 6:6-11

4. Selection of the Twelve Apostles   Chapter 6:12-19

5. The Beatitudes   Chapter 6:20-26

6. Rules of Kingdom Life   Chapter 6:27-38

7. Parable of the Blind Leading the Blind   Chapter 6:39-45

8. Parable of Two Foundations   Chapter 6:46-49

Introduction: Fishing on the Sea of Galilee was a big business. This now-famous body of water, eight miles wide and 13 miles long, lay beside a fertile plain renowned for its agriculture. In Jesus's day, nine cities crowded its shorelines, each with no less than 15,000 citizens, possibly making the region's total population greater than Jerusalem's.

The names of the Galilean towns reflect the importance of fishing to the life and economy of the area. For example, at Tarichaea, "the place of salt fish," workers packed fish for shipment to Jerusalem and export to Rome. Bethsaida—from which at least four fishermen left their nets to follow Jesus— (Matthew 4:18-22; John 14:40) means "fish town." Most of the town was employed in the fishing industry.

Shoals offshore were a fisherman's paradise in Jesus's day; hundreds of fishing boats trawled the lake. Galileans ate little meat besides fish. It came highly salted as there was no other way of preserving the "catch of the day." The fisherman's day did not end with the return to shore. Mending and washing nets, preserving fish, maintaining boats and supplies, training and supervising crews, and negotiating with merchants and others in the shipping industry made for long tiring hours.

The center of Jesus's Galilean ministry, two of Jesus's apostles—Simon Peter and Andrew—(Mark 1:29-31; Luke 4:38) are known to have come from the city of Capernaum. Capernaum was one of the most important, prosperous cities on the northwestern shore of the Sea of Galilee. It was an economic and political hub of the Galilean region of the first century A.D. It was the crossroads of international trade and commerce and was near the border between the tetrarchies of Philip and Herod Antipas. The region was blessed with fertile land and a mild climate. The area grew date palms, walnut trees, olives, figs. wheat, and wildflower, and even today grows bananas.

The city offered many options for employment: agriculture, trade, fishing, even tax collection, a lucrative but not well-respected enterprise (Matthew 9:9-13).

II Chronicles 7:14

If my people, which are called by my name, shall humble themselves, and pray, and seek my face, and turn from their wicked ways; then will I hear from heaven, and will forgive their sin, and will heal their land.

Psalm 122:6

Pray for the peace of Jerusalem; they will prosper who love thee.

Lesson Plan 30

The Book of Luke

Chapter 7

Objective: To acquaint us with the detailed account of Luke's Gospel and how it portrays a message that reaches out to people of every class and background

Objective Breakdown:

1. Introduction

2. A Centurion's Great Faith	Chapter 7:1-10
3. A Dead Man is Raised at Naim	Chapter 7:11-17
4. He Who is Least in the Kingdom	Chapter 7:18-35
5. A Sinner at Simon's Dinner	Chapter 7:36-50

Introduction: Luke recorded two miracles in chapter seven. A centurions' servant healed and a dead boy raised–as a basis for belief in authority (Chapter 7:22-23). After Jesus's sermon (Luke 6:17-49), which was given outside of town, He entered Capernaum, His adopted hometown, where He performed many of His messianic signs.

A centurion in the Roman army was a commander of a century, a group of 100 soldiers. This centurion in Capernaum, unlike most Roman soldiers, was well-liked and respected by the Jewish people in and around Capernaum, because he loved them, and had built them a synagogue (Luke 7:4-5).

The Centurion's servant was extremely sick and about to die (Luke 7:2). The centurion had faith that Jesus would heal the servant. Perhaps he sent Jewish elders to present his request because he doubted that Jesus would have heeded a Roman soldier's request.

Matthew Chapter 8:5-13 records the same event, but Matthew did not record the sending of messengers. He presented the account as if the centurion were present himself. Matthew was reflecting what the centurion meant when he noted that his messengers do his bidding as if he were there himself (Luke 7:8).

Luke 7:11-17: In addition, Luke recorded the raising of the widow's son from the dead so that the ensuing interchange between Jesus and John the Baptist's disciples (Luke 7:18-23) would have more force.

II Chronicles 7:14

If my people, which are called by my name, shall humble themselves, and pray, and seek my face, and turn from their wicked ways; then will I hear from heaven, and will forgive their sin, and will heal their land.

Psalm 122:6

Pray for the peace of Jerusalem; they shall prosper that love thee.

Lesson Plan 31

The Book of Luke

Chapter 8

Objective: To acquaint us with the detailed account of Luke's Gospel and how it portrays a message that reaches out to people of every class and background.

Objective Breakdown:

1. Introduction

2. Many Woman Provide for Jesus   Chapter 8:1-3

3. A Parable About a Sower   Chapter 8:4-8

4. The Purpose of Parables   Chapter 8:9-10

5. The Parable of the Sower Explained   Chapter 8:11-15

6. A Lamp on a Lamp Stand   Chapter 8:16-18

7. Jesus's Mother and Brothers Come to Him   Chapter 8:19-21

8. A Great Storm Obeys Jesus   Chapter 8:22-25

9. A Demon Possessed Man is Healed   Chapter 8:26-39

10. A Life is Restored and a Woman is Healed   Chapter 8:40-55

Introduction: Nearly every society and every city in biblical times had a large underclass–people scraping by on the margins of society. Tending to congregate in cities, the underclass indeed included the poor, the sick, the disabled, the lepers, the blind, the insane, the demon-possessed, widows, orphans, runaways, castaways, and refugees. Lacking resources to provide for even their basic needs, many turned to begging, stealing, menial labor, slavery, and prostitution. Few cultures made provision for these desperate, destitute wanderers, and so they remained largely powerless to change their condition.

The incident in Luke 7:36–50 contrasts a respectable Pharisee, Simon, against a disreputable woman. Luke describes her as a sinner (Luke 7:37), a general term describing both those who failed to keep the ritual law as well as those who flaunted moral laws. How she gained entrance to Simon's feast is unclear.

The religious leader was probably restricted from even talking to the woman. Extensive Jewish law had developed in the first century to ensure moral purity. Many men suspected women of being sexually aggressive and eager to trap unsuspecting men. So Jewish men in general and teachers of the Law in particular such as Simon and Jesus were to have as little to do with women as possible. Jesus knew what kind of life the woman lived, but He accepted anyway, violating taboos against speaking with her or allowing her to touch Him. In return, she gave to Jesus what Simon, the host should have given– a kiss of welcome, a washing of the feet, and oil for the skin. These comforts were not merely symbolic, but practical expressions of hospitality.

There are six women named Mary in the New Testament: (1) Mary the mother of Jesus (Luke 1–2); (2) Mary Magdalene whom Jesus cast out seven demons. This Mary (Magdalene) has been associated with the woman who washed Jesus's feet, but there is no scriptural basis for this; (3) Mary of Bethany, sister of Martha and Lazarus (Luke 10:38–42); (4) Mary, the mother of the disciple James and Jose (Matthew 27:55–61); (5) Mary the mother of John Mark (Acts 12:12); (6) Mary of Rome (Romans 16:6). All we know about this latter Mary is found in Paul's salutation: "Greet Mary, who labored much for us."

Anointing of Jesus: There are three separate anointings of Jesus in the New Testament.

(1) Luke 7:36-45, Jesus's feet were anointed at the Pharisee house by unnamed women; (2) John 12:1-8, Jesus is anointed (His feet) by Mary, sister of Lazarus (for Jesus's burial); (3) Mark 14:3, Jesus's head is anointed in Simon the leper's house in Bethany. Also described in Matthew 26:2-10.

II Chronicles 7:14

If my people, which are called by my name, shall humble themselves, and pray, and seek my face, and turn from their wicked ways; then will I hear from heaven, and will forgive their sin, and will heal their land.

Psalm 122:6

Pray for the peace of Jerusalem; they will prosper that love thee.

Lesson Plan 32

The Book of Luke

Chapter 9

Objective: To acquaint us with the detailed account of Luke's Gospel and how it portrays a message that reaches out to people of every class and background.

Objective Breakdown:

1. Introduction

2. Jesus Sends Out the Twelve   Chapter 9:1-6

3. Herod Seeks to See Jesus   Chapter 9:7-9

4. Jesus Feeds the Five Thousand   Chapter 9:10-17

5. Peter Recognizes Jesus as Christ   Chapter 9:18-20

6. Jesus Predicts His Death   Chapter 9:21-27

7. The Transfiguration   Chapter 9:28-36

8. A Man's Demon Possessed Son Is Healed   Chapter 9:37-42

9. Jesus Again Predicts His Death   Chapter 9:43-45

10. Teaching About Rank   Chapter 9:46-50

11. Samaritans Reject Jesus   Chapter 9:51-56

12. The Cost of Discipleship   Chapter 9:57-62

Introduction: Heading South from Galilee to Jerusalem (Luke 9:51), Jesus traveled with His disciples through Samaria (Luke 9:52). Prejudiced against the Samaritans (John 4:9), Jews commonly bypassed the region by journeying down the east bank of the Jordan River. But Jesus deliberately chose the more direct route, as if to seek out conflict rather than avoid it.

A confrontation erupted at the first village. The Samaritans did not want Jesus or His followers there, nor did the disciples want to be there. Neither group could see past the other's ethnic identity. But the disciples turned exceptionally ugly. Insulted by the villagers' rejection of their Lord, they were itching to call down fire from heaven–with the justification (according to most manuscripts), "just as Elijah did."

Their response shows how destructive centuries of hatred and bitterness can be. No wonder Jesus utterly rebuked this response. He realized that His followers were blinded by their presumption of religious and ethnic superiority. In rebuke, He reminded them of His mission: to save lives–not to destroy them.

We as Jesus's followers today need to consider this incident carefully. Who do we regard with condemnation rather than compassion? It is someone of another race or a different ideology? Our differences may arise from legitimate concerns. But, if we would just as soon see someone eliminated to reinforce our feelings of ethnic, racial, moral, theological, or spiritual superiority, then we need the rebuke of Jesus's words: "You do not know what manner of spirit you are of" (Luke 9:55).

II Chronicles 7:14

If my people, which are called by my name, shall humble themselves, and pray, and seek my face, and turn from their wicked ways; then will I hear from heaven, and will forgive their sin, and will heal their land.

Psalm 122:6

Pray for the peace of Jerusalem; they will prosper that love thee.

Lesson Plan 33

The Book of Luke

Chapters 10 & 11

Objective: To acquaint us with the detailed account of Luke's Gospel and how it portrays a message that reaches out to people of every class and background.

Objective Breakdown:

1. Introduction

2. Paul Sends Out Seventy Workers   Chapter 10:1-16

3. The Joy of Jesus   Chapter 10:17-24

4. The Parable of The Good Samaritan   Chapter 10:25-37

5. Jesus at Mary & Martha's House   Chapter 10:38-42

6. Instructions on Prayer   Chapter 11:1-13

7. Jesus is Called Satanic   Chapter 11:14-26

8. Obedience Is More Important than Family Ties   Chapter 11:27-28

9. Jesus Warns the Crowds   Chapter 11:29-36

10. Pharisees and Lawyers Are Rebuked   Chapter 11:37-54

Whatever Became of Demon Possession? For all the good they've contributed to the healing professions and pastoral care, some theories of psychology have done a great disservice by casting doubt on the objective reality of evil and the devil. That presents a problem for those who read the Bible's account of demon possession (for example, Luke 9:38–42) and believes that demonic powers can play a hand in physical illnesses.

Some schools of psychology reduce religious experience to nothing but unconscious drives projected onto the external world. Satan, they say, is no more than a personification of one's deepest, darkest emotions. Likewise, God is reduced to the embodiment of a fully authenticated self, parental ideals, social mores, or universal symbols of goodness.

Without question, a genuine encounter with God or with Satan may involve intense emotional and psychological experiences. But, that does not make either one any less real. The existence of Satan and demons is affirmed in scores of scriptural texts. (A demon is a fallen angel or spirit that has joined with Satan in his futile rebellion against God) At war with Jesus and His followers, these evil powers have played a major role in such events as the Fall, the Flood, and Jesus's crucifixion, and will figure in the tribulations that will someday wrack the earth and the final judgment.

The gospel records several dozen encounters between Jesus and the powers of evil. In many of those instances, demon possession had produced any number of physical maladies and manifestations, such as deafness (Mark 9:25); muteness (Matthew 12:22; Mark 9:17-25); bodily deformity (Luke 13:10-27); blindness (Matthew 12:22); and epileptic seizures (Luke 9:39).

Ailments like these did not automatically imply demon possession. In fact, distinctions were made between possession and physical illness unrelated to evil spirits (Matthew 4:24; 10:8; Mark 1:32; Luke 6:17-18).

By casting out demons and restoring people both physically and spiritually, Jesus showed that the kingdom of God was as real as, and more powerful than, the forces of Satan (Matthew 10:7-8; 12:28). Today the same work has been delegated to the church (Luke 10:17; Acts 16:18). Psychology is often helpful in the task, but it is no match for the kingdom of darkness. Only the "whole armor of God" can help believers prevail (Ephesians 6:10-18).

II Chronicles 7:14

If my people, which are called by my name, shall humble themselves, and pray, and seek my face, and turn from their wicked ways; then will I hear from heaven, and will forgive their sin, and will heal their land.

Psalm 122:6

Pray for the peace of Jerusalem; they will prosper that love thee.

Lesson Plan 34

The Book of Luke

Chapter 12

Objective: To acquaint us with the detailed account of Luke's Gospel and how it portrays a message that compliments the other two synoptic gospels (Matthew and Mark).

Objective Breakdown:

1. Introduction

2. Hypocritical Leaders Are Warned Against   Chapter 12:1-12

3. A Parable About a Rich Fool   Chapter 12:13-21

4. Priorities and Comforts of the Kingdom   Chapter 12:22-40

5. A Parable About a Faithful Manager   Chapter 12:41-53

6. The Signs of the Times   Chapter 12:54-59

Introduction: Every culture seems afraid of someone. The Hebrews feared the Romans because of their ruthless might of their occupation troops. Eventually, those fears were realized as Rome viciously destroyed Jerusalem in A. S. 70 (Luke 21-20). In recent years, the west feared destruction from Soviet nuclear missiles. Today, there is growing alarm over China, Iran, and drug-related gang violence in our cities.

But in Luke 12:4-7, we see that Jesus redefines fear by rearranging our view, so we look at things from God's perspective. He draws upon the Old Testament concept of the "fear of the Lord" (Proverb 1-7). This is not a fawning, cringing dread that keeps us wallowing in anxiety, but a respect for who God is—the One who holds the ultimate power.

When we have a balanced view of God, it puts our thinking in a proper framework. We view everybody and everything in relation to God's holiness, righteousness, and love. We can't ignore physical threats and violence, but we dare not ignore the One who holds sway over our eternal destiny.

How about you? Are you up on current affairs, yet unaware of God's global works and purposes? Are you ignorant of the signs of the times?

Signs of The Times

1. Knowledge Shall Increase

2. Moral Decline

3. Environmental Signs

4. Scientific Signs

5. Spiritual Signs

6. Economic Signs

7. Political Signs

8. Social Signs

9. Religious Signs

II Chronicles 7:14

If my people, which are called by my name, shall humble themselves, and pray, and seek my face, and turn from their wicked ways; then will I hear from heaven, and will forgive their sin, and will heal their land.

Psalm 122:6

Pray for the peace of Jerusalem; they will prosper that love thee.

Lesson Plan 35

The Book of Luke

Chapters 13 & 14

Objective: To acquaint us with the detailed account of Luke's Gospel and how it portrays a message that compliments the other two synoptic gospels (Matthew and Mark).

Objective Breakdown:

1. Introduction

2. The Need for Repentance   Chapter 13:1-9

3. A Crippled Woman Finds Help   Chapter 13:10-17

4. A Parable About a Mustard Seed   Chapter 13:18-19

5. A Parable About a Hidden Leaven   Chapter 13:20-21

6. The Exclusivity of the Kingdom   Chapter 13:22-30

7. Jesus Mourns over Jerusalem   Chapter 13:31-35

8. Jesus Heals on the Sabbath   Chapter 14:1-6

9. A Parable About Seating at a Dinner   Chapter 14:7-14

10. A Parable About a Slighted Invitation   Chapter 14:15-24

11. More About the Costs of Discipleship   Chapter 14:25-35

Introduction: Good Men Cry. Jesus cried out as He came upon Jerusalem, mourning the lost children of Israel (Luke 13:34). He was speaking of "children" in spiritual terms. But spiritual desolation is often reflected in outward ways. The fastest-growing category of street people today is the children of the homeless in our cities. What would Jesus cry upon seeing them? What is our own response? This was not the last time that Jesus would weep over Jerusalem (Luke 19:41).

Sorting out membership. Do you try to sort out who is saved and who is not? Do you find yourself making judgments about people's faith and its quality? One of Jesus's followers asked Him how many others were being saved (Luke 13:23). The Lord's response turned the questioner's attention away from others and toward his own quality of faith and the implications of that (Luke 13:26-27). And He warned that those who seem to be the least likely candidates for the kingdom will enter ahead of others (Luke 13:30).

The Sabbath-day controversy (Luke 14:1-6) shows tension between the letter of the law and its spirit. The Old Testament was clear about keeping the Sabbath holy by resting from work (Exodus 20:8-11). But Jesus was known for doing the "work" of healing on the Sabbath (Luke13:10-17). Was He breaking the Law or not? The lawyers and the Pharisees could not say (Luke 14:6). Jesus let them stew over the issue, but clearly He was convinced that He was acting well within the Law.

II Chronicles 7:14

If my people, which are called by my name, shall humble themselves, and pray, and seek my face, and turn from their wicked ways; then will I hear from heaven, and will forgive their sin, and will heal their land.

Psalm 122:6

Pray for the peace of Jerusalem; they will prosper that love thee.

Lesson Plan 36

The Book of Luke

Chapters 15 & 16

Objective: To acquaint us with the detailed account of Luke's Gospel and how it portrays a message that compliments the other two synoptic gospels (Matthew and Mark).

Objective Breakdown:

1. Introduction

2. A Parable About a Lost Sheep   Chapter 15:1-7

3. A Parable About a Lost Coin   Chapter 15:8-10

4. A Parable About a Lost Son   Chapter 15:11-32

5. A Parable About an Unjust Servant   Chapter 16:1-13

6. Jesus Denounces the Pharisees   Chapter 16:14-18

7. The Rich Man and Lazarus   Chapter 16:19-31

Introduction Confused Value: In Luke chapter 15, Jesus tells three parables, about a lost sheep (Luke 15:4-7), a lost coin (Luke 15:8-10), and a lost son (Luke15:11-32). Each story reflects God's concern for lost people, the tremendous value He places on every individual, and the great joy He feels "over one sinner who repents" (Luke 15:10).

In the first two stories, Jesus points out the natural value that humans place on their possessions. A shepherd loses one sheep out of a hundred (only one percent of his flock), yet he goes out and scours the countryside until he finds it and returns it to the fold.

Likewise, when a woman loses one coin out of ten (only 10 percent of her collection), yet she searches high and low until she finds it.

But in the third story, the loss is a worthless son–not unlike the tax collectors and sinners listening to Jesus (Luke 15:1). We can imagine that Jesus's critics, the Pharisees, found it easy to write off such unrighteous people. Surely, they were hopelessly lost in sin and shame.

But Jesus's parable shows that God views every sinner with compassion, not merely as a possession, but as a person–indeed, as a lost but loved son. He longs for each one to return to Him.

If you grew up in the church or have been a believer for many years, it is worth looking carefully at the prodigal son's older brother (Luke 15:25). He is one of the most intriguing characters in all of Jesus's parables. A case study in what can happen to people who have been around religion for a long time and who are not getting fed the Word of God but are surviving on tradition and ritual.

II Chronicles 7:14

If my people, which are called by my name, shall humble themselves, and pray, and seek my face, and turn from their wicked ways; then will I hear from heaven, and will forgive their sin, and will heal their land.

Psalm 122:6

Pray for the peace of Jerusalem; they will prosper that love thee.

Lesson Plan 37

The Book of Luke

Chapter 17

Objective: To acquaint us with the detailed account of Luke's Gospel and how it portrays a message that compliments the other two synoptic gospels (Matthew and Mark).

Objective Breakdown:

1. Introduction

2. Forgiveness   Chapter 17:1-4

3. About Faith & Faithfulness   Chapter 17:5-10

4. Ten Lepers Are Healed in Samaria   Chapter 17:11-19

5. The Kingdom of God & The Day of the Lord   Chapter 17:20-37

Doing Your Duty: Jesus's words in Luke 17:6-10 raise many puzzling questions. Did He intend that we should never thank people for doing what is expected of them? Should workers never expect praise for doing their jobs? Why are the workers "unprofitable" if they did their duty? Should we always do more than expected? Was this a sermon on initiative and creativity? Who was Jesus addressing bosses or employees?

He was responding to His disciples' request for more faith (Luke Chapter 17:5). That is a key to understanding this passage. Jesus had just challenged His followers to forgive others freely and repeatedly (Luke 17:1-4). But they replied, "Give us more faith," as if took great faith to forgive.

But it does not. Forgiveness is not some supernatural ability that only God can give. It is not the product of great faith, but rather of simple obedience. That is what the servant in the parable must do—obey his master. It doesn't take great trust on the part of a servant to get a meal prepared; it just takes doing it. In the same way, forgiveness is expected of Christ's followers. Since Christ has forgiven us, we are obliged to forgive others. There is no reward attached to it.

The disciples expected a payoff for following Jesus (Luke 9:46–48; Matthew 20:20–28). But Jesus wanted them to see that following Him was a reward in itself!

II Chronicles 7:14

If my people, which are called by my name, shall humble themselves, and pray, and seek my face, and turn from their wicked ways; then will I hear from heaven, and will forgive their sin, and will heal their land.

Psalm 122:6

Pray for the peace of Jerusalem; they will prosper that love thee.

Lesson Plan 38

The Book of Luke

Chapter 18

Objective: To acquaint us with the detailed account of Luke's Gospel and how it portrays a message that compliments the other two synoptic gospels (Matthew and Mark).

Objective Breakdown:

1. Introduction

Introduction: Jesus warned His followers to remember Lot's wife (Luke 17:31). By including this instruction in His Gospel, Luke made sure we would do that! Mrs. Lot was forced to leave her prosperous home in Sodom, taking only what she could carry. Angels had come to warn her and her husband of God's impending judgment on the city. They told her not to look back, not to linger, not to long for her old way of life. But she did, and as a result, judgment fell on her as well. She was turned into a pillar of salt (Genesis 19:15-26).

The example of Lot's wife reminds us that the return of Christ will be just as sudden as the judgment on Sodom–and the consequences of longing for the old ways of life just as severe.

Comparisonitis will kill you. How do you establish your identity? Are you always comparing yourself to others? If so, you suffer from "comparisonitis" a malady that can kill you! Consider the Pharisee in Jesus's parable (Luke 18:9-14). He started his prayer with a comparison: "God

I thank you that I am not like other men."

In contrast to the Pharisee, the second man in Jesus's parable looked to God in order to see himself properly. Doing so exposed his sin, but also brought about God's forgiveness and restoration. This man shows us the path of true identity. It is based on honesty about ourselves and becoming Christ-like.

Holding Wealth or Serving Others: Do you feel that your life would be better if only you were wealthy? Would your friends describe you as generous? These two issues were at stake in the encounter between Jesus and the rich young ruler (Luke 18:18–30). The young man was confident that he was wealthy for this life, but he was fearful of his destiny and came seeking security for his future.

Jesus made service to others the indication of fitness for eternal life. Real wealth involves following Jesus, living not to be served, but to serve others and to give one's life for others (Matthew 20:28). Where is your attention focused—on accumulation or servanthood?

II Chronicles 7:14

If my people, which are called by my name, shall humble themselves, and pray, and seek my face, and turn from their wicked ways; then will I hear from heaven, and will forgive their sin, and will heal their land.

Psalm 122:6

Pray for the peace of Jerusalem; they will prosper that love thee.

Lesson Plan 39

The Book of Luke

Chapter 19

Objective: To acquaint us with the detail account of Luke's Gospel and how it portrays a message that compliments the other two synoptic gospels (Matthew and Mark).

Objective Breakdown:

1. Introduction:

2. Zacchaeus Believes   Luke 19:1-10

3. A Parable About an Unfaithful Servant   Luke 19:11-27

4. Jesus' Triumphal Entry into Jerusalem   Luke 19:28-40

5. Jesus Weeps over Jerusalem   Luke 19:41-44

6. Jesus Purges the Temple   Luke 19:45-48

Introduction: Luke describes Zacchaeus as a tax collector (Luke 19:2). His first century reader would have understood that to mean that Zacchaeus was a cheating, corrupt lackey of the Roman government. In fact, he was the chief tax collector, which probably meant he was public enemy number one to the Jews in Jericho, even worse than the notorious bandits on the city's main highway.

But Jesus reached out to the curious Zacchaeus, prompting him to change his ways. In fact, Zacchaeus came with his own formula for making restitution on the tax fraud he had practiced: a 400% rebate to those he had knowingly cheated, plus half of his net worth to go to the poor (Luke 19:8). By paying restitution, he showed his new respect for the Old Testament law (Exodus 22:1). Giving away his possessions was not a requirement of the Law, but it revealed his change of heart.

Imagine a corrupt public official or shady corporate financier today following that formula. Imagine a pastor challenging a business person in his congregation to repay four times what was made on a crooked deal. It sounds simplistic, but Zacchaeus was truly repentant. He was like the tax collector, Jesus had recently mentioned in a parable who cried out, "God be merciful to me a sinner!" (Luke 18:13).

A Job to Do: The parable recorded in Luke 19:12-27 describes a case of absentee ownership and onsite management. Actually, it reflected the government in Palestine, in which Rome "owned" the region but left it in the hands of local governors, such as the infamous Herod (see Acts 12:1-2).

The reason that Jesus told this story is given in Luke 19:11: The kingdom of God would be delayed, and He wanted his followers to know some of the implications of that delay.

Chief among them is that we as believers have a job to do. We have been given resources to manage until the Lord returns (Luke 19:13). These include our skills, jobs, time, wealth, mental capacities, physical bodies, and so on. Eventually we will give a full accounting for how we have used these (Luke 19:15). Jesus delivered this lesson in the form of a parable and was obviously talking about more than the management of money. Yet it is clear, that He expects His followers to live out their everyday temporal lives with an eye toward His return. He will ask us what we have done with our lives and reward us accordingly.

II Chronicles 7:14

If my people, which are called by my name, shall humble themselves, and pray, and seek my face, and turn from their wicked ways; then will I hear from heaven, and will forgive their sin, and will heal their land.

Psalm 122:6

Pray for the peace of Jerusalem; they will prosper that love thee.

Lesson Plan 40

The Book of Luke

Chapter 20

Objective: To acquaint us with the detailed account of Luke's Gospel and how it portrays a message that compliments the other two synoptic gospels (Matthew and Mark).

Objective Breakdown:

1. Introduction

2. Jesus's Authority Us Questioned   Luke 20:1-8

3. A Parable About Wicked Vine Dressers   Luke 20:9-19

4. Jesus Is Tested About Tax Payment   Luke 20:20-26

5. Jesus Is Tested About Resurrection   Luke 20:27-38

6. The Scribes Are Confounded   Luke 20:39-47

Introduction: Are we owners or tenants? Are we owners of possessions like money, houses, land, cars, clothing, TV sets, and so forth? Our culture tells us that we are. Many messages tell us that significance is determined by how much we own and how much those possessions are worth.

But the parable of the vineyard owner (Luke 20:9-19) challenges that perspective. Jesus tells of tenants or workers who scheme to steal a vineyard from its owner rather than return its produce to him. They value the land, trees, and the fruit more than people—they beat the owner's representatives (Luke 20:10-12) and even more than life itself—they kill the owner's son (Luke:14-15).

In the same way, the community leaders among Jesus's listeners harbored the same desire to kill Him (Luke 20:19). Just as their forebears had rejected the prophets that God had sent, they would also reject God's own Son in a futile effort to keep the nation under their control.

When Highly competitive people are overshadowed or intimidated, they often resort to ugly tactics to try and regain their superiority. An unhealthy need for importance, success, and power can bring the worst in anyone.

As community leaders saw Jesus once again gaining popularity and influence, they schemed to ensnare Him (Luke 20:9-19). They even enlisted agents for their plot (Luke 20:20). There always seems to be a ready supply of help for evil designs.

But Jesus refused to stoop to their methods (Luke 20:23-25). As they tried to undo Him, He foiled their plans with grace and truth. Do you know how to respond to trickery or evil when it is intended for you?

II Chronicles 7:14

If my people which are called by my name, shall humble themselves, and pray, and seek my face, and turn from their wicked ways; then I will hear from heaven, and will forgive their sin, and will heal their land."

Psalm 122:6

Pray for the peace of Jerusalem; they will prosper that love thee.

Lesson Plan 41

The Book of Luke

Chapter 21

Objective: To acquaint us with the detailed account of Luke's Gospel and how it portrays a message that compliments the other two synoptic gospels (Matthew and Mark).

Objective Breakdown:

1. Introduction

2. A Poor Widow's Contribution   Luke 21:1-4

3. Jesus's Teaches About the End Times   Luke 21:5-38; Matthew 24:1-51;
                                               Mark 13:1-37

Introduction: Those living in Jerusalem at the time of Christ had reason to believe Jesus's predictions that the city would eventually fall to an invading army Luke 21:20; see also Luke 19:41-44). Political tensions were at a breaking point.

The Jews bitterly resented Rome's occupation to their homeland, which brought the corrupting influence of Greek culture, crushing taxes, and cruel government. Some, like the Zealots, fanned the flames of revolution by leading tax revolts and launching terrorist strikes against Roman troops and officials.

The final chapter in drama began in A.D. 66 when a skirmish broke out between Jews and Gentiles over the desecration of the synagogue at Caesarea. Unable to prevail politically, the Jews retaliated religiously by banning all sacrifices on behalf of foreigners, even for the emperor himself. Furthermore, access to the temple grounds at Jerusalem would be limited to Jewish countrymen.

Meanwhile, the Roman procurator ordered an enormous payment from the temple treasury. The Jews balked and assumed that the ruler would back down. Instead, he unleashed troops on the city who raped and pillaged at will, even resorting to flogging and crucifixion. The slaughter claimed about 3,600 Jewish lives, including children.

The city rioted. Arsonists torched official buildings along with the home of the high priest, long suspected of collusion with the empire. Elsewhere, Jews overran Roman fortresses and ambushed a legion of reinforcements, capturing arms for the revolt at Jerusalem. In the end, the Romans retreated, leaving the Holy City in the hands of the rebels.

Yet no matter how brave or committed the Jewish revolutionaries may have been, they were no match for the professional armies of Rome. Emperor Nero dispatched Vespasian, his top general, to the region. Beginning in Galilee and working his way south, he systematically cut off Jerusalem's lines of supply and escape. By A.D. 70 he was poised to launch the final assault on Jerusalem.

However, Vespasian returned to Rome to succeed Nero as emperor, leaving his son Titus to complete the campaign. Advancing on the city from the north, the east, and the west, his legions erected a siege wall and finally took the city, fulfilling Jesus's prophecy. Herod's temple was destroyed only three years after its completion (compare Luke 21:5-6), the priesthood and the council were abolished, and all Jews were expelled from the remains of the city. Jesus wept to think of such carnage (Matthew 23:37-39). Yet it was one of the prices His generation paid for rejecting Him as its Messiah.

Luke 21

1. As he looked up, Jesus saw the rich putting their gifts into the temple treasury.

2. He also saw a poor widow put in two very small copper coins.

3. "I tell you the truth," he said, "this poor widow has put in more than all the others.

4. All these people gave their gifts out of their wealth; but she out of her poverty put in all she had to live on."

Jesus Teaches About the End Times

5. Some of his disciples were remarking about how the temple was adorned with beautiful stones and with gifts dedicated to God. But Jesus said,

6. "As for what you see here, the time will come when not one stone will be left on another; every one of them will be thrown down."

7. "Teacher," they asked, "when will these things happen? And what will be the sign that they are about to take place?"

8. He replied: "Watch out that you are not deceived. For many will come in my name, claiming, 'I am he' and, 'The time is near.' Do not follow them.

9. When you hear of wars and revolutions, do not be frightened. These things must happen first, but the end will not come right away."

10. Then he said to them: "Nation will rise against nation, and kingdom against kingdom.

11. There will be great earthquakes, famines, and pestilence in various places, and fearful events and great signs from heaven.

12. "But before all this, they will lay hands on you and persecute you. They will deliver you to synagogues and prisons, and you will be brought before kings and governors, and all on account of my name.

13. This will result in your being witnesses to them.

14. But make up your mind not to worry beforehand how you will defend yourselves.

15. For I will give you words and wisdom that none of your adversaries will be able to resist or contradict.

16. You will be betrayed even by parents, brothers, relatives and friends, and they will put some of you to death.

17. All men will hate you because of me.

18. But not a hair of your head will perish.

19. By standing firm you will gain life.

20. "When you see Jerusalem being surrounded by armies, you will know that its desolation is near.

21. Then let those who are in Judea flee to the mountains, let those in the city get out, and let those in the country not enter the city.

22. For this is the time of punishment in fulfillment of all that has been written.

23. How dreadful it will be in those days for pregnant women and nursing mothers! There will be great distress in the land and wrath against these people.

24. They will fall by the sword and will be taken as prisoners to all the nations. Jerusalem will

be trampled on by the Gentiles until the times of the Gentiles are fulfilled.

25. There will be signs in the sun, moon, and stars. On the earth, nations will be in anguish and perplexity at the roaring and tossing of the sea.

26. Men will faint from terror, apprehensive of what is coming on the world, for the heavenly bodies will be shaken.

27. At that time they will see the Son of Man coming in a cloud with power and great glory.

28. When these things begin to take place, stand up and lift up your heads, because your redemption is drawing near.

29. He told them this parable: "Look at the fig tree and all the trees.

30. When they sprout leaves, you can see for yourselves and know that summer is near.

31. Even so, when you see these things happening, you know that the kingdom of God is near.

32. I tell you the truth, this generation will certainly not pass away until all these things have happened.

33. Heaven and earth will pass away, but my words will never pass away.

34. Be careful, or your hearts will be weighed down with dissipation, drunkenness and the anxieties of life, and that day will close on you unexpectedly like a trap.

35. For it will come upon all those who live on the face of the whole earth.

36. Be always on the watch, and pray that you may be able to escape all that is about to happen, and that you may be able to stand before the Son of Man."

37. Each day Jesus was teaching at the temple, and each evening he went out to spend the night on the hill called the Mount of Olives, and all the people came early in the morning to hear him at the temple.

Matthew 24

1. Jesus Predicts the Temple's Destruction

2. Jesus left the temple and was walking away when his disciples came up to him to call his attention to its buildings.

3. "Do you see all these things?" he asked. "I tell you the truth, not one stone here will be left

on another; every one will be thrown down."

4. As Jesus was sitting on the Mount of Olives, the disciples came to him privately. "Tell us," they said, "When will this happen, and what will be the sign of your coming and of the end of the age?"

5. Jesus answered: "Watch out that no one deceives you.

6. For many will come in my name, claiming, `I am the Christ, ' and will deceive many.

7. You will hear of wars and rumors of wars, but see to it that you are not alarmed. Such things must happen, but the end is still to come.

8. Nation will rise against nation, and kingdom against kingdom. There will be famines and earthquakes in various places.

9. All these are the beginning of birth pains."

Terrible Times to Come

1. "Then you will be handed over to be persecuted and put to death, and you will be hated by all nations because of me.

2. At that time many will turn away from the faith and will betray and hate each other, and many false prophets will appear and deceive many people.

3. Because of the increase of wickedness, the love of most will grow cold, but he who stands firm to the end will be saved.

4. And this gospel of the kingdom will be preached in the whole world as a testimony to all nations, and then the end will come.

5. "So when you see standing in the holy place `the abomination that causes desolation,' spoken of through the prophet Daniel--let the reader understand-- then let those who are in Judea flee to the mountains.

6. Let no one on the roof of his house go down to take anything out of the house.

7. Let no one in the field go back to get his cloak.

8. How dreadful it will be in those days for pregnant women and nursing mothers!

9. Pray that your flight will not take place in winter or on the Sabbath.

10. For then there will be great distress, unequaled from the beginning of the world until now--and never to be equaled again.

11. If those days had not been cut short, no one would survive, but for the sake of the elect those days will be shortened.

12. At that time if anyone says to you, `Look, here is the Christ!' or, `There he is!' do not believe it.

13. For false Christs and false prophets will appear and perform great signs and miracles to deceive even the elect--if that were possible.

14. See, I have told you ahead of time.

15. "So if anyone tells you, `There he is, out in the desert,' do not go out; or, `Here he is, in the inner rooms,' do not believe it.

16. For as lightning that comes from the east is visible even in the west, so will be the coming of the Son of Man.

17. Wherever there is a carcass, there the vultures will gather.

18. "Immediately after the distress of those days, the sun will be darkened, and the moon will not give its light; the stars will fall from the sky, and the heavenly bodies will be shaken.'

19. "At that time the sign of the Son of Man will appear in the sky, and all the nations of the earth will mourn. They will see the Son of Man coming on the clouds of the sky, with power and great glory.

20. And he will send his angels with a loud trumpet call, and they will gather his elect from the four winds, from one end of the heavens to the other.

21. "Now learn this lesson from the fig tree: As soon as its twigs get tender and its leaves come out, you know that summer is near.

22. Even so, when you see all these things, you know that it is near, right at the door.

23. I tell you the truth, this generation will certainly not pass away until all these things have happened.

24. Heaven and earth will pass away, but my words will never pass away."

Faithful and Foolish Living

1. "No one knows about that day or hour, not even the angels in heaven, nor the Son, but only the Father.

2. As it was in the days of Noah, so it will be at the coming of the Son of Man.

3. For in the days before the flood, people were eating and drinking, marrying and giving in marriage, up to the day Noah entered the ark; and they knew nothing about what would happen until the flood came and took them all away. That is how it will be at the coming of the Son of Man.

4. Two men will be in the field; one will be taken and the other left.

5. Two women will be grinding with a hand mill; one will be taken and the other left.

6. "Therefore keep watch, because you do not know on what day your Lord will come.

7. But understand this: If the owner of the house had known at what time of night the thief was coming, he would have kept watch and would not have let his house be broken into.

8. So you also must be ready, because the Son of Man will come at an hour when you do not expect him.

9. "Who then is the faithful and wise servant, whom the master has put in charge of the servants in his household to give them their food at the proper time?

10. It will be good for that servant whose master finds him doing so when he returns.

11. I tell you the truth, he will put him in charge of all his possessions.

12. But suppose that servant is wicked and says to himself, 'My master is staying away a long time,' and he then begins to beat his fellow servants and to eat and drink with drunkards.

13. The master of that servant will come on a day when he does not expect him and at an hour he is not aware of.

14. He will cut him to pieces and assign him a place with the hypocrites, where there will be weeping and gnashing of teeth.

Mark 13 Jesus Predicts the Temple's Destruction

1. As he was leaving the temple, one of his disciples said to him, "Look, Teacher! What

massive stones! What magnificent buildings!"

2. "Do you see all these great buildings?" replied Jesus. "Not one stone here will be left on another; everyone will be thrown down."

Signs of the End

1. As Jesus was sitting on the Mount of Olives opposite the temple, Peter, James, John and Andrew asked him privately,

2. "Tell us, when will these things happen? And what will be the sign that they are all about to be fulfilled?"

3. Jesus said to them: "Watch out that no one deceives you.

4. Many will come in my name, claiming, `I am he,' and will deceive many.

5. When you hear of wars and rumors of wars, do not be alarmed. Such things must happen, but the end is still to come.

6. Nation will rise against nation, and kingdom against kingdom. There will be earthquakes in various places, and famines. These are the beginning of birth pains.

7. "You must be on your guard. You will be handed over to the local councils and flogged in the synagogues. On account of me, you will stand before governors and kings as witnesses to them.

8. And the gospel must first be preached to all nations.

9. Whenever you are arrested and brought to trial, do not worry beforehand about what to say. Just say whatever is given you at the time, for it is not you speaking, but the Holy Spirit.

10. "Brother will betray brother to death, and a father his child. Children will rebel against their parents and have them put to death.

11. All men will hate you because of me, but he who stands firm to the end will be saved.

12. "When you see `the abomination that causes desolation' standing where it does not belong—let the reader understand—then let those who are in Judea flee to the mountains.

13. Let no one on the roof of his house go down or enter the house to take anything out.

14. Let no one in the field go back to get his cloak.

15. How dreadful it will be in those days for pregnant women and nursing mothers!

16. Pray that this will not take place in winter, because those will be days of distress unequaled from the beginning, when God created the world, until now--and never to be equaled again.

17. If the Lord had not cut short those days, no one would survive. But for the sake of the elect, whom he has chosen, he has shortened them.

18. At that time if anyone says to you, `Look, here is the Christ!' or, `Look, there he is!' do not believe it.

19. For false Christs and false prophets will appear and perform signs and miracles to deceive the elect--if that were possible.

20. So be on your guard; I have told you everything ahead of time.

21. "But in those days, following that distress, "`the sun will be darkened, and the moon will not give its light; the stars will fall from the sky, and the heavenly bodies will be shaken.'

22. "At that time men will see the Son of Man coming in clouds with great power and glory.

23. And he will send his angels and gather his elect from the four winds, from the ends of the earth to the ends of the heavens.

24. "Now learn this lesson from the fig tree: As soon as its twigs get tender and its leaves come out, you know that summer is near.

25. Even so, when you see these things happening, you know that it is near, right at the door.

26. I tell you the truth, this generation will certainly not pass away until all these things have happened.

27. Heaven and earth will pass away, but my words will never pass away.

28. "No one knows about that day or hour, not even the angels in heaven, nor the Son, but only the Father.

29. Be on guard! Be alert! You do not know when that time will come.

30. It's like a man going away: He leaves his house and puts his servants in charge, each with

his assigned task, and tells the one at the door to keep watch.

31. "Therefore keep watch because you do not know when the owner of the house will come back--whether in the evening, or at midnight, or when the rooster crows, or at dawn.

32. If he comes suddenly, do not let him find you sleeping.

33. What I say to you, I say to everyone: 'Watch!'"

II Chronicles 7:14

If my people which are called by my name, shall humble themselves, and pray, and seek my face, and turn from their wicked ways; then I will hear from heaven, and will forgive their sin, and will heal their land."

Psalm 122:6

Pray for the peace of Jerusalem; they will prosper that love thee.

Lesson Plan 42

The Book of Luke

Chapter 22

Objective: To acquaint us with the detailed account of Luke's Gospel and how it portrays a message that compliments the other two synoptic gospels (Matthew and Mark).

Objective Breakdown:

1. Introduction

2. Judas Conspires to Betray Jesus   Luke 22:1-6

3. Jesus and the Twelve Eat the Passover   Luke 22:7-38

4. Jesus Prays in Gethsemane   Luke 22:39-46

5. The Arrest of Jesus   Luke 22:47-53

6. Peter Denies Knowing the Lord   Luke 22:54-62

7. Jesus is Beaten   Luke 22:63-65

8. Jesus is Condemned by the Council   Luke 22:66-71

Introduction: The Passover and Feast of the Unleavened Bread (Luke 22:7) was the first of three great festivals of the Hebrews. The name Passover recalls the deliverance of Israel from slavery in Egypt (Exodus 12:1–13:6). God sent His angels to kill all the firstborn sons of the Egyptians in order to persuade Pharaoh to let His people go. Hebrew families were instructed to sacrifice a lamb and smear its blood on the doorpost of their houses as a signal to God that His angel should "pass over" them during judgment.

Passover was observed on the fourteenth day of the first month, Abib (March-April), with the service beginning in the evening (Leviticus 23:6). It was on the evening of this day that Israel left Egypt in haste. Unleavened bread was used in the celebration as a reminder that the people had no time to leaven their bread before they ate their final meal as slaves in Egypt.

In New Testament times, Passover became a pilgrim festival. Large numbers gathered in Jerusalem to observe the annual celebration. Thus, an unusually large crowd was on hand to take part in the events surrounding Jesus's entry into the city (Luke 19:37-39) and His arrest, trial, and crucifixion (Luke 23:18, 27, 35,48). Many stayed until the Feast of Pentecost, when they heard Peter's persuasive sermon (Acts 2:1-41).

Like the blood of the lambs which saved the Hebrews from destruction in Egypt, the blood of Jesus, the ultimate Passover Lamb, saves us from the power of sin and death.

II Chronicles 7:14

If my people, which are called by my name, shall humble themselves, and pray, and seek my face, and turn from their wicked ways; then will I hear from heaven, and will forgive their sin, and will heal their land.

Psalm 122:6

Pray for the peace of Jerusalem; they will prosper that love thee.

Lesson Plan 43

The Book of Luke

Chapter 23

Objective: To acquaint us with the detailed account of Luke's Gospel and how it portrays a message that compliments the other two synoptic gospels (Matthew and Mark).

Objective Breakdown:

1. Introduction

2. Jesus Is Brought to Pilate & Herod   Luke 23:1-12

3. Pilate sentences Jesus to Death   Luke 23:13-25

4. The Crucifixion   Luke 23: 26-49

5. Friends Bury Jesus in a Borrowed Tomb   Luke 23:50-56

Introduction: The Romans used one the most painful methods of torture ever devised to put Jesus to death (Luke 23:33). Crucifixion was used by many nations of the ancient world, including Assyria, Media, and Persia. The idea may have originated from the practice of hanging up the bodies of executed persons on stakes for public display. This discouraged civil disobedience and mocked defeated military foes (Genesis 40:19; 1 Samuel 31:8–13).

Crucifixion on a stake or cross was practiced by the Greeks, notably Alexander the Great, who hung 2000 people on crosses when the city of Tyre was destroyed. During the period between Greek and Roman control of Palestine, the Jewish ruler Alexander Jannaeus crucified 800 Pharisees who opposed him. Such executions were condemned as detestable and abnormal even in that day as well as by the latest Jewish historian Josephus.

From the early days of the Roman Republic, death on the cross was used for rebellious slaves and bandits, although Roman citizens were rarely subjected to it. To the Jewish people, crucifixion represented the most disgusting form of death: "He who is hanged is accursed of God" (Deuteronomy 21:23). Yet the Jewish council sought and obtained Roman authorization to have Jesus crucified (Mark 15:13–15). Medical experts who have studied crucifixion report that it was designed to maximize the victim's pain.

He did it for you! To what extent have you ever sacrificed for someone else? Sacrifice can mean giving up something you want so someone else can have it. But an even greater sacrifice involves taking on something that you do not want so that someone else will not have to bear it.

That is what Jesus did when He was "wounded for our transgressions" and "bruised for our iniquities" (Isaiah 53:5). He took on Himself the "chastisements" or punishment, that we deserved for our sins so that we would not have to bear it. He did not want us to suffer, but He submitted to suffering because of His great love.

Hundreds of years before Jesus came, Isaiah described in remarkable detail how the Messiah would suffer on behalf of others.

II Chronicles 7:14

If my people, which are called by my name, shall humble themselves, and pray, and seek my face, and turn from their wicked ways; then will I hear from heaven, and will forgive their sin, and will heal their land.

Psalm 122:6

Pray for the peace of Jerusalem; they will prosper that love thee.

Lesson Plan 44

The Book of Luke

Chapter 24

Objective: To acquaint us with the detailed account of Luke's Gospel and how it portrays a message that compliments the other two synoptic gospels (Matthew and Mark).

Objective Breakdown:

1. Introduction

2. Resurrection   Chapter 24:1-12

3. Jesus Appears on the Road to Emmaus   Chapter 24:13-35

4. Jesus Appears to His Apostles   Chapter 24:36-43

5. Final Instructions   Chapter 24:44-49

6. The Ascension   Chapter 24:50-53

Introduction: Would you be able to explain to someone where the scriptures speak about Jesus, "beginning at Moses and all the prophets" (Luke 24:27)? That is what the Lord did with two of His disciples on the road to Emmaus. He explained how the Old Testament—the only inspired scriptures in existence at that time—foretold His coming as the Messiah.

An entire list of the Old Testament texts to which Jesus probably referred would be too lengthy to list here. But one book that He undoubtedly spent a lot of time on was Isaiah. No other Old Testament prophet made as many references to the coming Messiah as did Isaiah. Notice on the attached graphs Isaiah's emphasis on the Messiah as a suffering servant, a role Jesus fulfilled.

What would you like to be your last words to your closest family and friends? Whatever they might be, imagine the impact if you returned from the grave to speak them!

Jesus did. He came back from the dead to give His followers a final word. As a result, His instructions carry unusual weight and have come to be known as the "Great Commission," because Jesus charged His followers with a mighty task. All four writers of His life provide a version of His mandate (Matthew 28:18-20; Mark 16:15-16; Luke 24:45-49; John 20:21-23; Acts 1:6–8). Jesus gives the privilege and responsibility of telling the good news about His provision of forgiveness and eternal life to all who will listen.

Do your friends know what Christ has done for them? Do they know what He has done and is doing in your life? Can you afford to deprive them of having good news so they can consider it for themselves?

II Chronicles 7:14

If my people, which are called by my name, shall humble themselves, and pray, and seek my face, and turn from their wicked ways; then will I hear from heaven, and will forgive their sin, and will heal their land.

Psalm 122:6

Pray for the peace of Jerusalem; they will prosper that love thee.

The Book of John

Scripture Focus Chapters 1 - 21

Objective: To gain an understanding of the Book of John, which is the most powerful case in all the Bible for the Deity of the Incarnate Son of God -- the man called Jesus, also called Christ, Son of the living God.

Objective Breakdown:

1. The Deity of Christ	Chapter 1:1-2
2. The Preincarnate Work of Christ	Chapter 1:3-5
3. The Forerunner of Christ	Chapter 1:6-8
4. The Rejection of Christ	Chapter 1:9-11
5. The Acceptance of Christ	Chapter 1:12-13
6. The Incarnation of Christ	Chapter 1:14-18
7. John's Witness to the Priests and Levites	Chapter 1:19-28
8. John's Witness as Christ's Baptism	Chapter 1:29-34
9. Andrew and Peter Follow Christ	Chapter 1:35-42
10. Phillip and Nathaniel Follow Christ	Chapter 1:43-51
11. Christ Changes Water to Wine	Chapter 2:1-10
12. The Disciples Believe	Chapter 2:11-12
13. Christ Cleanses the Temple	Chapter 2:13-25
14. Christ Witnesses to Nicodemus	Chapter 3:1-21
15. John the Baptist Witnesses Concerning Christ	Chapter 3:22-36
16. Christ Witnesses to the Woman at the Well	Chapter 4:1-26
17. Christ Witnesses to the Disciples	Chapter 4:27-38

Lesson Plan 45

The Book of John

Chapter 1

Objective: To obtain a thorough understanding of the Book of John, the Deity of Jesus, and the author John as he walked with the Creator of the Universe.

Objective Breakdown:

1. Introduction

2. The Word   Chapter 1:1-18

3. The Testimony of John the Baptist   Chapter 1:19-34

4. Jesus Recruits His Followers   Chapter 1:35-51

Introduction: John and his brother James came from the prosperous family of Zebedee, a successful fisherman who owned his own boat and had hired servants (Mark 1:19–20). Together with Simon and Andrew, with whom they were in partnership (Luke 5:10), the brothers became loyal followers of Jesus. Their mother Salome also joined the fellowship and supported Jesus's ministry (Mark 15:40-41; Luke 8:3).

Modern Christians regard John as the "apostle of love" because of the frequent appearance of that theme in his writings and because the Gospel of John refers to him as the disciple whom Jesus loved (John 13:23). But he certainly didn't start as a model of charity.

John and his brother were headstrong and opinionated, and Jesus dubbed them Sons of Thunder (Mark 3:17). On one occasion they created a storm of protest and indignation from the other disciples by asking if they could sit on Jesus's right and left hands in glory (Mark 10:35–45). On another occasion they suggested calling down fire from heaven on an unreceptive Samaritan village; Jesus rebuked them (Luke 9:51-56).

Somehow John's exposure to Jesus worked an amazing change in his life. After the Lord's departure, he became a leader of the Christian movement, as might be expected. But now his perspective was different. When the word came that the gospel had spread to the Samaritans,

John was sent with Peter to investigate. Whereas before he had wanted to destroy Samaritans, now he helped bring them the Holy Spirit (Acts 8:14–25). The son of thunder had become a son of love.

II Chronicles 7:14

If my people who are called by my name will humble themselves and pray, and seek my face, and turn from their wicked ways, then I will hear from heaven and will forgive their sin and heal their land.

Psalm 122:6

Pray for the peace of Jerusalem; they shall prosper who love thee.

Lesson Plan 46

The Book of John

Chapters 2 & 3

Objective: To obtain a thorough understanding of the Book of John, the Deity of Jesus, and the author John as he walked with the Creator of the universe.

Objective Breakdown:

1. Introduction

2. A Marriage Feast at Cana   Chapter 2:1-12

3. Merchants Are Evicted from The Temple   Chapter 2:13-25

4. Nicodemus Visits Jesus by Night   Chapter 3:1-21

5. John the Baptist Teaches About Jesus   Chapter 3:22–36

Introduction: In the first four chapters of the Book of John, the Son of God (John 1:19 – 4:54) is under careful consideration and scrutiny by Israel. He is introduced by John the Baptist who directs his disciples to Christ. Shortly the author begins listing the seven signs, which continue through to the 11th chapter. John carefully selects seven miracles out of the many that Christ accomplished (John 21:25) in order to build a concise case for His deity. They are called signs because they symbolize the life-changing results of belief in Jesus.

The signs are:

1. Water into Wine: the ritual of the law is replaced by the reality of grace   (John 2:1-11);

2. Healing the nobleman's son: the gospel brings spiritual restoration   (John 4:46–54);

3. Healing the paralytic: weakness is replaced by strength   (John 5:1–16);

4. Feeding the multitude: Christ satisfies spiritual hunger   (John 6:1–13);

5. Walking on water: The Lord transforms fear to faith   (John 6:16–21);

6. Sight to the man born blind: Jesus overcomes darkness and brings in light (John 9:1–7);

7. Raising of Lazarus: the gospel brings people from death to life (John 11:1–44).

The above signs combine to show that Jesus is indeed the Son of God.

And truly Jesus did many other signs in the presence of His disciples, which are not written in this book, but these listed above are written that you may believe that Jesus is the Christ, the Son of God, and believe you may have life in His name (John 20:30-31).

Cana was about 4 miles northeast of Nazareth. Nathaniel was of Cana (21:2). He did not have a very high opinion of his neighbor town Nazareth (1:46). The marriage took place in the home of some friend or relative of either Jesus or Nathaniel. They ran out of wine, and the mother of Jesus said to Him, "They have no wine." (John 2:3). Jesus said to her, "Woman, what does your concern have to do with Me? My hour has not come."

"Woman" (John 2:4) was a title of respect in the usage of that day. Jesus used it again on the cross, at a time when there could have been no possible savor of disrespect. The point of this remark seems to be: "Suppose the wine is gone; what have I to do with it? It is not my affair. My time to work miracles has not yet come."

Brief Sojourn in Capernaum.   (Chapter 2:12)

This was sort of a family visit, including his mother and brothers, probably to the home of John or Peter to lay plans for his future work. About a year later, Capernaum became his main residence. He did no more miracles in Galilee till after his return from the Judean Ministry (4:54).

The Early Judean Ministry.   (Chapter 2:13 to 4:3)

This is told only in John's gospel. It lasted 8 months, beginning at the Passover time (2:13),

April, and ending "four months" before harvest (4:3, 35), December. It includes Cleansing of the Temple, Visit of Nicodemus, and Ministry by the Jordan.

Jesus Cleanses the Temple   (Chapter 2:13-25)

There were two cleansings, three years apart: this one at the beginning of His public ministry (note the word "after" 3:22), the other at the close during His last week (Matthew 21:12-16; Mark11:15-18; Luke 19:45-46). In this, He drove out the cattle; in the other, He drove out the traders. In this, He called the Temple "a house of merchandise;" in the other, "a den of robbers."

II Chronicles 7:14

If my people, which are called by my name, shall humble themselves, and pray, and seek my face, and turn from their wicked ways; then will I hear from heaven, and will forgive their sin, and will heal their land.

Psalm 122:6

Pray for the peace of Jerusalem; they will prosper that love thee.

Lesson Plan 47

The Book of John

Chapters 4 & 5

Objective: To obtain a thorough understanding of the Book of John, the Deity of Jesus, and the author John as he walked with the Creator of the universe.

Objective Breakdown:

1. Introduction

2. Jesus Encounters a Samaritan Woman   Chapter 4:1-42

3. Jesus Heals the Nobleman's Son   Chapter 4:43-54

4. Jesus Heals a Paralyzed Man   Chapter 5:1-15

5. Jesus Responds to His Critics   Chapter 5:16-47

Introduction: Samaria was the central province of Palestine under the Romans. Its key city, also called Samaria, had been the capital of the Northern Kingdom of Israel before it fell to Assyria (722 B.C.). It was noted for rich, fertile farmlands that produced valuable grain crops, olives, and grapes. Served by five major roads, which encouraged trade with Phoenicia, Syria, and Egypt. Historically it was a prime target of invaders due to its reputation of prosperity.

The disciples marveled that their rabbi was speaking to a woman (John 4:27). In their day it was considered disreputable and beneath the dignity for a rabbi to speak to a woman in public. But Jesus chose a more inclusive posture than His religious peers.

The Nobleman's Son: The key to understanding the significance of Jesus's second miracle (John 4:46-54) is geography. The nobleman and his dying son lived in Capernaum, the main city of the Galilee region (see Luke 4:31). But Jesus was 20 miles away at Cana (where significantly, His first sign miracle had taken place: John 2:1–12). That means the nobleman walked 40 miles round trip–a two-day trek by foot–to implore Jesus to heal his son. But Jesus merely spoke a word (John 4:50), producing results 20 miles away, in a world that knew nothing about phones, faxes, or modems. We can see how the incident produced faith (John

4:53). Jesus was the master of distance.

Sychar was a Samaritan city mentioned only once in the Bible (John 4:5). Its exact location is unknown, but it could be the same as ancient Askar, one mile north of Jacob's well, or possibly Shechem, a city of great historical significance (Genesis 33:18). Today some 300 Samaritans' descendants live in Nablus, the site of ancient Shechem.

Building the Temple: During Jesus's time, the temple at Jerusalem was undergoing extensive reconstruction and renovation. Desiring favor among the Jews, King Herod pledged to build a magnificent temple that would perhaps recall some of the glory of Solomon's temple (1Kings 6:1). Work began in 19 B.C. and was carried on until A.D. 64. At first, the priests opposed Herod, suspicious that this real intent was to either do away with the temple altogether or erect something profane in its place. But Herod proved he was serious, hiring 10,000 labors and ordering 1000 wagons for hauling cream-colored stone. When finished the structure shone so brightly in the Mediterranean sun that it was difficult to look at directly. (Source: Word of Life Bible NKJV pg. 1864)

II Chronicles 7:14

If my people who are called by my name will humble themselves and pray, and seek my face, and turn from their wicked ways, then I will hear from heaven and will forgive their sin and heal their land.

Psalm 122:6

Pray for the peace of Jerusalem; they shall prosper who love thee.

Lesson Plan 48

The Book of John

Chapter 6

Objective: To obtain a thorough understanding of the Book of John, the Deity of Jesus, and the author John, as he walked with the Creator of the Universe.

Objective Breakdown:

1. Introduction

2. Jesus Feeds the Five Thousand   Chapter 6:1-14

3. Jesus Walks on Water   Chapter 6:15-21

4. I Am the Bread of Life   Chapter 6:22-40

5. Jesus's Listeners Are Confounded   Chapter 6:41-59

6. Many Followers Abandon Jesus   Chapter 6:60-67

7. Peter Declares That Jesus Is the Christ   Chapter 6:68-71

Introduction: John writes that the crowd followed Jesus did so in response to His miracles (John 6:2), a link to the healing of the lame man in (John 5:1-17). This leads to a fourth sign (miracle), the feeding of the 5,000.

What Jesus did was remarkable in every way. Consider, for example, that even today very few facilities in the United States can accommodate 5,000 people for a sit-down meal. Yet Jesus miraculously provided or at least that many—with leftovers! John mentions that they filled 12 baskets—perhaps one for each disciple, or perhaps one for each of the twelve tribes of Israel. The overall result of this sign was faith: Jesus must be the Messiah, the crowd concluded.

Yet, doubt and rejection were soon to follow. Detractors pointed out that Jesus's lunch m ay have been impressive, but it was only one meal. By contrast, Moses had fed Israel in the wilderness for 40 years (John 6:30-31). Incredibly, they missed the point of the sign. Jesus was not merely a deliveryman, He was the "Bread of Life itself" (John 6:32-58).

The fifth sign (miracle) that John included in his Gospel was a private affair for the disciples alone (John 6:15-21). What happened on the troubled Sea of Galilee revealed Jesus as master of the elements. John makes no explanatory comment on this incident, but its impact on the disciples is evident in Peter's words: "We have come to believe and know that you are the Christ, the Son of the living God" (John 6:69).

Do you stagger under a heavy load of expectation that we alone (or that we primarily) are responsible for bringing our friends and coworkers to faith? Do you feel guilty because you can't get them converted? If so, you may be surprised to discover that not even Jesus felt that kind of load for the lost!

While explaining how people enter the kingdom, Jesus declared that it is God the Father who draws them (John 6:44). That means that people's response to the Gospel does not primarily depend on you. Jesus taught elsewhere that: "All that the Father gives Me will come to Me: (John 6:37). And, "No one can come to Me unless it has been granted to him by My Father (John 6:65).

The responsibility for conversion ultimately belongs to the Father. Then is there anything we can do as Christ's followers to motivate others toward the Savior? Yes, we can give evidence of how God works in our lives as we grow. We can offer clear, truthful information about the Gospel as we have the opportunity. We can invite and even urge others to believe.

But the ultimate responsibility for salvation is God's, not ours. So live the faith, talk about it, and offer the "Born Again Procedure" to others. But let the dynamics of conversion be from God alone.

Bread of Life: When Jesus called Himself the "bread of life" (John 6:35; also John 6:32-33, 41, 48), He was using an image more than a staple of the diet; He was drawing on a rich symbol of Jewish life.

Bread played an important role in Israel's worship. During the celebration of Pentecost, two loaves of leavened bread were offered as sacrifices (Leviticus 23:17). In the tabernacle, and later in the temple, the Levites placed twelve loaves of unleavened bread, or bread without yeast, before the Lord each week to symbolize God's presence with the twelve tribes of Israel

(Exodus 25:30).

Throughout the Exodus, God miraculously sustained His People by sending manna from Heaven each morning (Exodus 16). The bread-like manna was a "small round substance as fine as frost" (Exodus 16:14). It looked "like coriander seed" and tasted like "wafers made with honey" (Exodus 16:31) or pastry prepared with oil (Numbers 11:8).

It was the manna that Jesus was recalling when He called Himself "the true bread from Heaven" (John 6:32), "the bread that came down from Heaven" (John 6:41), and the "bread of life"

(John 6:48-51, 58). Symbolically, Jesus is the heavenly manna, the spiritual or supernatural food given by the Father to those who ask, seek, and knock (John 6:45; Matthew 7:7-8). He was indicating that He was God's provision for the people's deepest spiritual needs.

II Chronicles 7:14

If my people, which are called by my name, shall humble themselves, and pray, and seek my face, and turn from their wicked ways; then will I hear from heaven, and will forgive their sin, and will heal their land.

Psalm 122:6

Pray for the peace of Jerusalem; they will prosper that love thee.

Lesson Plan 49

The Book of John

Chapter 7

Objective: To obtain a thorough understanding of the Book of John, the Deity of Jesus, and some insight on the Holy Spirit and the inspired author John as he walked with the "Creator of the Universe."

Objective Breakdown:

1. Introduction

2. Jesus's Brothers Doubt Him   Chapter 7:1-9

3. Jesus Attends the Feast of Tabernacles   Chapter 7:10-36

4. Jesus Provides Living Water   Chapter 7:37-53

Introduction: Does anyone believe you when you witness? If you ever feel dis- courage because family, friends, or co-workers refuse to accept the gospel, you may take some comfort that even Jesus's own brothers did not believe that He was the Christ (John 7:5). Even though they had seen His miracles and listened to His teaching, they still balked at the idea of placing faith in Jesus as the Son of God.

This is important to notice. The person who hears the gospel bears the responsibility for responding in faith, while the person who shares the gospel bears the responsibility for communicating with faithfulness. If we as believers ever start holding ourselves responsible for whether unbelievers accept or reject the message of Christ, we are headed for trouble.

That is not to suggest that we can be careless in our witness or ignore our credibility. Notice that Jesus's brothers rejected Him despite His works and words. Is that true of us? Or do people dismiss our faith because our lives show little evidence that what we say we believe is true or that it makes little difference to us?

Eventually, some of Jesus's brothers did believe in Him. James, probably the oldest, became a leader in the Church (Acts 15:13-21) and wrote the New Testament letter that bears his name.

Likewise, the author of Jude may have been the half-brother of Jesus. Ultimately, both urged Christians to practice and defend their faith (James 2:2-26; Jude 3).

Who is Jesus Christ?

Jesus is called "The Son of God" in all four Gospels:

Matthew 3:17; 4:3; 6; 8;29; 14:33; 16:16; 17:5; 26:63; 27:54.

Mark 1:1; 1:11; 3:11; 5:7; 9:7; 14:61, 62.

Luke 1:32, 35; 3:32; 4:41; 9:35; 22:70.

John 1:34; 1:49; 3:16,18; 5:25; 9:35; 10:36; 19:7; 20:31.

Jesus called himself "The Son of God" (John 5:25); "making himself equal with God" (John 5:18). Three times Jesus categorically said, "I AM THE SON OF GOD" Mark 14;61-62; John 9:35-37; 10:36).

Jesus repeatedly used expressions about himself that can be predicated only of Deity:

"I am the Truth" (John 14:6).

"I am the Way" (To God) (John 14:6).

"I am the Door" (John 10:9). By me, if any man shall enter he shall be saved, and shall go in and out and shall find pasture.

"No one can come unto the Father but by Me" (John 14:6).

"I am the Bread of Life" (John 6:35, 38).

"I am the Life" (John 11:25; 14:6).

"I am the Resurrection" (John 11:25)

"I am the Messiah" (John 4:25-26)

"Before Abraham was, I am" (John 8:58). This is an amazing statement, beyond the reach of finite conception, eliminating the passage of time, and resolving the past and future into one Eternal Now.

"Father, glorify Me with the glory I had with Thee before the world was" (John 17.5). A clear recollection of his pre-incarnation existence.

"He that has seen Me has seen the Father" (John 14:9).

"I and the Father are One" (John 10:30).

"All Power on earth and in heaven had been given unto me" (Matthew 28:20).

"I am with you always, even to the end of the world" (Matthew 28:20).

Who else could have said such things about himself? Of whom else could we say them?

In addition:

Mark called Jesus "The Son of God" (Mark 1:1).

John called Jesus "The Son of God" (John 3:16,18; 20:31).

John the Baptist called Jesus "The Son of God" (John 1:34).

Nathanael called Jesus "The Son of God" (John 1:49).

Peter called Jesus "The Son of God" (Matthew 16:16).

Martha called Jesus "The Son of God" (John 11:17).

The Disciples called Jesus "The Son of God" (Matthew 14:33)

Gabriel called Jesus "The Son of God" (Luke 1;32.35).

GOD HIMSELF called Jesus His Own "Beloved Son" (Matt 3:17; Mark 1:11; Luke 3:22; 9:35).

Even Evil Spirits called Jesus "The Son of God" (Matthew 8:29; Mark 3:11, 5:7; Luke 4:41).

It was commonly recognized that He made the claim: "He said I am the "Son of God" (Matthew 27:43)

"Truly this was the "Son of God"" (Matthew 27:54).

"Of a truth you are the "Son of God"" (Matthew 14:33).

"If you are the "Son of God" come down from the cross" Matthew 27:40).

"He made himself the "Son of God"" (John 19:7).

The Old Testament prophets foretold His Deity: "His name shall be called Mighty God, Everlasting Father" (Isaiah 9:6); "This is the name whereby He shall be called, God our

155

Righteousness" (Jeremiah 23:6; 33:16); "In that day the house of David shall be as God" (Zechariah 12:8).

The "Rock" on which Jesus said He would build his church (Matthew 16:18), was the Truth that He is the Son of God.

Jesus is Himself called "God" (John 1:1; 10:33; 20:28; Romans 9:5; Colossians 1:16; 2:9; I Timothy 1:17; Hebrews 1:8; I John 5:20; Jude 25).

Thus, neither Jesus himself nor the scriptures leave any possible doubt as to the nature of Jesus's Person. We should accept the record as it is. Amen. Amen.

II Chronicles 7:14

If my people who are called by my name will humble themselves and pray, and seek my face, and turn from their wicked ways, then I will hear from heaven and will forgive their sin and heal their land.

Psalm 122:6

Pray for the peace of Jerusalem; they shall prosper who love thee.

Lesson Plan 50

The Book of John

Chapter 8

Objective: To obtain a thorough understanding of the Book of John, the Deity of Jesus, and some insight on the Holy Spirit and the inspired author John as he walked with the "Creator of the Universe."

Objective Breakdown:

1. Introduction

2. A Woman Caught in Adultery   Chapter 8:1-11

3. I am the Light of the World   Chapter 8:12-59

Introduction: John in chapter eight records a heated, even bitter, confrontation between Jesus and the Jews, led by the Pharisees. The Lord became particularly blunt with the religious leaders because they refused to accept His claims, imperiling not only their own spiritual standing but that of Israel.

Jesus chose to keep a low profile at this year's festival (John 7:2-10). He taught in the temple (John 7:14) but waited for the right moment to declare Himself publicly. It came on the last day of the feast (John 7:37), probably at the climax of the daily processional.

A double standard? The woman presented to Jesus (John 8:3) must have been utterly humiliated at being dragged into the temple by self-righteous men who were only using her to try and trick the Teacher they hated. According to the law, adultery required capital punishment of both parties (Leviticus 20:10). Did the accusers forget to bring the man? Or had they allowed a double standard to creep in? If so, Jesus refrained from challenging their hypocrisy, but He did set a new standard for judgment: Let someone perfect decide the case (John 8:7; compare Matthew 5:48). Ironically, He was the only one who fit that qualification, and He did decide the case–declining to condemn the woman, but admonishing her to "go and sin no more."

II Chronicles 7:14

If my people who are called by my name will humble themselves and pray, and seek my face, and turn from their wicked ways, then I will hear from heaven and will forgive their sin and heal their land.

Psalm 122:6

Pray for the peace of Jerusalem; they shall prosper who love thee.

Lesson Plan 51

The Book of John

Chapters 9 & 10

Objective: To obtain a thorough understanding of the Book of John, the Deity of Jesus, and some insight on the Holy Spirit and the inspired author John as he walked with the "Creator of the Universe."

Objective Breakdown:

1. Introduction

2. Jesus Heals a Man Born Blind   Chapter 9:1-41

3. I Am the Good Shepherd   Chapter 10:1-21

4. Jesus Attends the Feast of Dedication   Chapter 10:22-39

5. Jesus Returns to The River Jordan   Chapter 10:40-42

Introduction:

Throughout John's Gospel, there is a cycle of "I am" sayings. Jesus said, "I am the Light of the World"; I am the Bread of Life"; "I am the Good Shepherd." The phrase "I AM" is very significant in the Old Testament. It is the Divine Name revealed to Moses at the burning bush. The name Yahweh (Jehovah) is built on the verb "I AM." These "I AM" sayings are identifying Jesus with God of the Covenant; the God who brought Israel out of Egypt; the God of Abraham, Isaac, and Jacob.

Early Christian Jews identified Jesus with God the Father Creator: "I and the Father are one," Jesus said: "He that hath seen me hath seen the Father." John is also the only Gospel that uses the powerful concept of the miracles of Jesus as signs. For example, Jesus teaches that he is the light of the world. However, he communicates that even more powerfully when he heals a man who was blind from birth and literally gives light to the blind! Jesus gives the 5,000 bread in the great miracle of five loaves and two fishes. But he is really saying, "I am the bread of life come down from heaven. You must eat the bread of life from heaven so that your spiritual life may be nourished."

Jesus Heals a Man Born Blind   Chapter 9:1-41

On a previous visit to Jerusalem (5:9), Jesus had healed an impotent man on the Sabbath and claimed that he was the Son of God, so they attempted to stone him (John 8:52-59). He now proceeds to work a still more notable Sabbath miracle (9:14).

The John Gospel uses the beautiful combination of Signs (miracles) and "I AM" sayings that make it so distinctive. He is also the only one who tells about the coming of the Paraclete or Comforter. In the upper room, at the time of the Last Supper, Jesus gave us the most important teachings in all the Bible about the Holy Spirit or Paraclete who would come. Jesus said that the Paraclete would bear witness of Him, but the Paraclete's ministry would not begin until Jesus went away. Therefore Jesus said it was better that he go away so that the Father could send the Paraclete, whom the world could not receive, but who would abide with his followers forever!

I Am the Good Shepherd Chapter 10:1-21

Jesus declares himself to be the Shepherd of Mankind; that is, for as many of mankind as will accept him as their Shepherd.

Jesus Attends the Feast of Dedication Chapter 10:22-39

There is an interval of two months between verses 21 and 22. The Feast of Tabernacles was in October. Jesus's visit to that Feast is covered by John 7:2 to 10:21. Now it is the Feast of Dedication (December). In the interval, it seems Jesus had gone back to Galilee, and north, and was transfigured.

Jesus Returns to The River Jordan Chapter 10:40-42

Where Jesus had spent eight months at the opening of his public ministry (John 3:22). He was there probably about two months. It was a thickly populated region, with many prosperous Roman cities under Herod's rule, out of reach of the Jerusalem authorities. (Covered by Luke 11 to 18 inclusive.)

II Chronicles 7:14

If my people who are called by my name will humble themselves and pray, and seek my face, and turn from their wicked ways, then I will hear from heaven and will forgive their sin and heal their land.

Psalm 122:6

Pray for the peace of Jerusalem; they shall prosper who love thee.

Lesson Plan 52

The Book of John

Chapter 11

Objective: To obtain a thorough understanding of the Book of John, the Deity of Jesus, and some insight on the Holy Spirit and the inspired author John as he walked with the "Creator of the Universe."

Objective Breakdown:

1. Introduction

2. Lazarus is Raised from the Dead   Chapter 11:1-44

3. Leaders Plot to Destroy Jesus   Chapter 11:45-57

Introduction: The intensity of the Jews hostility can be seen in their readiness to stone Him (John 10:31; 8:59). Stoning was an ancient method of capital punishment reserved for the most serious crimes against the Mosaic Law, including child sacrifice (Leviticus 20:2); consultation with mediums and occultist (Leviticus 20:27); blasphemy (Leviticus 24:16); Sabbath-breaking (Numbers 15:32-36); the worship of false gods (Deuteronomy 13:10); rebellion against parents Deuteronomy 21:21); adultery (Ezekiel 16:40) and certain cases against God's express command (Joshua 7:25).

Stoning was usually carried out by the men of the community (Deuteronomy 21:21) upon the testimony of at least two witnesses, who were to cast the first stones (Deuteronomy 17:5-7). The execution usually took place outside the camp or city (Leviticus 24:14, 23; 1 Kings 21:10, 13). Jesus must have known He was headed for trouble when His enemies "surrounded" Him literally, "closed in on Him" as He walked on Solomon's porch (John 10:23-24). In the same way, a victim of stoning would be surrounded as the executioners cut off all means of escape from their fury.

The final sign miracle in John's Gospel is the climax of Jesus's signs: He raised Lazarus from the dead (John 11:41-44), proving to all that He was master even over death. The amazing thing was that this miracle led directly to the plot to arrest Him and put Him to death (John

11:46–53), along with Lazarus (John 12:10–11).

It was after the raising of Lazarus from the dead that the chief priests, Pharisees, and other religious leaders finally determined to put Jesus to death (John 11:53). Until now, the conflict between them and the upstart rabbi had been little more than a war of words. But the raising of Lazarus was an incredible miracle, witnessed by many. Jesus had raised a least two others, but those events had taken place in faraway Galilee (Mark 522–24, 35-43; Luke 7:11–17). By contrast, Lazarus's resurrection occurred in Bethany, a suburb of Jerusalem (John 11:18), a village about 2 miles east of Jerusalem on the southeast slope of the Mount of Olives, on the road to Jericho

II Chronicles 7:14

If my people who are called by my name will humble themselves and pray, and seek my face, and turn from their wicked ways, then I will hear from heaven and will forgive their sin and heal their land.

Psalm 122:6

Pray for the peace of Jerusalem; they shall prosper who love thee.

Lesson Plan 53

The Book of John

Chapter 12 & 13

Objective: To obtain a thorough understanding of the Book of John; the Deity of Jesus; and some insight on the Holy Spirit and the inspired author John as he walked with the "Creator of the Universe."

Objective Breakdown:

1. Introduction

2. Mary Anoints Jesus with Costly Oil   Chapter 12:1-8

3. The Curious Gather   Chapter 12:9-11

4. A Parade Welcomes Jesus to Jerusalem   Chapter 12:12-19

5. Jesus Sums up His Teaching   Chapter 12:20-36

6. Unbelief Persists   Chapter 12:37-43

7. Jesus Makes His Final Claim   Chapter 12:44-50

8. Jesus Washes the Disciples' Feet   Chapter 13:1-20

9. Judas Leaves to Betray Jesus   Chapter 13:21-30

10. A New Commandment   Chapter 13:31-35

11. Jesus Predicts Peter's Denial   Chapter 13:36-38

Introduction: Funeral Preparations

Jesus told the dinner crowd that Mary was preparing Him for His burial (John 12:7). It's difficult for us today to appreciate the significance that burial rituals had in ancient peoples. Nearly every ancient religion gave explicit and sometimes elaborate instructions for preparing and burying the dead.

For Hebrews at the time of Christ, women and men participated in the mourning ritual, but women likely prepared the body for internment. First they washed the body, then scented it with fragrant oil, an act of devotion that might be repeated at the tomb.

The oil that Mary used on Jesus (John 12;30 was probably nard, a perfume used by women, imported from India, it was extremely costly and was known for its strong fragrance. It was the same perfume used by the woman that Solomon praised in his Song of Solomon (Song of Solomon 1:12; 4:13).

Washed and scented, the body was dressed in the person's own clothes or else wrapped in specially prepared sheets. Then as soon as possible, it was carried upon a bier to the tomb. Relatives, friends, and professional mourners (see Matthew 9:23) formed a procession, and anyone meeting it was obliged to show honor to the deceased and the relatives by joining. A eulogy was often delivered at the gravesite.

The body was placed on a shelf in the tomb, which was then sealed by a heavy, tight fitting slab. Jews were expected to visit the tomb often, partly as a precaution against burying someone who only seemed dead.

There are five Marys in our gospels: (1) Mary of Bethany (2) Mary, the mother of Jesus (Luke 1:26-56); (3) Mary of Magdala (Luke 8:2); (4) Mary the mother of James and Joses (Matthew 27:55-61); and (5) Mary the mother of John Mark (Acts 12:12).

Scripture records only one sentence spoken by Mary of Bethany (John 11:31), and even that wasn't original; her sister Martha had already said the same thing (John 11:21)! But what Mary may have lacked in outspokenness, she more than made up for in devotion to Jesus. All three portraits of her in the Gospels show her at the Lord's feet:

- During one of Jesus's visits to her home, Mary sat at His feet, listening (Luke 10:38-42).

- When Jesus came to Bethany after Lazarus's death, Mary fell at His feet, completely broke over the tragedy (John 11:32).

- During a Passover meal just before Jesus's death, Mary poured fragrant oil on his head and feet and wiped His feet with her hair (Matthew 26:6; Mark 14:3–9; John 12:1-8).

On each of these occasions, this quiet woman was criticized by others. But apparently, she didn't notice or didn't care. Mary seemed to be a woman who made choices based on a commitment to Jesus that went to the core of her being. In return, Jesus defended her actions, giving her freedom to be His disciple.

Mary is a model for anyone who lives in the shadow of a strong sibling or parent, or who prefers to listen rather than speak. She demonstrates that preaching sermons or leading movements are not the only ways to follow Jesus. One can also show devotion by listening to the Lord's voice and worshiping at His feet.

II Chronicles 7:14

If my people, which are called by my name, shall humble themselves, and pray, and seek my face, and turn from their wicked ways; then will I hear from heaven, and will forgive their sin, and will heal their land.

Psalm 122:6

Pray for the peace of Jerusalem; they will prosper that love thee.

Lesson Plan 54

The Book of John

Chapters 14 & 15

Objective: To obtain a thorough understanding of the Book of John, the Deity of Jesus, and some insight on the Holy Spirit inspired author, John, as he walked with the "Creator of the Universe."

Objective Breakdown:

1. Review

2. Introduction

3. I Am the Way and the Truth and the Life   Chapter 14:1-31

4. I Am the Vine   Chapter 15:1-10

5. Love One Another   Chapter 16:11-27

Review of the First Fifteen Chapters of the Book of John

Chapter 1.

- Describes the Word   Chapter 1:1-18

- The Testimony of John the Baptist   Chapter 1:19-34

- Jesus Recruits His First Followers   Chapter 1:35-51

Chapter 2.

- A Marriage Feast at Cana   Chapter 2:1-12

- Merchants Are Evicted from The Temple   Chapter 2:13-24

Chapter 3.

- Nicodemus Visits Jesus by Night   Chapter 3:1-21

- John the Baptist Teaches About Jesus   Chapter 3:22-36

Chapter 4.

Chapter 5.

Chapter 6.

Chapter 7.

Chapter 8.

Chapter 9.

Chapter 10.

Introduction: It was the raising of Lazarus from the dead that the chief priests, Pharisees, and other religious leaders finally determined to put Jesus to death (John 11:53). The conflict between them (the leaders) had been a little more than a war of words. But the raising of Lazarus was an incredible miracle, witnessed by many. Jesus had raised at least two others, but those had taken place in faraway Galilee (Mark 5:22-24, 35-43; Luke 7:11-17). By contrast, Lazarus's resurrection occurred in Bethany, a suburb of Jerusalem (John 11:18), only a mile and half away.

Not surprisingly, the miracle caused many to believe in Jesus (John 11:45). It provided undeniable proof that Jesus's bold claim must be true: "I am the resurrection and the life... and whoever lives and believes in Me shall never die" (John 11:25). Indeed Lazarus became something of a curiosity, drawing numerous onlookers who wanted to see for themselves the man who Jesus brought back to life (John 12:9). Lazarus was living evidence of Jesus's power. Thus, Jesus became a threat to the religious and political status of the High Priests and Pharisees, and from their point of view must be dealt with.

II Chronicles 7:14

If my people, which are called by my name, shall humble themselves, and pray, and seek my face, and turn from their wicked ways; then will I hear from heaven, and will forgive their sin, and will heal their land.

Psalm 122:6

Pray for the peace of Jerusalem; they will prosper that love thee.

Lesson Plan 55

The Book of John

Chapters 16 & 17

Objective: To obtain a thorough understanding of the Book of John, the Deity of Jesus, and some insight on the Holy Spirit and the inspired author John as he walked with the "Creator of the Universe."

Objective Breakdown:

1. Introduction

2. The Work of the Spirit   Chapter 16:1-15

3. Temporary Sorrow Then Permanent Joy   Chapter 16:16-33

4. Jesus Prays for His Followers   Chapter 17:1-26

Introduction:

The ideas appearing in these precious chapters are that the disciples love one another: that they keep Christ's Commandments; that they abide in Him; that they must expect pruning and persecution; that they Abide in Him; that it was necessary for Him to go away; that the Holy Spirit would take His place; that their sorrow would be turned to Joy; and that in His absence wondrous answers to their prayers would be granted. And while Jesus was going into the depths of His own sorrow and suffering, He was doing His best to also comfort His bewildered disciples.

He closes His tender farewell by commending them to God, praying both for Himself and for them, as He turns away to tread the winepress alone. Remembrance of His pre-human existence, and its "glory" (verse 5), gave Him courage. He prayed for His own (verse 9), not for the world. He came to save the world, but His special interest was in those who believed in Him. He drew a definite line between His and those who were not. This idea is prevalent throughout John's writings.

After leaving the upper room (John 17:1-26). Jesus offers a nine-fold review of the past concerning what the Son has done.

a. He has given eternal life to all the elect (John 17:2)

b. He has glorified the Father (John 17:4)

c. He has completed His assignment (John 17:4)

d. He has revealed the Person of God to man (John 17:6, 26)

e. He has declared the Word of God to Man (John 17:8, 14)

f. He asked the Father to protect them from evil (John 17:15)

g. He asked the Father to sanctify them (John 17: 17)

h. He asked the Father to guide them in the world (John17:23)

i. He asked the Father to gather them in the heavens (John 17:24)

j. He asked the Father to fill them with love (John 17:26)

In summary: In this prayer, Jesus prays for Himself (John 17:1-5), for the disciples (John 17:5-19), and for the church (John 17:20-26).

II Chronicles 7:14

If my people, which are called by my name, shall humble themselves, and pray, and seek my face, and turn from their wicked ways; then will I hear from heaven, and will forgive their sin, and will heal their land.

Psalm 122:6

Pray for the peace of Jerusalem; they will prosper that love thee.

Lesson Plan 56

The Book of John

Chapters 18 & 19

Objective: To obtain a thorough understanding of the Book of John, the Deity of Jesus, and some insight on the Holy Spirit inspired author John as he walked with the "Creator of the Universe."

Objective Breakdown:

1. Introduction

2. Jesus Is Arrested   Chapter 18:1-14

3. Peter Denies Knowing Jesus   Chapter 18:15-27

4. Jesus Is Taken to Pilate   Chapter 18:28-40

5. Pilate Sends Jesus to be Crucified   Chapter 19:1-16

6. Jesus is Crucified   Chapter 19:17-37

7. Jesus's Body Laid in Joseph's Tomb   Chapter 19:38-42

Introduction: Jesus's arrest is told also in Matthew 26:47-56; Mark 14:43-50 and Luke 22:47-53. It was about midnight. The Roman garrison, consisting of a cohort of soldiers led by the chief captain, with emissaries from the high priest evidently thinking they were on a dangerous mission, were guided by Judas to the place of Jesus's retreat. As they streamed out of the East Gate and down the Kedron road with lanterns, torches, and weapons, they were visible from the garden where Jesus was. As they approached, Jesus, by some unseen power, caused them to fall to the ground, to make them understand that they could not take him against his will. To make Jesus's identification certain, Judas pointed him out by kissing him.

Peter's Denial

It occurred in the court of the high priest, as Jesus was being condemned. Peter had just been willing to fight the whole Roman garrison alone. He was not a coward by any means. He does deserve some credit. We can never know the whirl of emotions that tore at Peter's soul that night.

As Peter was vehemently denying that he knew Jesus, Jesus turned and looked at him. That look must have broken Peter's heart knowing the disappointment of Jesus being denied by him a trusted friend.

Jesus is Crucified. See Matthew 27:33-56; Mark 15:21-41 and Luke 23:32-49. The legs of the robbers were broken (32) to hasten death, which otherwise might have occurred for four or five days.

The "Blood and Water." Jesus was already dead when the spear pierced his side, after being on the cross for 6 hours. Some medical authorities have said that in the case of heart rupture, and in that case only, the blood collects in a clot and watery serum. If this is a fact, then the actual immediate physical cause of Jesus's death was heart rupture. Under intense pain, and the pressure of his wildly raging blood, his heart burst open. It may be that Jesus literally, died of a broken heart over the sin of the world. It may be that the suffering for human sin is more than the human constitution can stand.

Burial. Joseph and Nicodemus, both members of the Sanhedrin, secret disciples—secret to the hour of Jesus's popularity—now in the hour of his humiliation, came out boldly to share with Jesus the shame of His cross.

The "Holy Shroud." The Scientific American of March 1937 contained an article by a French scientist about a sheet of linen cloth that was in a Roman Catholic Church at Turin, Italy. He believes this cloth to be the actual winding sheet of Jesus's body. He further described it as being 14 feet long, 3 feet 7 inches wide, with negative images of the front and back of a full-grown human body, indicating that the man was laid on one half, and on the other half was folded over lengthwise. The figures, he claimed, are not paintings, but images produced by ammoniac vapors, given off in great abundance in sweat produced by intense suffering. The scourge marks, the wound in the hands, on the head, and in the side are plainly visible, with evidence that serum and blood flowed from the wound.

It is unmistakably the image of a man crucified, with every detail dovetailing with the Scripture account and with the countenance of a man of noble appearance. It first appeared in France in 1355, with notices that it had been seen in Constantinople 1204. However, we do not know for sure whether it is the real shroud of Jesus.

Jesus's Body is Laid in Joseph's Tomb. "In the place where Jesus was crucified there was a garden; and in the garden a new tomb wherein was never man yet laid." This means that the tomb in which Jesus was buried was very close to the place where he was crucified. (See Mark 15: 21-41)

General Christian Gordon, 1881, found at the west foot of the "Skull Hill" a Garden. He set a team of men to digging, and under five feet of rubbish, he found a tomb of Roman times, cut in a wall of solid rock, with a trench in front, where the stone rolled to the door.

The tomb is 14 feet wide, 10 ft deep, 7 ½ feet high. As you enter, there are two graves on the right, one next to the front wall, and one next to the back wall. This place is called the "Garden Tomb" where Jesus was buried and is considered the holiest spot on earth, the place whence came the Assurance of Life that Shall Never End. (See Mark 15: 21-41)

II Chronicles 7:14

If my people who are called by my name will humble themselves and pray, and seek my face, and turn from their wicked ways, then I will hear from heaven and will forgive their sin and heal their land.

Psalm 122:6

Pray for the peace of Jerusalem; they shall prosper who love thee.

Lesson Plan 57

The Book of John

Chapters 20 & 21

Objective: To obtain a thorough understanding of the Book of John; the Deity of Jesus; and some insight on the Holy Spirit and the inspired author John as he walked with the "Creator of the Universe".

Objective Breakdown:

1. Introduction

2. The Resurrection   Chapter 20:1-10

3. Jesus Appears to Mary & the Disciples   Chapter 20:11-29

4. The Purpose of John's Gospel   Chapter 20:30-31

5. A Great Catch of Fish   Chapter 21:1-14

6. Jesus Commissions Peter   Chapter 21:15-25

Introduction:

Would you consider your life a success if, at its conclusion, you had only the clothes on your back? That was the sum total of Jesus's earthly wealth–and the soldiers took those away, leaving Him nothing (John 19:24). For many of us, that kind of poverty would mark us as failures. "Jesus–a homeless man?" (Matthew 8:20) addresses the Lord's lack of earthly possessions and what that means for us today. But oh, what a mark Jesus made on mankind. His ministry is thriving two years later and mankind's future depends on their belief in Jesus the man and Jesus the Son of God. Wow!! What an accomplishment and what a gift He has given us…forgiveness of our sins and eternal life for those who believe.

Old Testament Quotations in the Book of John

Note: Some of the Old Testament quotations are cited as prophecies which are future events. Those quotations are designated with a "P."

Old Testament	Subject	New Testament
Isaiah 40:3P	Voice in the Wilderness	John 1:23
Psalm 69:9	Holiness of God's house	John 2:17
Exodus 16:4	Bread from Heaven	John 6:31
Nehemiah 9:15	Bread from Heaven	John 6:31
Psalm 78:24	Bread from Heaven	John 6:31
Isaiah 54:13P	Revelation of Christ	John 6:45
Psalm 82:6	Christ the Son of God	John 10:34
Psalm 118:26P	Blessing God's Messiah	John 12:13
Zechariah 9:9P	Jesus's Entrance into Jerusalem	John 12:15
Isaiah 53:1P	The Spirit of the Lord	John 12:38
Isaiah 6:10P	Unbelief	John 12:40
Psalm 41:9P	Betrayal of Christ	John 13:18
Psalm 64:4P	Hatred of Christ	John 15:25
Psalm 22:18P	Crucifixion of Christ	John 19:24
Exodus 12:46P	Sacrifice of Christ	John 19:36
Numbers 9:12P	Sacrifice of Christ	John 19:36
Psalm 34:20P	Sacrifice of Christ	John 19:36
Zechariah 12:10P	Crucifixion of Christ	John 19:37

II Chronicles 7:14

If my people, which are called by my name, shall humble themselves, and pray, and seek my face, and turn from their wicked ways; then will I hear from heaven, and will forgive their sin, and will heal their land.

Psalm 122:6

Pray for the peace of Jerusalem; they will prosper that love thee.

The Book of Acts

Scripture Focus Chapters 1 - 28

Objective: To gain an understanding of the Book of Acts. Acts is a Biblical Book of Transition from the Gospels to the Epistles (History), from Judaism to Christianity (Religion), from Law to Grace (Divine Dealings), from Jews alone to Jews and Gentiles (People of God), and from Kingdom to Church (Program of God).

Objective Breakdown:

1. Prologue to Acts	Chapter 1:1-2
2. Appearance of the Resurrected Christ	Chapter 1:3-8
3. Ascension of Christ	Chapter 1:9-11
4. Anticipation of the Spirit	Chapter 1:12-14
5. Appointment of Matthias	Chapter 1:15-26
6. Filling with the Holy Spirit	Chapter 2:1-4
7. Speaking with Other Tongues	Chapter 2:5-13
8. Peter Explains Pentecost	Chapter 2:14-41
9. Practices of the Early Church	Chapter 2:42-47
10. Peter Heals the Lame Man	Chapter 3:1-11
11. Peter's Second Sermon	Chapter 3:12-26
12. Peter and John Are Put in Custody	Chapter 4:1-4
13. Peter Preaches to the Sanhedrin	Chapter 4:5-12
14. Sanhedrin Commands Peter not to Preach	Chapter 4:13-22
15. Apostles Prayer for Boldness	Chapter 4:23-31
16. Early Church Voluntarily Shares	Chapter 4:32-37

Lesson Plan 58

The Book of Acts

Chapter 1

Objective: To gain a good understanding of the Book of Acts, and its story of the expansion of the Gospel throughout Palestine, northward to Antioch, and thence westward through Asia Minor, Greece to Rome, covering the region that then constituted the backbone of the Roman Empire.

Objective Breakdown:

1. Introduction

2. Prologue to Acts   Chapter 1:1-2

3. Appearances of the Resurrected Christ   Chapter 1:3-8

4. Ascension of Christ   Chapter 1:9-11

5. Anticipation of the Spirit   Chapter 1:12-14

6. Appointment of Matthias   Chapter 1:15-20

7. Let Another Take His Office   Chapter 1:21-26

Introduction:

Luke begins the Book of Acts where he left off in his gospel. Acts records the initial fulfillment of the Great Commission of Matthew 28:19, 20 as it records the beginnings and growth of the New Testament Church. This growth can be seen in Acts 1:15, 2:41, 47; 4:4;5:14; 6:7; 9:31; 12:24; 13:49; 16:5; 19:20. Acts also traces the important events in the early history of Christianity from the Ascension of Christ to the outpouring of the Holy Spirit to the rapid progress of the gospel, beginning in Jerusalem and spreading throughout the Roman Empire.

Acts is a pivotal book of transitions: from the gospels to the epistles (history), from Judaism to Christianity (religion), from law to grace (divine dealing), from Jews alone to Jews and Gentiles (people of God), and from kingdom to church (program of God).

The three movements of Acts follow its key verse (Acts 1:8); Witness in Jerusalem (Acts 1:1–8:4); Witness in Judea and Samaria (Acts 8:5–12:5); Witness to the Ends of the Earth (Acts 13–28).

II Chronicles 7:14

If my people, which are called by my name, shall humble themselves, and pray, and seek my face, and turn from their wicked ways; then will I hear from heaven, and will forgive their sin, and will heal their land.

Psalm 122:6

Pray for the peace of Jerusalem; they will prosper that love thee.

Lesson Plan 59

The Book of Acts

Chapters 2 & 3

Objective: To gain a good understanding of the Book of Acts, and its story of the expansion of the Gospel throughout Palestine, northward to Antioch, and thence westward through Asia Minor, Greece to Rome, covering the region that then constituted the backbone of the Roman Empire.

Objective Breakdown:

1. Introduction

2. Filling with the Holy Spirit   Chapter 2:1-4

3. Speaking with Other Tongues   Chapter 2:5-13

4. Peter Explains Pentecost   Chapter 2:14-41

5. Practices of the Early Church   Chapter 2:42-47

6. Peter Heals a Lame Man   Chapter 3:1-10

7. Peter Speaks Again   Chapter 3:11-26

Introduction:

What happened at Pentecost began to reverse what happened at ancient Babel (Genesis 11:1-9). At Babel God confused the languages of the peoples and dispersed the nations abroad to stop their evil from multiplying. At Pentecost, He brought Jews from many nations together in Jerusalem. Once again there was confusion (Acts 2:6), this time it came from the fact that everyone heard ordinary men and women, filled with the Holy Spirit, speaking in the various languages of the ancient world. Then an international, multilingual church was born when the onlookers heard the gospel preached and believed it.

Pentecost: Chapter 2:1-13

A.D. Birth-Day of the Church. 50th Day after Jesus's Resurrection. 10th Day after his Ascension to Heaven. Beginning of the Gospel Era. That particular Pentecost was on Sunday.

Pentecost was also called Feast of First Fruits, and Feast of Harvest. Jesus, in John 16:7-14, had spoken of the Coming of the Holy Spirit Era. It is now inaugurated in a Miraculous Manifestation of the Holy Spirit, with the sound of a Roaring Wind, and with Tongues as of Fire parting asunder, upon each of the Apostles.

It was the opening Public Proclamation to the world of the Resurrection of Jesus, to the Jews and Jewish proselytes assembled in Jerusalem for Pentecost, from all the countries of the known world. Fifteen nations are named (Acts 2:9-11) --- The Galilean Apostle speaking to them in their own language.

Peter's Sermon: Chapter 2:14-26

The amazing spectacle of the Apostle speaking under Tongues of Fire, in languages of all nations there represented.

Fulfillment of Prophecy:

Betrayal by Judas (1:16,20); Crucifixion (3:18); Resurrection (2:25-28); Ascension of Jesus (2:33-35); Coming of the Holy Spirit (2:17).

The Resurrection of Jesus:

The Resurrection was the pivotal point of Peter's sermon (2:25-28) And also in his second sermon (3:15). And in his defense before the council (4:2,10).

The New Born Church:

3000 the first day (2:41). This is a testimony to Unmistakable Evidence of the Resurrection of Jesus and the working of the Holy Spirit.

II Chronicles 7:14

If my people, which are called by my name, shall humble themselves, and pray, and seek my face, and turn from their wicked ways; then will I hear from heaven, and will forgive their sin, and will heal their land.

Psalm 122:6

Pray for the peace of Jerusalem; they will prosper that love thee.

Lesson Plan 60

The Book of Acts

Chapters 4 & 5

Objective: To gain a good understanding of the Book of Acts, and its story of the expansion of the Gospel throughout Palestine, northward to Antioch, and thence westward through Asia Minor, Greece to Rome, covering the region that then constituted the backbone of the Roman Empire.

Objective Breakdown:

1. Introduction

2. Peter & John Arrested; More Respond   Chapter 4:1-4

3. Peter & John Face the Council   Chapter 4:5-22

4. Peter & John Are Released   Chapter 4:23-37

5. Ananias & Sapphira Sell their Property   Chapter 5:1-11

6. Growing Respect Among the People   Chapter 5:12-16

7. Religious Leaders Try to Stop the Apostles   Chapter 5:17-42

Introduction: We ought to obey God rather than men. What should Christians do when faced with a conflict between human authority and God's authority? Notice what Peter and the other apostles did (Acts 5:22-32):

They aimed to serve and glorify God. They were not motivated by ego or out to protect their own power.

Their point of disobedience was specific and particular They did not resist the authority of the Jewish Council in total.

They approached the situation with a spirit of submissiveness toward both the Council and God. They did not harbor rebellious anger toward authority in general.

They delivered a positive, factual message about God's plan and power in loving truth. They did not slander or show disrespect to their superiors.

They accepted the cost of being loyal to the truth without rancor or bitterness.

Wealth–hold it lightly! Whether we own land, buildings, things, or cash, wealth is tricky to handle. How we hold these assets speaks volumes about our values. If we hold them too tightly, the results are likely to be possessiveness, stinginess, manipulation, and elitism.

Barnabas converted some land that he owned into a cash gift for needy believers (Acts 4:36-37). He laid it at the Apostle's feet to be administered by them. By contrast, Ananias and Sapphira practiced a similar transaction for the same need, but lied about it (Acts 5:1-2).

They wanted to look good among the believers, but they also wanted to secretly hold on to some of their money from the sale. God calls us as believers to hold our resources lightly. After all, everything that we have comes from Him. He gives it to us as a trust to be managed– not a treasure to be hoarded.

II Chronicles 7:14

If my people, which are called by my name, shall humble themselves, and pray, and seek my face, and turn from their wicked ways; then will I hear from heaven, and will forgive their sin, and will heal their land.

Psalm 122:6

Pray for the peace of Jerusalem; they will prosper that love thee.

Lesson Plan 61

The Book of Acts

Chapters 6 & 7

Objective: To gain a good understanding of the Book of Acts, and its story of the expansion of the Gospel throughout Palestine, northward to Antioch, and thence westward through Asia Minor, Greece to Rome, covering the region that then constituted the backbone of the Roman Empire.

Objective Breakdown:

1. Introduction

2. Ethnic Tensions   Chapter 6:1-7

3. Stephen Is Arrested   Chapter 6:8-15

4. Stephen Addresses the Council   Chapter 7:1-8

5. The Israelites Were Slaves in Egypt   Chapter 7:9-22

6. God Raised Up Moses   Chapter 7:23-34

7. The People Rejected Moses –And God   Chapter 7:35-43

8. The Council Also Has resisted God   Chapter 7:44-53

9. Stephen Is Stoned to Death   Chapter 7:54-60

Introduction:

Up until this time the Apostles had been administering the business affairs of the Church (4:37). Because the Church, in a few months or possibly a year or two, had grown enormously, waiting on tables was absorbing too much of the Apostles' time.

The Apostles were the ones who had first-hand knowledge of the precious story of Jesus. Therefore, their first and primary business, from morning to night, in public and in private, was to keep telling the story of Jesus to the multitudes coming and going. So seven assistants were appointed to take the administrative and serving the needs of the widows as reflected in

(6:5-6).

Of the seven, two were great preachers: Stephen and Philip. Stephen had the honor of being the Church's first Martyr. Philip carried the Gospel to Samaria and west Judea. Stephen's particular sphere of labor seems to have been among the Greek Jews. At that time there were about 460 Synagogues in Jerusalem some of which were built by Jews of various countries for their own use. Five of these were for sojourners from Cyrene, Alexandria, Cilicia, Asia, and Rome (Acts 6:9). Tarsus being in Cilicia, Saul may have been in this very group. Some of the foreign-born Jews brought up in centers of Greek culture, felt themselves to be superior to the Jews of the homeland. But they met their match in Stephen. Unable to withstand him in an argument, they hired a false witness and brought him before the Council. Stephen must have been a very brilliant man. Then again, God was with him and helped him through many miracles.

Stephen's Trial and Murder. Ethnic tension played a decisive role in the trial and death of Stephen, the church's first martyr. Other members of the early church faced the council (Acts 6:12; 4:1-23), but it was Stephen, probably a Hellenist, who first died for his faith. Hellenist Jews born outside of Palestine were among those first attracted by the gospel. Treated as second-class citizens by native-born Jews, many found acceptance in the early church. But it could be that as the new faith threatened to further alienate Hellenistic Jews as from the full-blooded majority, some Hellenists (Acts 6:9) had a motive to discredit the Christian movement.

Their opposition focused on Stephen, a dynamic, emerging leader who enjoyed in the church a prominence that would have been denied him in the Hebrew community. His trial and murder (Acts chapter 7) show that the Hellenists were willing to sacrifice one of their own as a demonstration to the ruling system.

The strategy worked. Stephen's death precipitated great persecution of believers, sanctioned by the council and led by a new young leader, Saul of Tarsus (Acts 8:1-3; 9:1-2).

Stephen's Martyrdom: He was before the same council that had crucified Jesus, and that had just recently attempted to stop the Apostles speaking in the name of Jesus (Acts 4:18). The same Annas and Caiaphas were there (Acts 4:6). Stephen's address before the council was mainly a recital of Old Testament history, climaxing in a stinging rebuke for their murder of Jesus (Acts 7:51-53). As he spoke, his face shone as the face of an Angel (Acts 6:15). They rushed upon him like wild beasts. As the stones began to fly, he looked steadfastly up into heaven and saw the Glory of God, and Jesus standing at the right hand of God, as if Heaven were reaching its hand across the border to welcome him home. He died as Christ had died, without resentment toward his contemptible murders, saying Lord lay not this sin to their charge (Acts 7:60).

A Young Man Named Saul: (Acts 7:58) Here is one of the Turning Points of History. Young Saul seems already to have been a member of the Sanhedrin (Acts 26:10). He may have been present at one or both of the Sanhedrin meetings in which they tried to stop the Apostles from preaching Christ (Acts 4:1-22); 5:17-40) and may himself have witnessed Peter's bold and defiant refusal. But now in all his life, he had never seen a death like Stephen's. Though its immediate effect was to start Saul on his rampage of persecuting disciples, yet it may be that Stephen's dying words went straight to the mark, and lodged deep in Saul's mind, there quietly working to make him ready and receptive for the Great Vision on the road to Damascus (Acts 26:14). Saul, now named Paul, the one man, who more than any other who established Christianity in the main centers of the then known world and altered the course of history. He wrote about a third of the New Testament.

II Chronicles 7:14

If my people, which are called by my name, shall humble themselves, and pray, and seek my face, and turn from their wicked ways; then will I hear from heaven, and will forgive their sin, and will heal their land.

Psalm 122:6

Pray for the peace of Jerusalem; they will prosper that love thee.

Lesson Plan 62

The Book of Acts

Chapters 8 & 9

Objective: To gain a good understanding of the Book of Acts, and its story of the expansion of the Gospel throughout Palestine, northward to Antioch, and thence westward through Asia Minor, Greece to Rome, covering the region that then constituted the backbone of the Roman Empire.

Objective Breakdown:

1. Introduction

2. Persecution by Saul Scatters Believers   Chapter 8:1-3

3. The Message Spreads to Samaria   Chapter 8:4-25

4. An Ethiopian Official Receives the Gospel   Chapter 8:26-40

5. Jesus Stops Saul Near Damascus   Chapter 9:1-9

6. Ananias Reaches Out Cautiously   Chapter 9:10-19

7. Believers Doubt Saul's Conversion   Chapter 9:20-31

8. Peter Heals Aeneas and Raises Tabitha   Chapter 9:32-43

Introduction: The message spreads to Africa. The Ethiopian treasurer was probably a convert to Judaism. He had a great yearning to know the God of Israel, as demonstrated by his reading of Isaiah 53 (Acts 8:23-33) and by the fact that he had to travel 750 miles one way to worship in Jerusalem. The trip would have taken him and his servants 30 days by chariot. How long would he have stayed? Then he faced a return trip. So he spent a least a quarter of a year traveling to Jerusalem to worship God.

What the Ethiopian treasurer heard in Jerusalem about the followers of Jesus and their persecution is not recorded. But he warmly responded to Phillip and the message about Christ and became the first known witness–black or white–to Africa. For the second time in Acts 8, the gospel moved outside of the narrow confines of Jerusalem and Judea.

Once again God used Phillip, the Greek-speaking Hellenist table server, to accomplish the task rather than Peter, John, or the other Apostles, who were beginning to realize that the gospel reaches out to all peoples–Hellenists, Samaritans, even Gentiles of all colors and races.

Ananias–scared but obedient. Saul's reputation as a ruthless persecutor of Christians preceded him to Damascus (Acts 9:1, 10). Perhaps hearing that Saul was headed that way, Ananias mentally prepared himself to be hunted down, arrested, imprisoned, and ultimately martyred for the following the new movement called "the Way." In any case, he was no doubt stunned by the Lord's command to go and meet this dangerous enemy face-to-face! But, God commanded, "Go" (Acts 9:11, 15), and to his credit, Ananias–scared as he may have been–went obediently to lay hands on Saul that he might receive the Holy Spirit, and to baptize him. As a result, he witnessed the spiritual birth of early Christianity's greatest spokesperson.

II Chronicles 7:14

If my people, which are called by my name, shall humble themselves, and pray, and seek my face, and turn from their wicked ways; then will I hear from heaven, and will forgive their sin, and will heal their land.

Psalm 122:6

Pray for the peace of Jerusalem; they will prosper that love thee.

Lesson Plan 63

The Book of Acts

Chapters 10 & 11

Objective: To gain a good understanding of the Book of Acts, and its story of the expansion of the Gospel throughout Palestine, northward to Antioch, and thence westward through Asia Minor, Greece to Rome, covering the region that then constituted the backbone of the Roman Empire.

Objective Breakdown:

1. Introduction/Background

2. Cornelius Sends for Peter   Chapter 10:1-8

3. Peter See the Great Sheet   Chapter 10:9-22

4. Peter Preaches to the Gentiles   Chapter 10:23-43

5. Gentiles Are Converted and Speak in Tongues   Chapter 10:44-48

6. Peter Defends His Visit to Gentiles   Chapter 11:1-18

7. The Witness of the Antioch Church   Chapter 11:19-26

8. Famine Relief for Judea   Chapter 11:27-30

Introduction:

The conversion of Saul: He was of the tribe of Benjamin (Philippians 3:5), a Pharisee; a native of Tarsus, the Third University Center of the World, being surpassed at the time only Athens and Alexandria, born a Roman citizen (Acts 22:28) of an influential family, and of Jewish, Greek, and Roman background. Saul had determined to destroy the Church. Having crushed and scattered the Jerusalem Church, he had set out for Damascus to ferret out Christians who had fled there.

On the way, the Lord appeared to Saul. His conversion is told three times, here and also in Chapter Acts 22:5-16 and Chapter Acts 26:12-18. It was a real vision and not just a dream.

He was blinded (Acts 9:8, 9, 18). His attendants heard the voice (Acts 9:7). Subsequently, he served the Christ he had sought to destroy with a devotion unmatched in history. He spent many days in Damascus, preaching Christ (9:23). Then the Jews sought to kill him. He went away to Arabia. He then returned to Damascus and was in Damascus and Arabia for 3 years. Then he returned to Jerusalem (Galatians 1:18) and was there for 15 days. They sought to kill him (Acts 9:29), and he returned to Tarsus (Acts 9:30). Some years later, Barnabas brought him to Antioch (Acts 11:25, 26).

Peter in Joppa:

In Lydda, Peter healed Aeneas. In Joppa, he raised Dorcas from the dead: miracles that led many to believe (35, 42). Peter abode in Joppa for many days (43). Thus, in the Providence of God, Peter was nearby when God was ready for the Gospel door to be opened to the Gentiles in Caesarea, about 30 miles to the North.

Extension of the Gospel to the Gentiles:

Cornelius was the first Gentile Christian. Up until this time, the Gospel had been preached only to the Jews and Jewish proselytes, and Samaritans who observed the Law of Moses.

The Apostles must have understood from Jesus's Final Commission (Matt 28:19) that they were to preach the gospel to All Nations. But it had not been revealed to them that Gentiles were to be received as Gentiles. They felt that the Gentiles had to be circumcised, become Jewish Proselytes, and Keep the Law of Moses before they could be accepted into the Household of God as Christians. Jews were scattered among all nations and the Apostles thought their mission was to them. For a while, they preached only to Jews (11:19). But now Judea, Samaria, and Galilee having been evangelized, the time had come to offer the Gospel to the Gentiles.

Cornelius:

The first Gentile, chosen of God, to be offered the Gospel, was an officer of the Roman Army in Caesarea, named Cornelius. Caesarea on the sea coast, about 50 miles northwest of Jerusalem, was the Roman Capital of Palestine, the residence of the Roman Governor and Military Headquarters of the Province. The band of which Cornelius was Centurion is thought to have been a bodyguard to the Governor. Thus, next to the Governor, Cornelius must have been one of the most important and best-known men in the whole region. Cornelius was a good and devout man. He must have known something of God of the Jews and the Christians.

Caesarea Philip's home (as we noted in chapters 8:40; & 21:80). But, though Cornelius prayed to the God of the Jews, he was still a Gentile.

It was of God that Cornelius was chosen to be the first Gentile to whom the Gospel Door was opened. God Himself directed the whole proceedings. He told Cornelius to send for Peter (10:5). It took a special vision from God for Peter to go (9:23). And God put His seal of approval on the reception of Cornelius into the Church (Chapter 10:44-48), the First Fruits of the Gentile World.

This was probably about 5 to 10 years after the founding of the Church in Jerusalem, possibly about 40 AD.

Apostles Approval   Chapter 11:1-18

Peter's acceptance of Cornelius, the Gentile, into the church, without requiring Circumcision, was approved by the rest of the Apostles only after Peter explained it was all God's doing: God told Cornelius to send for Peter; God told Peter to go to Cornelius; God sealed the transaction by sending the Holy Spirit (12-15). But there arose a sect of Jewish Christians who refused to acquiesce (15:5).

The Church at Antioch   Chapter 11:19-26

Founded soon after the stoning of Stephen, by those who were scattered abroad in the Persecution that followed, probably about A.D. 32, consisting at first of only Jewish Christians (19). Some years later, probably about A.D. 42, certain Christians of Cyprus and Cyrene, possible having heard of the reception of Cornelius into the Church, came to Antioch and began to preach to the Gentiles that they could be Christians without becoming Jewish Proselytes, God Himself, in some way showing His approval (11:21).

The Jerusalem Church heard of it. Convinced by Peter's story of Cornelius that the work was of God, they sent Barnabas to carry the Blessing of the Mother Church. And multitudes of Gentiles were added to the Lord (11:24).

Barnabas went to Tarsus about 100 miles northwest of Antioch and found Saul and brought him to Antioch. This seems to have been some 10 years after Saul's conversion; 3 years of which he spent in Damascus and Arabia, and the rest as far as is known, in Tarsus. God had called Saul to carry the Gospel to the Gentiles (22:21).

Antioch

The third city of the Roman Empire. Population 500,000. Surpassed only by Rome and Alexandria. Mediterranean doorway to the Great Eastern Highways. 300 miles north of Jerusalem. Called "Queen of the East," and Antioch the Beautiful." Embellished with everything that "Roman Wealth, Great Aestheticism and Oriental Luxury could produce."

Its worship of Ashtaroth was accomplished with immoral indulgence and unbelievable indecency. Yet a multitude of its people accepted Christ. It became the birthplace of the name "Christian," and the center of an organized effort to Christianize the world.

Antioch Sends Relief to Jerusalem   Chapter 11:27-30

Relief was brought by Barnabas & Paul. This seems to have been Paul's second return to Jerusalem after his conversion (Galatians 2:1). On his first trip, they had attempted to kill him (Acts 9:26-30). His arrival in Jerusalem (11:30) would seem to place this visit in

A.D. 44, since it is mentioned before Herod's killing of James and imprisonment of Peter (Acts 12:1-4) and mention of his return to Antioch (12:25) just after Herod's death (Acts 12:23). Herod's death is known to have been in A.D. 44.

II Chronicles 7:14

If my people, which are called by my name, shall humble themselves, and pray, and seek my face, and turn from their wicked ways; then will I hear from heaven, and will forgive their sin, and will heal their land.

Psalm 122:6

Pray for the peace of Jerusalem; they will prosper that love thee.

Lesson Plan 64

The Book of Acts

Chapters 12 & 13

Objective: To gain a good understanding of the Book of Acts, and its story of the expansion of the Gospel throughout Palestine, northward to Antioch, and thence westward through Asia Minor, Greece to Rome, covering the region that then constituted the backbone of the Roman Empire.

Objective Breakdown:

1. Herod Executes James & Has Peter Arrested	Chapter 12:1-4
2. Peter Is Miraculously Released	Chapter 12:5-19
3. An Angel of God Strikes Down Herod	Chapter 12:20-24
4. Barnabas and Saul Are Sent Out	Chapter 12:25-13:3
5. A Governor Believes	Chapter 13:4-12
6. Barnabas & Paul Turn to the Gentiles	Chapter 13:13-52

Introduction/Background:

James Killed & Peter Imprisoned

This James is the brother of John, one of three in the inner circle of Jesus and was the first of the Twelve to die in A.D. 44. Another James, the stepbrother of Jesus, came to be recognized as the leading Bishop of Jerusalem.

When Herod imprisoned Peter, God Himself took a hand and delivered Peter (12:7) and smote Herod (11:23). This Herod was the son of Herod who had killed John the Baptist and mocked Christ.

The Herod's were an Edomite line of kings, who under Rome got control of Judea shortly before Christ. Herod the Great (37-3 B.C.), got his throne and kept it by crimes of unspeakable brutality. He murdered his wife and two sons. He was cruel, cunning, cold-blooded. It was he who slew the children of Bethlehem in an effort to kill Christ.

His son Herod Antipas some 33 years later killed John the Baptist (Mark 6:14-29) and mocked Christ (Luke 23:7-12). His grandson Herod Agrippa I, 14 years later, killed James the Apostle (Acts 12:1-2). His great-grandson, Herod Agrippa II, 16 years later was the king before whom Paul was tried (Acts 25:13-26;32).

Paul's Missionary Journey: Chapters 13:45-48

Antioch rapidly became the leading center of Gentile Christianity. One of its teachers was the foster-brother of Herod (13:1). Antioch became Paul's headquarters for his missionary work. From Antioch, he started on his missionary journeys and to Antioch, he returned to report.

Paul had been a Christian now for some 12 to 14 years. He had become a leader in the Antioch Church. The time had now come for him to set forth on the work of bearing the name of Christ far hence to the Gentile world (22:21).

The Galatian region, in central Asia Minor, where Paul went was about 300 miles northwest of Antioch. It was a rather a long journey when we consider there were no railroads, automobiles, or airplanes; only horses, donkeys, camels, or on foot; or by sail and oar boats.

Cyprus: Chapter 13:4-12

The route would have been more direct by land, going through Tarsus, the southeastern gateway to Asia Minor, but the Holy Spirit sent them down to Seleucia and from there they sailed to Cyprus. They went through the island of Cyprus and north into central Asia Minor.

In Cyprus, the Roman Governor was a convert. A miracle did the work (13:11-12). The blinding of the sorcerer was an act of God administered by Paul. From here on Saul, is called Paul (13:9). Paul was the Roman form of the Hebrew name Saul. Up to this point, it was Barnabas and Paul. From here on it is Paul and Barnabas, henceforth Paul is the Leader.

Antioch, Iconium, Lystra, Derbe: Chapter 13:43-52

In Antioch of Pisidia, Paul as his custom started his work in the Jewish synagogue. Some Jews believed, plus many Gentiles in the region around and about (Chapter13:43, 48, 49). But some unbelieving Jews stirred up persecution and drove Paul and Barnabas out of the city.

In Iconium about 100 miles east of Pisidian Antioch, they stayed a long time (14:3); wrought signs and wonders; and a great multitude thought Paul was a god. Later they stoned him and left him for dead. Lystra as the home of Timothy (16:1). Perhaps Timothy saw the occurrence II Timothy 3:11).

In Derbe, about 30 miles southeast of Lystra, they made many disciples. And then they returned through Lystra, Iconium, and Antioch. Paul's thorn in the flesh (II Corinthians 12:2,7), came upon him 14 years before he wrote II Corinthians. That was about the time he entered Galatia (Galatians 4:13).

II Chronicles 7:14

If my people, which are called by my name, shall humble themselves, and pray, and seek my face, and turn from their wicked ways; then will I hear from heaven, and will forgive their sin, and will heal their land.

Psalm 122:6

Pray for the peace of Jerusalem; they will prosper that love thee.

Lesson Plan 65

The Book of Acts

Chapters 14 & 15

Objective: To gain a good understanding of the Book of Acts, and its story of the expansion of the Gospel throughout Palestine, northward to Antioch, and thence westward through Asia Minor, Greece to Rome, covering the region that then constituted the backbone of the Roman Empire.

Objective Breakdown:

1. Introduction

2. Conflicts at Iconium   Chapter 14:1-7

3. Enthusiasm Turns to Violence   Chapter 14:8-20

4. Paul & Barnabas Retrace Their Steps   Chapter 14:21-28

5. A Controversy Over Doctrine Boils Over   Chapter 15:1-21

6. A Letter of Reconciliation Is Sent   Chapter 15:22-35

7. Paul & Barnabas Part   Chapter 15:36-41

Introduction: An encounter with a different culture can sometimes force believers to evaluate what they believe and why. In Antioch, the church ran into a pluralistic society made up of several different groups, prompting the question, "what about circumcision and the law?" The council at Jerusalem came together to address the issue and formulate a biblical response (Acts 15:2, 6). In this sense, Antioch could be called the mother not only of Christian missions and church government but of biblical theology as well.

Even though first-century Christians made regular pilgrimages to Jerusalem and met annually in the Upper Room, the city of Antioch–not Jerusalem –was the center of early Christianity. In fact, modern churches might consider Antioch as a model for when God's people ought to be and do.

Like most cities today, Antioch was racially diverse and culturally pluralistic. As a result, when the scattered believers arrived there (Acts 11:10-20), they had to wrestle with how to make the gospel meaningful for a diversity of groups. Four factors help to account for their success.

They saw ethnic division as a barrier to overcome rather than a status quo to be maintained. Antioch walled off the four dominant groups of its population, Greek, Syrian, African, and Jewish. But the Gospel breaks down walls of separation and hostilities (Ephesians 2:14–22) and brings diverse groups together in Christ. We know that because the Antioch believers broke through the ethnic barriers because: They soon had multi-ethnic leadership. The church employed and deployed pastors, teachers, and evangelists who reflected the composition of the community. Notice the cross-section of the city represented by the leadership team in Acts 13:1.

Barnabas, a Hellenist from Cyprus raised in a priestly family. Appropriately, he was the first major leader of the new group (Acts 4:36; 11:22-23)

Simeon (Niger), an African.

Lucius of Cyrene, also of African descent.

Manaen, a childhood companion of Herod Antipas (the ruler who killed John the Baptist, Mark 6:17–28), perhaps even a relative, surely a privileged member of society.

Saul, a Hellenist Jew from Tarsus with rabbinical training who had Roman citizenship. Note how Barnabas intentionally recruited this untried leader for work (Act11:25-26).

II Chronicles 7:14

If my people, which are called by my name, shall humble themselves, and pray, and seek my face, and turn from their wicked ways; then will I hear from heaven, and will forgive their sin, and will heal their land.

Psalm 122:6

Pray for the peace of Jerusalem; they will prosper that love thee.

Lesson Plan 66

The Book of Acts

Chapters 16 & 17

Objective: To gain a good understanding of the Book of Acts, and its story of the expansion of the Gospel throughout Palestine, northward to Antioch, and thence westward through Asia Minor, Greece to Rome, covering the region that then constituted the backbone of the Roman Empire.

Objective Breakdown:

1. Introduction

2. Timothy Is Recruited for the Work   Chapter 16:1-5

3. The Holy Spirit Directs the Team Westward   Chapter 16:6-10

4. A Clothier Turns to Christ   Chapter 16:11-15

5. A Slave Girl Finds Faith & Freedom   Chapter 16:16-24

6. A Jailer and His Family Believe   Chapter 16:25-34

7. Paul & Silas Are Released   Chapter 16:35-40

8. Converts & Conflicts in Thessalonica   Chapter 17:1-9

9. More Conflict in Berea   Chapter 17:10-15

10. Distress and Debate in Athens   Chapter 17:16-34

Introduction: The early church was a diverse, grassroots, from-the-ground-up movement that drew people together in surprising ways. It turned them inside out, toward one another in service and love. Its example challenges believers today to ask: How are we allowing for cultural differences in our pluralistic society.

Individual converts came from many diverse backgrounds. Dorcas, who possibly worked in the tailoring and garment industry (Acts 9:39). Simon was employed in leather tanning (Acts 9:43). Cornelius, a centurion from the Italian Regiment of the Roman Military (Acts 10:1-

48). Rhoda, a domestic, Acts 12:12-17). Lydia, who manufactured, imported, and exported clothing for the rich (Acts 16:13-15, 40). Tentmakers, Priscilla and Aquila Acts18:1-3).

Iconium, Lystra, Derbe, Philippi, Corinth, Antioch, Athens. For most people today, these are merely dots on a map, but they were major cities in the Roman world. They were centers of influence that attracted Christian messengers such as Paul (Acts16:4). The message of Christ was a message for the city–for its marketplace, arts, academies, councils, courts, prisons, temples, and synagogues.

Paul could use a common language, Greek. Older ethnic languages prevailed among rural peoples, but multi-cultural city dwellers spoke to each other in koine ("common") Greek.

Urban people were perhaps most likely open to entertain new ideas and consider change. He could anticipate greater receptivity and influence networks since he was dealing in the crossroads of communication and commerce. Cities tended to amplify the Christian message to surrounding areas. Cities brought into close proximity Jews and Gentiles, men and women, rich and poor. The message of Christ brought them together.

II Chronicles 7:14

If my people, which are called by my name, shall humble themselves, and pray, and seek my face, and turn from their wicked ways; then will I hear from heaven, and will forgive their sin, and will heal their land.

Psalm 122:6

Pray for the peace of Jerusalem; they will prosper that love thee.

Lesson Plan 67

The Book of Acts

Chapters 18 & 19

Objective: To gain a good understanding of the Book of Acts, and its story of the expansion of the Gospel throughout Palestine, northward to Antioch, and thence westward through Asia Minor, Greece to Rome, covering the region that then constituted the backbone of the Roman Empire.

Objective Breakdown:

1. Introduction

2. Partnership with Priscilla and Aquila   Chapter 18:1-4

3. A Synagogue Ruler Believes   Chapter 18:5-11

4. Jewish Leaders Oppose the Gospel   Chapter 18:12-17

5. Paul Returns to Antioch   Chapter 18:18-23

6. Apollos Is Mentored in the Faith   Chapter 18:24-28

7. Paul Arrives at Ephesus   Chapter 19:1-7

8. Lectures in the Synagogue and the School of Tyrannus   Chapter 19:8-10

9. Occultists Are Converted   Chapter 19:11-20

10. The Gospel Challenges the Economy   Chapter 19:21-41

Introduction: At Athens, Paul addresses the Greeks in three different settings: the synagogue, the Areopagus (the supreme tribunal), and the Agora, or marketplace. This required three different approaches and points to Paul's great ability in the rhetorical arts.

Interestingly, Paul spoke out in the marketplace. As there were few if any believers in Athens, he had to work "from the outside in" to present the gospel to Athenian workers. By contrast, believers today work in all levels of industry and commerce.

Paul's example raises a challenging question: Are you willing –and prepared— to represent Christ and His message and values where you are? Your faith cannot be a purely personal affair. God has appointed you to your workplace to carry the message of Christ to your family, friends, extended family, and neighbors, just as he appointed Paul to go to the Agora of Athens.

Apparently, none of the Epicurean or Stoic philosophers of Athens responded to Paul's message about Christ, but Luke does name a council member (Dionysius) and a woman (Damaris) as the nucleus of a group that did believe (Acts 17:34).

II Chronicles 7:14

If my people, which are called by my name, shall humble themselves, and pray, and seek my face, and turn from their wicked ways; then will I hear from heaven, and will forgive their sin, and will heal their land.

Psalm 122:6

Pray for the peace of Jerusalem; they will prosper that love thee.

Lesson Plan 68

The Book of Acts

Chapters 21 & 22

Objective: To gain a good understanding of the Book of Acts, and its story of the expansion of the Gospel throughout Palestine, northward to Antioch, and thence westward through Asia Minor, Greece to Rome, covering the region that then constituted the backbone of the Roman Empire.

Objective Breakdown:

1. Background/Introduction

2. Paul Is Warned to Avoid Jerusalem   Chapter 21:1-16

3. Paul Arrives in Jerusalem   Chapter 21:17-26

4. A Mob Seeks to Kill Paul   Chapter 21:27-39

5. Paul Is Allowed to Address the People   Chapter 21:40-22:1-29

6. Paul Is Brought Before the Jewish Leaders   Chapter 22:1-30

Background/Introduction:

Scripture mentions Alexandria only four times (all in Acts: 6:9; 18:24; 27:6; 28:11). However, the city's influence on the New Testament and the church was far greater than these few references might lead one to believe. Alexandria was the birthplace of the Greek Old Testament translation known as the Septuagint.

Scattered among the cities of the Alexandrians, Greek, and Roman empires were millions of Hebrews. By the first century, more than one million lived in Egypt. In Alexandria, they had separate districts from their Gentile neighbors, but isolation from Jerusalem took its toll. Each successive generation moved further away from Judaism, adopting Hellenist ways of Alexandrian society.

The Septuagint was a response to cultural assimilation. Tradition holds that Jewish leaders in Alexandria invited some 70 Greek-speaking elders from Israel to translate the Hebrew

Scripture into Koine, the Greek that was commonly spoken as a trade language throughout the ancient world. The Septuagint was completed in the second century B.C. This Alexandrian Greek Urban Bible became the Bible of the early church. It is the Bible that Peter quoted at Pentecost and the Bible that Apollos had grown up with. Conceived in a world-class pluralistic city, it was the first Bible translated into the language of the people and encouraged the use of koine for the New Testament.

One purpose of the journey to Jerusalem was to deliver the Offering of Money which he had gathered from Gentile Churches in Greece and Asia Minor for the poor saints in Jerusalem (Acts 24:17; Romans 15:25, 26; I Corinthians 16:11-4; II Corinthians 8:10; 9:1-15). It was a great offering. He had spent over a year gathering it. A crowning demonstration of the spirit of Brotherly Kindness, to encourage a feeling of Christian Love between Jew & Gentile.

Another purpose of the journey was to keep a Vow (Acts 21:24-25). A Vow had brought him to Jerusalem at the close of his Second Journey (Acts 18:18). These Vows he had made to show to the Jews that while he taught Gentiles that they could be Christians without keeping the law of Moses, he himself, as a Jew, was zealous to observe all Jewish Laws.

From the start of the journey, he was warned not to go. The Holy Spirit in every city warned him (Acts 20:23). In Caesarea, while he was at Philip's house, the warning was repeated with graphic emphasis (Acts 21:10,11). Even Luke begged him not to go (Acts 21:12).

But it was settled in Paul's mind, even if it meant death (Acts 21:13). Why these warnings from God? Could it be that Paul was mistaken and God was trying to tell him so? Or could it be that God was testing him? Or preparing him? Could it be that Paul may have thought his own martyrdom at Jerusalem would have been a fitting climax, in the same city where he himself martyred many Christians?

Paul arrives in Jerusalem. He arrived there about June, A.D. 58 (Acts 20:16). It was his 5th recorded visit to Jerusalem after his conversion. In intervening years he won vast multitudes of Gentiles to the Christian faith for which unbelieving Jews hated him. After he had been there nearly a week, fulfilling his vow in the Temple, certain Jews recognized him.

Also, when Paul declared, "I must also see Rome" (Acts 19:21), he wasn't talking about a tourist excursion. He was stating his bold intentions to penetrate the capital of the world with the gospel. To him, Rome was a symbol of the center of power, the system that was driving the world. Jerusalem may have been important as a starting point, but the goal was Rome.

Ephesians 4:29-32:

29. Let no corrupt communication proceed out of your mouth, but that which is good to the use of edifying, that it may minister grace unto the hearers.

30. And grieve not the Holy Spirit of God, whereby ye are sealed unto the day of redemption.

31. Let all bitterness, and wrath, and anger, and clamour, and evil speaking, be put away from you, with all malice:

32. And be ye kind one to another, tenderhearted, forgiving one another, even as God for Christ's sake hath forgiven you.

II Chronicles 7:14

If my people, which are called by my name, shall humble themselves, and pray, and seek my face, and turn from their wicked ways; then will I hear from heaven, and will forgive their sin, and will heal their land.

Psalm 122:6

Pray for the peace of Jerusalem; they will prosper that love thee.

Lesson Plan 69

The Book of Acts

Chapters 23, 24, & 25

Objective: To gain a good understanding of the Book of Acts, and its story of the expansion of the Gospel throughout Palestine, northward to Antioch, and thence westward through Asia Minor, Greece to Rome, covering the region that then constituted the backbone of the Roman Empire.

Objective Breakdown:

1. Introduction/Background

2. Paul Is Brought Before the Jewish Leaders   Chapter 23:1-11

3. A Murder Plot Is Uncovered   Chapter 23:12-35

4. Paul Faces Felix the Governor   Chapter 24:1-27

5. Paul Faces Festus the Governor   Chapter 25:1-12

6. Paul Appears Before King Agrippa and Bernice   Chapter 25:13-27

Introduction/Background: (Two Years, from Summer of A.D. 58 to Fall of A.D. 60.)

Paul had just been in Caesarea a week before, in Philip's house, on his way to Jerusalem, where a prophet, named Agabus, had come from Jerusalem to warn him (Acts 21:8-14).

Caesarea was the Roman Capital of Judea, chosen of God, for the reception of the First gentile into the Church, Cornelius, an Officer of the Roman Army, some 20 years before.

Here, in this most important Roman city of Palestine, Paul spent two years as a prisoner in the Palace of the Roman Governor (Acts 23:35) with the privilege of visitors. What an opportunity to make Christ known!

Paul Is Brought Before the Jewish Leaders   Chapter 23:1-11

A Murder Plot Is Uncovered   Chapter 23:12-25

Paul Faces Felix the Governor   Chapter 24:1-27

Felix had been Roman Governor of Palestine for many years. He knew something about Christians, for there were multitudes of them under his jurisdiction. Now he was to sit in judgment on the most noted of all Christian teachers. Paul made a deep impression on Felix. Felix sent for him often. But his covetousness kept him from accepting Christ or releasing Paul (26). Drusilla was the sister of Agrippa (25:13).

Paul Faces Festus the Governor   Chapter 25:1-12

Festus succeeded Felix as Governor, A.D. 60. The Jews were still plotting to murder Paul. Festus, though convinced of Paul's innocence, was disposed to turn him over to the Jews, which Paul knew would mean death. So Paul appealed to Caesar (11), which, as a Roman Citizen, he had a right to do, and which appeal Festus had to honor.

Paul's Roman Citizenship, probably conferred on his father for some service to the State, saved his life more than once.

Paul Appears before King Agrippa II   Chapter 25:13-27

This Agrippa was Herod Agrippa II, and was the son of Herod Agrippa I, who 16 years before had killed James (Acts:12:2); he was the grandson of Herod Antipas who had killed John the Baptist and mocked Christ; and the great-grandson of Herod the Great who had murdered the children of Bethlehem.

King Agrippa II was tetrarch over the Province on the northeast border of Palestine. He is now asked to aid Festus. Bernice was his sister and was living with him as his wife. A woman of rare beauty, she had already been married to two kings and had come back to be her own brother's wife. Later she became mistress to Emperor Vespasian and Emperor Titus. Think of Paul making his defense before a pair like that.

Even so, King Agrippa II was profoundly impressed (Acts 26:28). But to Festus, the idea of a Resurrection from the Dead was so unthinkable that he cried out that Paul must be crazy (Acts 26:24). However, they all agreed that Paul was innocent of any wrong (Acts 26:31).

II Chronicles 7:14

If my people, which are called by my name, shall humble themselves, and pray, and seek my face, and turn from their wicked ways; then will I hear from heaven, and will forgive their sin, and will heal their land.

Psalm 122:6

Pray for the peace of Jerusalem; they will prosper that love thee.

Lesson Plan 70

The Book of Acts

Chapters 26, 27, & 28

Objective: To gain a good understanding of the Book of Acts, and its story of the expansion of the Gospel throughout Palestine, northward to Antioch, and thence westward through Asia Minor, Greece to Rome, covering the region that then constituted the backbone of the Roman Empire.

Objective Breakdown:

1. Introduction/Background

2. Paul Speaks to King Agrippa   Chapter 26:1-32

3. Shipwreck on the Way to Rome   Chapter 27:1-42

4. A Friendly Exchange at Malta   Chapter 28:1-10

5. Paul Arrives at Rome   Chapter 28:11-16

6. Some Jews Believe and Some Do Not   Chapter 28:17-29

7. Paul Teaches and Preaches   Chapter 28:30-31

Introduction: Festus was the successor to Felix as governor of Judea (A.D. 59-61 see Acts 23:24). Festus is best known today for insisting that Jewish leaders meet with Paul in Caesarea where the Apostle Paul was protected, thereby foiling a plot to kill him. Later though, Festus suggested a retrial in Jerusalem as a favor to the Jews.

The diplomatic visit of King Agrippa and Bernice to Caesarea proved timely (Acts 25:13). As a new, relatively inexperienced Roman governor of Judea, Festus faced a delicate religious conflict between the Jews, led by council, and the growing Christian movement, represented by Paul. Just as Festus began to rule on the case, Agrippa and Bernice arrived. Festus, and the Jews, and Paul all benefited from the couple's expertise in Jewish history and affairs (Acts 25:23; 26:3). The brother and sister had watched their father govern Judea and its population for several years before Agrippa inherited the office himself.

Paul was competent in and comfortable with the Roman judicial system and its procedures. He knew how to address Roman officials, respecting their position. At this point, he respected the political system. The state had not yet become the beast that John described in Revelation 13.

The problems Paul did encounter were not with the system but with its leaders. He faced two politicians, one dealing with bribes (Acts 24:25-26), the other in political favors (Acts 25:9). Seeking justice, Paul got caught in the middle.

Paul found himself caught between Festus (Acts 25:1), a brand new local governor appointed by the Romans (Acts 24:27), and a well-established Jewish council, the supreme court of the Hebrews (Acts 25:2). The council could have outwitted the new official–at Paul's expense and to their own gain; particularly if the case had been moved to their home turf in Jerusalem (Acts 25:9). So Paul appealed to a higher court, Caesar, to regain a balance of power (Acts 25:11). In doing so, he exercised his rights as a Roman citizen. At this time the Caesar was Nero, and he had not yet begun to persecute the Christians, as he did later in A.D. 64 (Acts 25:12).

Paul's Voyage to Rome   Chapter 27:1-28:15

Began in the early fall of A.D. 60. Three inter-months in Melita. Arrived in Rome in early Spring of A.D. 61. The Trip was made in three different ships: one from Caesarea to Myra; another from Myra to Melita; and the third from Melita to Puteoli.

Soon after leaving Myra, they ran into fierce adverse winds, were driven off course, and after many days, when all hope was gone, God, who had two years before (back in Jerusalem) told Paul that he would see him to Rome (23:11), again appeared to Paul to assure him that He would make good His Word (27:24). And He did.

Paul in Rome   Chapter 28:16-31

Paul was in Rome for at least two years (28:30). Though a prisoner, he was allowed to live in his own hired house, with his guard (28:16), with the freedom to receive visitors and to teach Christ. Paul's two years in Rome were very fruitful, reaching even into the palace (Philippians 4:23). While in Rome, he wrote the Epistles to the Ephesians, Philippians, Colossians, Philemon, and possibly Hebrews.

Paul's Later Life

It is generally accepted that Paul was acquitted, about A.D. 63 or 64. Whether he went on to Spain, as he planned (Romans 15:28), is not known. Tradition intimates that he did, but if he did, he did not stay long. It seems fairly certain that he was back in Greece and Asia Minor about A.D. 65 to A.D. 67, in which period he wrote the Epistle to Timothy and Titus. Then rearrested, he was taken back to Rome and beheaded about 67 A.D.

Summary of Paul's Life

Paul first appears as a persecutor of Christians, resolutely determined to blot out the name of Jesus. No doubt he thought the resurrection of Jesus from the dead was a fixed-up story. Then on the road to Damascus, as by a stroke from heaven, he was smitten down. Jesus Himself spoke to him, (about A.D. 32). From that moment, he was a changed man with zeal and devotion unparalleled in history. He went up and down the highways of the Roman Empire crying out, "Jesus Did Rise from the Dead. It is true, it is true, it is true, He is risen, He is risen, HE IS RISEN."

In Damascus, they tried to kill him. He went into Arabia, then back to Damascus. Then he returned to Jerusalem in about A.D. 35 and they tried to kill him. Then he went to Tarsus.

In Antioch, about A.D. 42 to 44: he went up to Jerusalem in about A.D.44 with an offering of money for the poor.

First Missionary Journey, about A.D. 45 to 48. Galatia: Pisidian Antioch, Iconium, Lystra, Derbe. Returned to Antioch.

Conference at Jerusalem about Gentile Circumcision, about A.D. 50. Second Missionary Journey, about A.D. 50-53; Greece: Philippi, Thessalonica, Berea, Athens, Corinth: return to Jerusalem, Antioch.

Third Missionary Journey, about A.D. 54-57: Ephesus, Greece.

To Jerusalem, A.D. 58 with a great offering of money.

In Caesarea A.D. 58-60, a prisoner in the governor's castle.

In Rome, A.D. 61-63, a prisoner.

Back in Greece and Asia Minor about A.D. 65-67

Beheaded in Rome about A.D. 67.

His ministry lasted about 35 years. In those 35 years, he won vast multitudes to Christ.

At times, God helped him with miracles. In almost every city, he was persecuted. Again and again, he was mobbed and they tried to kill him. He was beaten, scourged, imprisoned, stoned, and driven from city to city. On top of all this, his "thorn in the flesh" (II Corinthians 12). His sufferings are almost unbelievable. He must have had an iron constitution. God used supernatural powers to keep him alive during his 35 years of ministry.

II Chronicles 7:14

If my people, which are called by my name, shall humble themselves, and pray, and seek my face, and turn from their wicked ways; then will I hear from heaven, and will forgive their sin, and will heal their land.

Psalm 122:6

Pray for the peace of Jerusalem; they will prosper that love thee.

The Book of Romans

Scripture Focus Chapters 1 - 16

Objective: To gain an understanding of the Book of Romans which is placed first among his fourteen Epistles in the New Testament. (I count the Book of Hebrew as written by Paul, thus a total of fourteen Epistles written by Paul.). The Book of Romans was probably written in Corinth about A.D. 57 and focuses on God's Plan of righteousness to everyone who comes to Christ by faith.

Objective Breakdown:

1. Introduction	Chapter 1:1-17
2. The Reason for Gentile Guilt	Chapter 1:18-23
3. Results of Gentile Guilt	Chapter 1:24-32
4. Jews Are Judged According to Truth	Chapter 2:1-5
5. Jews Are Judged by Their Works	Chapter 2:6-10
6. Jews Are Judged with Impartiality	Chapter 2:11-16
7. Jews Do Not Obey the Law	Chapter 2:17-29
8. Jews Do Not Believe the Oracles	Chapter 3:1-8
9. Conclusion: All Guilty Before God	Chapter 3:9-20
10. Description of Righteousness	Chapter 3:21-31
11. Abraham's Righteousness Apart from Works	Chapter 4:1-8
12. Abraham's Righteousness Apart from Circumcision	Chapter 4:9-12
13. Abraham's Apart from the Law	Chapter 4:13-15
14. Abraham's Righteousness Was by Faith	Chapter 4:16-25
15. Peace with God	Chapter 5:1-2
16. Joy in Tribulation	Chapter 5:3-8

Lesson Plan 71

The Book of Romans

Chapters 1 & 2

Objective: To give us insight and discernment on what we must do to be a Christian.

Objective Breakdown:

Introduction/Background

Greetings	Chapter 1:1-7
Paul Prays for His Readers:	Chapter 1:8-13
The Gospel Is the Power of God:	Chapter 1:16-17
God Will Judge Sin:	Chapter 1:18-32
All Are Guilty, Whether Jew or Gentile:	Chapter 2:1-16
Being Jewish Is Not Enough:	Chapter 2:17-29

Introduction/Background: Paul was chosen to be the chief expounder of the Gospel to the world, and his Epistle to the Romans is Paul's complete explanation of his understanding of the Gospel.

Date and Occasion of the Epistle: Winter of A.D. 57-58. Paul was in Corinth, at the close of his Third missionary Journey, on the eve of his departure to Jerusalem with the offering of money for the poor saints (Romans 15:22-27). A woman named Phoebe, of Cenchreae, a suburb of Corinth, was sailing for Rome (Romans 16:1-2). Paul availed himself of the opportunity to send this letter by her. There was no postal system in the Roman Empire except for official business. Personal letters had to be carried by friends or chance travelers.

Purpose of the Epistle: To let the Roman Christians know that he was on his way to Rome. He reached Rome three years after he wrote this Epistle. The nucleus of the Roman Church probably was formed by the Romans who were present at Jerusalem on the Day of Pentecost (Acts 2:10).

II Chronicles 7:14

If my people, which are called by my name, shall humble themselves, and pray, and seek my face, and turn from their wicked ways; then will I hear from heaven, and will forgive their sin, and will heal their land.

Psalm 122:6

Pray for the peace of Jerusalem; they will prosper that love thee.

Lesson Plan 72

The Book of Romans

Chapters 3 & 4

Objective: To give us insight and discernment on what we must do to be a Christian.

Objective Breakdown:

1. Introduction

2. Faith Alone Makes Heritage Valuable   Chapter 3:1-8

3. All Stand Condemned Before God   Chapter 3:9-20

4. The Way of Righteousness – By Faith   Chapter 3:21-31

5. Abraham Was Justified by Faith   Chapter 4:1-15

6. God Rewarded Abraham's Faith   Chapter 4:16-25

Introduction: The Bible is straightforward about the ultimate cause behind suffering and evil. It gives a sobering account of how we human beings, who were created as pure and noble creatures, have become wicked and hurtful toward each other. The Book of Romans speaks candidly about our condition, which it calls sin (Roman3:23). This separation from God has resulted in our thoughts become futile and our futile hearts being darkened (Romans 1:21). God has given us up to the full outworking of our rebellion against Him (Romans1:24). This rebellion has produced:

• Sexual immorality, wherein we dishonor the bodies that God gave us (Romans 1:24)

• Idolatry wherein we turn away from our Creator and exalt the works of our own hands (Romans 1:25).

• Vile passions, wherein we become irrational pleasure seekers, often dominated by a perverted sensuality, rather than thoughtful servants of each other and responsible stewards of God's good gifts (Romans 1:26-27).

- A debased mind, wherein we come under terrible spiritual bondage that makes us incapable of doing good; we become slaves to sin (Romans 1:28).

The candor of the above list is painful but honest.

Faith Alone Makes Heritage Valuable	Read Chapter 3:1-8
All Stand Condemned Before God	Read Chapter 3:9-20
The Way of Righteousness–By Faith	Read Chapter 3:21-31
Abraham Was Justified by Faith	Read Chapter 4:1-15
God Rewarded Abraham's Faith	Read Chapter 4:16-25

II Chronicles 7:14

If my people, which are called by my name, shall humble themselves, and pray, and seek my face, and turn from their wicked ways; then will I hear from heaven, and will forgive their sin, and will heal their land.

Psalm 122:6

Pray for the peace of Jerusalem; they will prosper that love thee

Lesson Plan 73

The Book of Romans

Chapters 5, 6, & 7

Objective: To give us insight and discernment on what it means to be a Christian.

Objective Breakdown:

1. Introduction

2. Through Faith, We Have Peace with God   Chapter 5:1-11

3. Through Faith, Christ Makes Us Alive Again   Chapter 5:12-21

4. Through Faith, We Can Obey God   Chapter 6:1-14

5. We Are No Longer Enslaved to Sin   Chapter 6:15-23

6. A New View of The Law   Chapter 7:1-12

7. A Terrible Inner Conflict   Chapter 7:13-25

Introduction: The happy effects of justification through faith in the righteousness of Christ. (Romans 5:1-5) That we are reconciled by His blood. (Romans 5:6-11). The fall of Adam brought all mankind into sin and death. (Romans 5:12-14). The grace of God, through the righteousness of Christ, has more power to bring salvation, than Adam's sin had to bring misery, (Romans 5:15-19) as grace did abound. (Romans 5:20, 21)

Romans 5:1-5: A blessed change takes place in the sinner's state, when he becomes a true believer, whatever he has been. Being justified by faith he has peace with God. The holy, righteous God cannot be at peace with a sinner, while under the guilt of sin. Justification takes away the guilt, and so makes way for peace. This is through our Lord Jesus Christ; through him as the great Peacemaker, the Mediator between God and man. The saints' happy state is a state of grace. Into this grace we are brought, which teaches that we were not born in this state.

Romans Chapter 6: Believers must die to sin and live to God. (Romans 6:1, 2). This is urged by their Christian baptism and union with Christ (Romans 6:3-10). They are made alive to

God. (Romans 6:11-15). And are freed from the dominion of sin (Romans 6:16-20). The end of sin is death and of holiness everlasting life (Romans 6:21-23). Romans 6:1- 2, the apostle is very full in pressing the necessity of holiness. He does not explain away the free grace of the gospel, but he shows that the connection between justification and holiness is inseparable. Let the thought be abhorred, of continuing in sin that grace may abound. True believers are dead to sin, therefore they ought not to follow it. No man can at the same time be both dead and alive. He is a fool who, desiring to be dead unto sin, thinks he may live in it.

Romans 6:3-10: Baptism teaches the necessity of dying to sin and being as it were buried from all ungodly and unholy pursuits, and of rising to walk with God in newness of life. Unholy professors may have had the outward sign of a death unto sin, and a new birth unto righteousness, but they never passed from the family of Satan to that of God. The corrupt nature, called the old man because it is derived from our first father Adam, is crucified with Christ, in every true believer, by the grace derived from the cross. It is weakened and in a dying state, though it yet struggles for life, and even for victory. But the whole body of sin, whatever is not according to the Holy Law of God, must be done away so that the believer may no more be the slave of sin, but live to God and find happiness in His service.

II Chronicles 7:14

If my people who are called by my name will humble themselves and pray, and seek my face, and turn from their wicked ways, then I will hear from heaven and will forgive their sin and heal their land.

Psalm 122:6

Pray for the peace of Jerusalem; they shall prosper who love thee.

Lesson Plan 74

The Book of Romans

Chapter 8

Objective: To give us insight and discernment on what it means to be a Christian.

Objective Breakdown:

1. Introduction

2. In Christ There Is No More Condemnation   Romans 8:1-8

3. Believers Are People of the Spirit   Romans 8:9-17

4. Believers Receive the Spirit's Help   Romans 8:18-30

5. Believers Are Loved by God   Romans 8:31:39

Introduction: The Liberation of Creation. In chapter 8 of Romans, Paul painted on a cosmic canvas a vast picture of the world, from its origin as God's beautiful creation to the impact of sin, and on to its ultimate restoration at the end of history. If you ever wondered what's ultimately going to happen to the world or if you ever worried about environmental disaster, if you ever wished that evil could somehow be vanquished, this passage is a must-read.

Paul recognized that the world is both delightful and disastrous, orderly and chaotic. He offered a good news/bad news scenario. The bad news is that all of creation, including human beings and their environment, is corrupted by sin. Sin is so prevalent and so destructive that we need more than just a better earth— we need a new earth. Sin is not just personal; it is global. It is infused in the bloodstream of the whole world, where sinful people create systems and cultures that promote and protect evil as well as good.

The good news is that God's salvation is equally universal in its availability and effect. His saving grace starts its work inside people but eventually works its way out. Through their influence, God's power and purposes begin to penetrate their values, worldview, relationships, career choices, and community involvements. As God's managers of the earth, we begin to reclaim the devil's territory by redirecting social systems and cultural values so that people and places benefit instead of being exploited. What begins as personal conversion results in societal change as God's people slowly impact their families, coworkers, churches, communities, culture, and environment.

But this liberation of creation will be partial and imperfect until Christ returns to redeem it personally. In the meantime, the world groans like a woman in labor (Romans 8:22), waiting for its delivery from sin. Christ calls His followers to participate in the world systems, to promote His values and love as we have the opportunity. In today's study, Paul teaches about God's mercy in salvation, extended surprisingly to the Gentile unbelievers of his day, who like all unbelievers did not deserve it.

Important Scriptures

2 Timothy 3:16

All scripture is given by inspiration of God, and is profitable for doctrine, for reproof, for correction, for instruction in righteousness.

2 Peter 1:20-21

Knowing this first, that no prophecy of the scripture is of any private interpretation. 21. For the prophecy came not in old time by the will of man: but holy men of God spake as they were moved by the Holy Ghost.

2 Peter 2:21-22

For it had been better for them not to have known the way of righteousness, than, after they have known it, to turn from the holy commandment delivered unto them.

22. But it is happened unto them according to the true proverb, the dog is turned to his own vomit again; and the sow that was washed to her wallowing in the mire.

1 John 4:1-3

Beloved, believe not every spirit, but try the spirits whether they are of God: because many false prophets are gone out into the world. 2. Hereby know ye the Spirit of God: Every spirit that confesseth that Jesus Christ is come in the flesh is of God: 3. And every spirit that confesseth not that Jesus Christ is come in the flesh is not of God: and this is that spirit of antichrist, whereof ye have heard that it should come; and even now already is it in the world.

James 5:20

Let him know, that he which converteth the sinner from the error of his way shall save a soul from death, and shall hide a multitude of sins.

Hebrews 6:4

For it is impossible for those who were once enlightened, and have tasted of the heavenly gift, and were made partakers of the Holy Ghost, 5. And have tasted the good word of God, and the powers of the world to come, 6. If they shall fall away, to renew them again unto repentance; seeing they crucify to themselves the Son of God afresh, and put him to an open shame.

Hebrews 10:26

For if we sin wilfully after that we have received the knowledge of the truth, there remaineth no more sacrifice for sins,

Galatians 1:6-9

I marvel that ye are so soon removed from him that called you into the grace of Christ unto another gospel: 7. Which is not another; but there be some that trouble you, and would pervert the gospel of Christ. 8. But though we, or an angel from heaven, preach any other gospel unto you than that which we have preached unto you, let him be accursed. 9. As we said before, so say I now again, If any man preach any other gospel unto you than that ye have received, let him be accursed.

1 Timothy 4:1-3

Now the Spirit speaketh expressly, that in the latter times some shall depart from the faith, giving heed to seducing spirits, and doctrines of devils; 2. Speaking lies in hypocrisy; having their conscience seared with a hot iron; 3. Forbidding to marry, and commanding to abstain from meats, which God hath created to be received with thanksgiving of them which believe and know the truth. 4. For every creature of God is good, and nothing to be refused, if it be received with thanksgiving: 5. For it is sanctified by the word of God and prayer.

Colossians 2:8

Beware lest any man spoil you through philosophy and vain deceit, after the tradition of men, after the rudiments of the world, and not after Christ.

Galatians 1:11-21

But I certify you, brethren, that the gospel which was preached of me is not after man.12. For I neither received it of man, neither was I taught it, but by the revelation of Jesus Christ. 13. For ye have heard of my conversation in time past in the Jews' religion, how that beyond measure I persecuted the church of God, and wasted it: 14. And profited in the Jews' religion above many my equals in mine own nation, being more exceedingly zealous of the traditions of my fathers. 15. But when it pleased God, who separated me from my mother's womb, and called me by his grace, 16. To reveal his Son in me, that I might preach him among the heathen; immediately I conferred not with flesh and blood: 17. Neither went I up to Jerusalem to them which were apostles before me; but I went into Arabia, and returned again unto Damascus. 18. Then after three years I went up to Jerusalem to see Peter, and abode with him fifteen days. 19. But other of the apostles saw I none, save James the Lord's brother. 20. Now the things which I write unto you, behold, before God, I lie not.21. Afterwards I came into the regions of Syria and Cilicia.

In Happy Moments, PRAISE GOD.

In Difficult Moments, SEEK GOD.

In Quiet Moments, WORSHIP GOD.

In Painful Moments, TRUST GOD.

Every Moment, THANK GOD.

II Chronicles 7:14

If my people, which are called by my name, shall humble themselves, and pray, and seek my face, and turn from their wicked ways; then will I hear from heaven, and will forgive their sin, and will heal their land.

Psalm 122:6

Pray for the peace of Jerusalem; they will prosper that love thee.

Lesson Plan 75

The Book of Romans

Chapters 9, 10, & 11

Objective: To give us insight and discernment on what it means to be a Christian.

Objective Breakdown:

1. Introduction

2. The Implication of Faith for Israel   Romans 9:1-13

3. God Is Sovereign   Romans 9:14-33

4. Paul Longs for Israel's Salvation   Romans 10:1-13

5. The Nation Needs to Hear the Gospel   Romans 10:14-21

6. God Has Not Given Up on His People   Romans 11:1-10

7. The Implications of Faith for Gentiles   Romans 11:11-24

8. Israel Will Eventually Be Saved   Romans 11:25-32

9. Paul's Prayer of Praise   Romans 11:33-36

Introduction: Have you ever wondered what happened to the special relationship between God and the nation of Israel (Romans 10:1). Are the Jews still God's "chosen people?" Are the promises that God made to Abraham, Moses, David, and other Old Testament Hebrews still in effect? Or did God reject Israel when the nation rejected His Son, Jesus God forbid? These issues that Paul addresses in Romans chapters 9-11. They are vitally important because they relate to whether or not God is to be trusted.

God's relationship with Israel goes back thousands of years to the Ancient Middle East. The Bible presents Abraham (Genesis 12:10) as the Father of the Nation. Abraham came from Ur, a city of ancient Sumer in Mesopotamia (Genesis 11:31), where he prospered before moving to the land of Canaan (Genesis 12:5).

There, God entered into a covenant with Abraham, promising to bless his descendants and make them a special people (Genesis 12:1-3). Abraham was to remain faithful to God and to serve as a channel through which God's blessings could flow to the rest of the world.

Abraham's son Isaac had two sons, Esau and Jacob. God chose Jacob for the renewal of His promise to Abraham (Genesis 28:13-15). Jacob's name was changed to Israel after a dramatic struggle with God (Genesis 32:24–30; 35:9–15). The name was later applied to Jacob's descendants of Jacob through his twelve sons, the Hebrew people. The twelve tribes were called "Israelites" "children of Israel," and "house of Israel," identifying them clearly as the descendants of Israel.

Note: God's covenant with Abraham was far more than a contract. A contract has an end date, while a covenant, in the biblical sense, is a permanent arrangement. This is good news for the Jews and Gentiles alike. For Jews it means that God has not abandoned His people, they still figure prominently in His plans and purposes. For Gentiles, it means that God can surely be trusted.

Israel's rejection of Christ is temporary. The days will come when all Israel shall be saved (Romans11:26). One of the darkest spots in the panorama of human history is the age-long suffering of these sorrowful, disobedient people. But one day it will end. Israel shall turn in penitence to the Lord. And all creation shall give thanks to God for the unsearchable wisdom of His providence.

Civil governments are ordained of God (Romans 13:1) to restrain the criminal elements of human society. However, many civil governments can often be run by evil men. Christians should be law-abiding citizens of the government under which they live, in all their attitudes and relations of life, governing themselves by the principles of the Golden Rule (Romans 13: 8-10), making a special effort to be honorable in all things, and always considerate to others. The only time that citizens should disobey the governmental authorities is when the government's edicts conflict with the Word and the laws of God.

See Acts 5:24-29.

II Chronicles 7:14

If my people, which are called by my name, shall humble themselves, and pray, and seek my face, and turn from their wicked ways; then will I hear from heaven, and will forgive their sin, and will heal their land.

Psalm 122:6

Pray for the peace of Jerusalem; they will prosper that love thee.

Lesson Plan 76

The Book of Romans

Chapters 12, 13, & 14

Objective: To give us insight and discernment on what it means to be a Christian.

Objective Breakdown:

1. Introduction

2. The Believer's Relationship to God   Chapter 12:1-2

3. The Believer's Position in the Body of Christ   Chapter 12:3-13

4. The Believer's Service to the Community   Chapter 12:14-21

5. Believers Submission to the State   Chapter 13:1-7

6. The Believers Conduct   Chapter 13:8-14

7. Controversial Practices   Chapter 14:1-13

8. Pursue Peace with Each Other   Chapter 14:14-23

Introduction: The Liberation of Creation. In chapter 8 of Romans, Paul painted a cosmic canvas a vast picture of the world, from its origin as God's beautiful creation to the impact of sin, and on to its ultimate restoration at the end of history. If you've ever wondered what ultimately is going to happen to the world; if you ever worried about environmental disaster; if you ever wished that evil could somehow vanish; then one needs to reread Romans chapter8 at a quiet time and in a quiet place.

Paul recognized that the world is both delightful and disastrous, orderly and chaotic. He offered a good news/bad news scenario. The bad news is that all of creation, including human beings and their environment, is corrupted by sin. Sin is so prevalent and so destructive that we need more than just a better earth— we need a new earth. Sin is not just local, it is global. It is infused in the bloodstream of the whole world, where sinful people create systems and cultures that promote and protect evil as well as good.

The good news is that God's salvation is equally universal in its availability and effect. His saving grace starts its work inside people but eventually works its way out through their influence. God's power and purposes begin to penetrate their values, worldview, relationships, career choices, and community involvements. As God's managers of the earth, we begin to reclaim the devil's territory, by redirecting social systems and cultural values so that people and places benefit instead of being exploited. What begins as personal conversion results in societal change as God's people slowly impact their families, coworkers, churches, communities, culture, and environment.

But this liberation of creation will be partial and imperfect until Christ returns to redeem it personally. In the meantime, the world groans like a woman in labor (Romans 8:22), waiting for its delivery from sin. Christ calls His followers to participate in the world systems, to promote His values and love as we have the opportunity.

In today's study, Paul is teaching about God's mercy in salvation, extended surprisingly to the Gentiles unbelievers of his day, who like all unbelievers did not deserve it. Paul begins by reflecting on his personal anguish over the lost condition of his Israelite kinfolks (Romans 9:1-5).

How strongly do you sense a burden for a lost person or group of persons?

If you sense no such burden, why not?

Are We One People? By the time Paul wrote his letter to the Christians at Rome, Gentiles were probably becoming the majority of believers throughout the church. Jews had less and less influence theologically, culturally, or politically. Gradually and tragically the attitudes of pride and prejudice with which the Jews had looked down on the Gentiles were coming back to haunt them, as Gentile believers began to turn away from their Jewish brothers.

In Romans chapters 9-11, Paul pleaded with his Gentile readers to remember that God has not forgotten Israel. God made promises to the nation that He cannot forsake (Romans 11:29). Furthermore, Gentiles have no room for arrogance: they were not originally included among God's people but were allowed in, like branches grafted onto a tree (Romans 11:17-18).

II Chronicles 7:14

If my people, which are called by my name, shall humble themselves, and pray, and seek my face, and turn from their wicked ways; then will I hear from heaven, and will forgive their sin, and will heal their land.

235

Pray for the peace of Jerusalem; they will prosper that love thee.

We should read Ephesians 4:29-32 daily.

29. Let no corrupt communication proceed out of your mouth, but that which is good to the use of edifying, that it may minister grace unto the hearers.

30. And grieve not the Holy Spirit of God, whereby ye are sealed unto the day of redemption.

31. Let all bitterness, and wrath, and anger, and clamor, and evil speaking, be put away from you, with all malice:

32. And be ye kind one to another, tenderhearted, forgiving one another, even as God for Christ's sake hath forgiven you.

Lesson Plan 77

The Book of Romans

Chapters 15 & 16

Objective: To give us insight and discernment on faith, salvation, and the need to hear the Gospel.

Objective Breakdown:

1. Introduction

2. Show Compassion to All   Chapter 15:1-13

3. Paul's Confidence in His Readers   Chapter 15:14-21

4. Paul Expects to Preach the Gospel at Rome   Chapter 15:22-33

5. Personal Greetings   Chapter 16:1-16

6. Warning Against False Teachers   Chapter 16:17-20

7. Final Greetings and a Benediction   Chapter 16:21-27

Introduction: Israel's rejection of Christ is temporary. The day will come when all Israel shall be saved (Romans11:26). One of the darkest spots in the panorama of human history is the age-long suffering of these sorrowful, disobedient people. But one day it will end. Israel shall turn in penitence to the Lord. And all creation shall give thanks to God for the unsearchable wisdom of His providence.

Civil governments are ordained of God (Romans 13:1) to restrain the criminal elements of human society. However, many civil governments can often be run by evil men. Christians should be law-abiding citizens of the government under which they live in all their attitudes and relations of life, governing themselves by the principles of the Golden Rule (Romans 13: 8-10), making a special effort to be honorable in all things, and always considerate to others. The only time that citizens should disobey the governmental authorities is when the government's edicts conflict with the Word and the laws of God. See Acts 5:24-29.

The largest employer in many nations is the government. That outrages some citizens, who see government as a massive, wasteful, scandal-plagued bureaucracy. But God takes a different view. If you work for the government—as an elected or appointed official, a letter carrier, police or military officer, a water meter reader—you'll want to pay special attention to Romans 13:1-7, which states:

1. "Let every soul be subject unto the higher powers. For there is no power but of God: the powers that be are ordained of God.

2. Whosoever therefore resisteth the power, resisteth the ordinance of God: and they that resist shall receive to themselves damnation.

3. For rulers are not a terror to good works, but to the evil. Wilt thou then not be afraid of the power? do that which is good, and thou shalt have praise of the same:

4. For he is the minister of God to thee for good. But if thou do that which is evil, be afraid; for he beareth not the sword in vain: for he is the minister of God, a revenger to execute wrath upon him that doeth evil.

5. Wherefore ye must needs be subject, not only for wrath, but also for conscience sake.

6. For this cause pay ye tribute also: for they are God's ministers, attending continually upon this very thing. 7. Render therefore to all their dues: tribute to whom tribute is due; custom to whom custom; fear to whom fear; honor to whom honor.

God refers to governmental authorities as God's ministers (Romans 13:4-6), meaning "servants". It is the same word translated elsewhere as "deacons." The point is that if you work for the government, you are ultimately God's worker. Your authority derives not just from the people, but from God Himself. (This is an amazing statement from Paul. He was not living under a democratically elected government, but under an imperial Roman system, probably headed by Nero!)

Government, then, is established by God. But good or bad, He chooses to allow them to exist and have authority. He works through them to accomplish His purposes.

Romans Road to Salvation

Romans 3:23 For all have sinned and fall short of the glory of God.

Romans 6:23 For the wages of sin is death, but the free gift of God is eternal life in Christ

Romans 5:8 But God demonstrates His own love toward us, in that while we were yet sinners, Christ died for us.

Romans 10:9 that if you confess with your mouth Jesus as Lord and believe in your heart that God raised Him from the dead, you shall be saved.

Romans 10:13 for "Whoever will call upon the Name of the Lord will be saved."

II Chronicles 7:14

If my people who are called by my name will humble themselves and pray, and seek my face, and turn from their wicked ways, then I will hear from heaven and will forgive their sin and heal their land.

Psalm 122:6

Pray for the peace of Jerusalem; they shall prosper who love thee.

<u>Words for Comfort of the Soul</u>

Ephesians 4:29 Let no corrupt word proceed out of your mouth, but what is good for necessary edification, that it may impart grace to the hearers.

Ephesians 4:30 Do not grieve the Holy Spirit of God, by whom you were sealed for the day of redemption.

Ephesians 4:31 Let all bitterness, wrath, anger, clamor, and evil speaking be put away from you, with all malice.

Ephesians 4:32 Be kind to another, tenderhearted, forgiving one another, even as God in Christ forgave you.

The Book of 1 Corinthians

Scripture Focus Chapters 1 - 16

Objective: To gain an understanding of the problems and the pressures and the struggles of the church in the most important city in Greece during Paul's day. This book is written in Ephesus in A.D. 56.

Objective Breakdown:

1.	Greeting of Grace	Chapter 1:1-3
2.	Prayer of Thanksgiving	Chapter 1:4-9
3.	Report of Divisions	Chapter 1:10-17
4.	The Gospel Is Not Earthly Wisdom	Chapter 1:18-31
5.	The Gospel Is Not Earthly Wisdom (cont.)	Chapter 2:1-5
6.	The Gospel Is Heavenly Wisdom	Chapter 2:6-16
7.	The Gospel Is Heavenly Wisdom (cont.)	Chapter 3:1-4
8.	Ministers Are Fellow Workers with God	Chapter 3:5-17
9.	Ministers Are Accountable to God	Chapter 3:18-23
10.	Ministers Are Accountable to God (cont.)	Chapter 4:1-5
11.	Misunderstanding of Paul's Ministry	Chapter 4:6-21
12.	Deliver the Fornicators for Discipline	Chapter 5:1-8
13.	Separate Yourselves from Immoral Believers	Chapter 5:9-13
14.	Concerning Litigation Between Believers	Chapter 6:1-11
15.	Warning Against Sexual Immorality	Chapter 6:12-20
16.	Principles for Married Life	Chapter 7:1-9
17.	Principles for the Married Believer	Chapter 7:10-16
18.	Principles of Abiding in God's Call	Chapter 7:17-24

Lesson Plan 78

The Book of 1 Corinthians

Chapters 1 - 3

Objective: To give us insight and discernment concerning the problems of the Corinthian church.

Objective Breakdown:

1. Introduction

2. A Word of Greeting   Chapter 1:1-9

3. The Corinthians Are Divided   Chapter 1:10-17

4. Wisdom Is Misunderstood   Chapter 1:18-31

5. Paul's Initial Visit in Weakness   Chapter 2:1-5

6. The Message Was God's Wisdom   Chapter 2:6-16

7. The Apostle Role Has Been Misunderstood   Chapter 3:1-8

8. A New Building for God   Chapter 3:9-23

Introduction: Corinth the most important city in Greece during Paul's day, was a bustling hub of worldwide commerce, degraded culture, and idolatrous religion. Paul founded a church in Corinth (Acts 18:1-17), and two of his letters are addressed "To the church of God which is at Corinth."

First Corinthians reveals the problems, pressures, and struggles of a church out of a pagan society. Paul addresses a variety of problems in the lifestyle of the Corinthian church: factions, lawsuits, immorality, questionable practices, abuse of the Lord's supper, and spiritual gifts.

As was noted, Corinth was a key city in ancient Greece until it was destroyed by the Romans in 146 B.C. Julius Caesar rebuilt it as a Roman colony in 46 B.C. and it grew and prospered, becoming the capital of the province of Achaia. Its official language was Latin, but the common language remained Greek. In Paul's day, Corinth was the metropolis of the

Peloponnesus, which was strategically located on a narrow isthmus between the Aegean Sea and the Adriatic Sea that connects the Peloponnesus with northern Greece. Because of its two seaports, it became a commercial center, and many small ships were rolled or dragged across the Corinthian isthmus to avoid the dangerous 200-mile voyage around southern Greece. Nero and others attempted to build a canal at the narrowest point, but this was not achieved until 1893.

The city was filled with shrines and temples, but most prominent was the Temple of Aphrodite on top of an 1800-foot promontory called the Acrocorinthus. Worshipers of the "goddess of love" made free use of the 1000 Hieroduli (consecrated prostitutes). Corinth became so notorious for its evils that the term Korinthiazomat (act like a Corinthian) became synonymous with debauchery and prostitution.

In Paul's day, the population was approximately 700,000, about two-thirds of whom were slaves.

Paul taught the Word of God in Corinth for eighteen months in A.D. 51 and 52. After Paul's departure, Apollos came from Ephesus to minister to the Corinthian church (1 Corinthians 3:6; Acts 18:24-28).

II Chronicles 7:14

If my people, which are called by my name, shall humble themselves, and pray, and seek my face, and turn from their wicked ways; then will I hear from heaven, and will forgive their sin, and will heal their land.

Psalm 122:6

Pray for the peace of Jerusalem; they will prosper that love thee.

Lesson Plan 79

The Book of 1 Corinthians

Chapters 4, 5, & 6

Objective: To give us Insight and Discernment Concerning Examples of Behavior, Idolatry, Head Coverings for Women, Impropriety in Worship, Proper Observance of the Lord's Supper, Spiritual Gifts and the Importance of Each Member.

Objective Breakdown:

1. Introduction

2. No Room for Boasting   Chapter 4:1-7

3. Fools for Christ   Chapter 4:8-13

4. Paul's Care for the Corinthians   Chapter 4:14-21

5. Immorality Must Be Dealt With   Chapter 5:1-13

6. Lawsuits Before Unbelievers   Chapter 6:1-11

7. Liberty Does Not Mean License   Chapter 6:12-20

Introduction: Corinth was a key city in ancient Greece until it was destroyed by the Romans in 146 B.C. Julius Caesar rebuilt it as a Roman colony in 46 B.C.

Paul taught the Word of God in Corinth for eighteen months in A. D. 51 & 52. After Paul's departure, Apollo came from Ephesus to minister in the Corinthian Church (1Corinthians 3:6; Acts 18:24-28). When Paul was teaching and preaching in Ephesus during his third missionary journey, he was disturbed by reports from the household of Chloe concerning quarrels in the of Corinth (1 Corinthians chapter 1:11). The church sent a delegation of three men (1 Corinthians 16:17) who apparently brought a letter that requested Paul's judgment on certain issues (1 Corinthians 7:1). Thus, Paul wrote this epistle as a response to the problems and questions of the Corinthians.

In this letter Paul authority is forced to exercise his apostolic authority as he deals firmly with problems of divisiveness, immorality, lawsuits, selfishness, abuses of the Lord's Supper and spiritual gifts, and denials of the Resurrection.

The three divisions of 1 Corinthians are: answer to Chloe's report of division (1 Corinthians 1-4); answer to report of fornication (1 Corinthians 1:5-6); and answer to letter of questions (1 Corinthians 1:7-16).

II Chronicles 7:14

If my people, which are called by my name, shall humble themselves, and pray, and seek my face, and turn from their wicked ways; then will I hear from heaven, and will forgive their sin, and will heal their land.

Psalm 122:6

Pray for the peace of Jerusalem; they will prosper that love thee.

Lesson Plan 80

The Book of 1 Corinthians

Chapters 7, 8, & 9

Objective: To give us insight and discernment concerning marriage, meat offered to idols, Christian liberty, and service.

Objective Breakdown:

1. Introduction

2. Instructions to Married Believers   Chapter 7:1-7

3. Instructions to Single Believers   Chapter 7: 8-9

4. Instructions to Those Married to Unbelievers   Chapter 7:10-16

5. Calling and Vocation   Chapter 7:17-24

6. Instructions Regarding Virgins   Chapter 7:25-38

7. Instructions Regarding Remarriage   Chapter 7:39–40

8. The Controversy of Meat Offered to Idols   Chapter 8:1-13

9. Paul's Example of Christian Liberty   Chapter 9:1-12

10. A Servant to All   Chapter 9:13-27

Introduction: What Controls You? As Christians, we live under grace and not under the law. We enjoy a certain freedom of choice and commitment. But Paul reminds us that our choices and commitments, while freely made, do not always bring freedom (1 Corinthians 6:12). Often they overpower us: we no longer possess our possessions—they possess us! We can be consumed by our jobs, our wealth, our houses, our hobbies even our churches, and yes, even golf and mah-jongg (Mah-Jongg). Are there any ways to manage this problem? Yes! Determine your limits, what you can handle and what is realistic. Manage the commitments you are taking on and what you are willing to give up. Taking on new responsibilities means trading one set of problems for another.

A New View of Sexuality. In an era when Greek women were often deprived both emotionally and sexually, Paul insisted that the Christian husband should recognize and fulfill the needs of the wife (1 Corinthians 7:3-6). He declared that marriage partners have authority over each other. That means that both husband and wife were forbidden from using sex as a means of control but were to enjoy mutuality in that aspect of their marriage.

Some believers in the early church had married before they became Christians. They wondered whether they should divorce their unbelieving spouses to remarry and live more wholeheartedly for Christ. But Paul didn't recommend that. He viewed the abandonment of the family as a very serious matter (1 Corinthians 7:10-11), arguing that the believer should stay in the marriage as long as possible (1 Corinthians 7:12-13). For how do you know if the believing spouse will save the unbelieving spouse? God desires peace in relationships (1 Corinthians 7:15), and that may not be possible in a family where Christian values are not shared. If the unbelieving spouse wants to leave, he or she should be allowed to do so (1 Corinthians 7:15).

II Chronicles 7:14

If my people, which are called by my name, shall humble themselves, and pray, and seek my face, and turn from their wicked ways; then will I hear from heaven, and will forgive their sin, and will heal their land.

Psalm 122:6

Pray for the peace of Jerusalem; they will prosper that love thee.

Lesson Plan 81

The Book of 1 Corinthians

Chapters 10 & 11

Objective: To give us insight and discernment concerning examples of behavior, idolatry, head coverings for women, impropriety in worship, proper observance of the Lord's supper, spiritual gifts, and the importance of each member.

Objective Breakdown:

1. Introduction

2. Warning Against Forfeiting Liberty   Chapter 10:1-13

3. Exhortation to Use Liberty to Glorify God   Chapter 10:14-33

4. Principles of Public Prayer   Chapter 11:1-16

5. Rebuke of Disorders at the Lord's Supper   Chapter 11:17-34

Introduction: Woman and Work in the Ancient World. Paul's observation that a married woman must care about "the things of the world" (1 Corinthians 7:34) hints at the busy lives that first-century women lived, especially in the large cities of the Roman Empire.

The New Testament shows that women carried out a wide range of tasks: for example, drawing water, grinding grain, manufacturing tents, hosting guests, governing and influencing civic affairs, making clothes, teaching, prophesying and filling other spiritual functions, burying the dead, and doing the work of slaves, to name but a few. Additional evidence from the period reveals women also served as wool workers, midwives, hairdressers, nurses, vendors, entertainers, political leaders, and even construction workers among other occupations.

In Jewish homes, women were responsible not only for carrying out household tasks, but also preparing the home for the Sabbath (Mark 1:29-31). Lydia was a successful businesswoman in the purple trade (Acts 16:14-15), and Priscilla manufactured tents with her husband (Romans 16:3-5).

Paul argued that food and drink do not determine our relationship to God (1 Corinthians 8: 8). Meat offered to idols is inconsequential because, ultimately, there is no such thing as an idol (1 Corinthians 8: 4-6). An idol is not God, so if a priest blesses meat and offers it to an idol means nothing. From that point of view, Christians should be able to enjoy whatever food they want.

However, if someone tells you that the meat has been offered to idols, then one should abstain to preclude a brethren to stumble or to cause division with fellow believers. As a member of Christ's family we are obligated not to be a stumbling block, but a loving neighbor.

II Chronicles 7:14

If my people, which are called by my name, shall humble themselves, and pray, and seek my face, and turn from their wicked ways; then will I hear from heaven, and will forgive their sin, and will heal their land.

Psalm 122:6

Pray for the peace of Jerusalem; they will prosper that love thee.

Lesson Plan 82

The Book of 1 Corinthians

Chapters 12, 13, & 14

Objective: To give us insight and discernment concerning examples of behavior, idolatry, spiritual gifts, and the importance of each member.

Objective Breakdown:

1. Introduction

2. The Spirit Gives Gifts to Each Believer   Chapter 12:1-11

3. Every Member Is Necessary   Chapter 12:12-31

4. The Way of Love   Chapter 13:1-13

5. The Value of Prophecy   Chapter 14:1-12

6. The Reason for Tongues   Chapter 14:13-25

7. Order of Worship   Chapter 14:26-40

Introduction: How many Christians realize that testament is just another word for covenant? Thus, the New Testament describes the New Covenant (1 Corinthians 11:25), or agreement, that God has made with humanity, based on the death and resurrection of Jesus Christ. In the Bible, a covenant involves more than a contract or simple agreement. A contract has an end date, but a covenant is a permanent arrangement.

The agreement with Israel was especially significant because it established a special relationship between God and the Hebrews. They were His "chosen people" through whom He would bring blessings and hope to the rest of the world. However, because the recipients of God's Law could not keep it perfectly, further provisions were necessary for them as well as the rest of humanity. That is why God promised a New Covenant through the prophet Jeremiah (Jeremiah 31:31-34). Under the new covenant, God would bestow His Law on human hearts. The work of Jesus Christ brought the promised New Covenant into being. When Jesus ate His final Passover meal with the twelve, He spoke of the cup as "the New Covenant in My Blood"

(Luke 22:20), the words that Paul quoted to the Corinthians to remind them of the need for purity and propriety in their worship (1 Corinthians 11-25-34).

When Paul writes that women should keep silent in the churches (1 Corinthians 14:34), we are led to ask why in light of previous statements in the letter. He has already mentioned that women prayed and prophesied, presumably during worship services (1 Corinthians 12:7,11), and presumably, some women received speaking gifts. So why would he exhort the women to keep silent?

One explanation is that the women in the congregation in Corinth probably had few opportunities for formal education and little exposure to large gatherings, except for the wild rites of their former religion. So when they came into the church, they may have assumed a similar approach to Christian worship. That would have been inappropriate, so Paul exhorted them to pursue a quieter, more orderly form of worship now that they were following the Lord.

II Chronicles 7:14

If my people, which are called by my name, shall humble themselves, and pray, and seek my face, and turn from their wicked ways; then will I hear from heaven, and will forgive their sin, and will heal their land.

Psalm 122:6

Pray for the peace of Jerusalem; they will prosper that love thee.

Lesson Plan 83

The Book of 1 Corinthians

Chapters 15 & 16

Objective: To give us insight and discernment concerning examples of behavior, idolatry, spiritual gifts, and the importance of each member.

Objective Breakdown:

1. Introduction

2. What the Gospel Is   Chapter 15:1-11

3. Who Says There Is No Resurrection   Chapter 15:12-34

4. A New Body   Chapter 15:35-58

5. A Collection for Believers at Jerusalem   Chapter 16:1-9

6. Greetings and Conclusions   Chapter 16:10-23

Introduction: Paul's doctrine of the resurrection (1 Corinthians 15:42) flew in the face of prevailing ideas about the afterlife. To the Greek mind, death released a person's spirit from the prison of the body. The last thing a Greek would want was to be reunited with a corruptible body (1 Corinthians 15:35).

Burial practices in Corinth and other cities in the Roman Empire were largely a function of one's status in life. If the deceased was a member of the upper class, the job of preparing the body was delegated to professional undertakers. They usually dressed the body in a toga adorned with badges and other tokens of personal accomplishments and offices. Professional mourners and musicians then led a possession to the burial site. Sometimes, actors were recruited to follow the cortege, wearing masks that depicted the family's ancestors. In Greek and Roman cultures, bodies were as likely to be cremated as buried. Either way, the rich tended to bury their dead in elaborate tombs. The poor, by contrast, laid their dead to rest in common, often unmarked graves. Or, if near Rome, they might use the catacombs. Christians were not permitted to use regular cemeteries, so they resorted to the catacombs for their funerals. As persecution increased, some eventually fled there for survival.

Among the Hebrews, bodies were laid either in a shallow grave covered with stones or in a cave hewn out of stone and secured by a circular stone rolled and sealed over the entrance. Graves were often marked with a large, upright stone.

Due to the hot climate of Palestine, dead bodies decayed rapidly, so burial usually took place within a few hours after death. If someone died late in the day, burial took place the next day, but always within 24 hours after death. The Hebrews did not follow the custom of cremation, except in emergencies, nor did they generally use coffins. And although they had historical ties to Egypt, they did not embalm their dead as the Egyptians did.

II Chronicles 7:14

If my people, which are called by my name, shall humble themselves, and pray, and seek my face, and turn from their wicked ways; then will I hear from heaven, and will forgive their sin, and will heal their land.

Psalm 122:6

Pray for the peace of Jerusalem; they will prosper that love thee.

The Book of 2 Corinthians

Scripture Focus Chapters 1 - 13

Objective: To gain an understanding of the problems and the pressures and the struggles of the church in the most important city in Greece during Paul's day. This book is written in Macedonia in A.D. 56 and the major theme is the defense of Paul's Apostolic credentials and authority.

Objective Breakdown:

1. Paul's Thanksgiving to God   Chapter 1:1-7

2. Paul's Trouble in Asia   Chapter 1:8-11

3. Paul's Original Plan   Chapter 1:12-22

4. Paul's Change of Plans   Chapter 1:23-24

5. Paul's Change of Plans (cont.)   Chapter 2:1-4

6. Paul's Appeal to Forgive   Chapter 2:5-13

7. Christ Causes Us to Triumph   Chapter 2:14-17

8. Changed Lives Prove Ministry   Chapter 3:1-5

9. New Covenant Is the Basis of Ministry   Chapter 3:6-18

10. Christ Is the Theme of the Ministry   Chapter 4:1-7

11. Trials Abound in the Ministry   Chapter 4:8-15

12. Motivation of Eternal Perspective   Chapter 4:16-18

13. Motivation of the Future Presence of Christ   Chapter 5:1-8

14. Motivation of Future Reward   Chapter 5:9-10

15. Motivation of the Love of Christ   Chapter 5:11-16

16. Motivation of the Message of Reconciliation   Chapter 5:17-21

17. Giving No Offense in the Ministry   Chapter 6:1-10

Lesson Plan 84

The Book of 2 Corinthians

Chapters 1 & 2

Objective: To give us insight and discernment concerning examples of accountability, image-consciousness, and a code of ethics for Christian witness.

Objective Breakdown:

1. Introduction

2. Date & Occasion of the Writing

3. Comfort in the Midst of Trouble   Chapter 1:1-11

4. Paul Defends His Integrity   Chapter 1:12-14

5. Paul Explains His Plans   Chapter 1:15-24

6. A Letter Instead of a Painful Visit   Chapter 2:1-4

7. Forgiving a Repentant Brother   Chapter 2:5-11

8. Christ Leads in Triumph   Chapter 2:12-17

Since Paul's First Letter, the Corinthians church had been swayed by false teachers who stirred up the people against Paul. They claimed he was fickle, proud, unimpressive in appearance and speech, dishonest, and unqualified as an apostle of Jesus Christ.

Paul sent Titus to Corinth to deal with these difficulties, and upon his return, rejoiced to hear that the Corinthians had a change in heart. Paul wrote this letter to express his thanksgiving for the repentant majority and to appeal to the minority to accept his authority. Throughout the book, he defends his conduct, character, and calling as an apostle of Jesus Christ.

Paul was in Ephesus when he wrote First Corinthians and expected Timothy to visit Corinth and return to him (1 Corinthians 16:10-11). Timothy brought Paul a report of the opposition that had developed against him in Corinth and Paul made a brief and painful visit to the Corinthians (this visit is not mentioned in Acts, but it can be inferred from 2 Corinthians 2:1;

12:14; 13:1, 2). Upon return to Ephesus Paul regretfully wrote his sorrowful letter to urge the church to discipline the leader of the opposition (2 Corinthians 2:1-11; 7:8). Titus carried this letter. Paul anxious to learn the results, went to Troas and then to Macedonia to meet Titus on his return trip (2 Corinthians 2:12, 13; 7:5-16). Paul was greatly relieved by Titus's report that the majority of the Corinthians had repented of their rebelliousness against Paul's authority. However, a minority of opposition persisted, evidently led by a group of Judaizers (2 Corinthians 10–13).

II Chronicles 7:14

If my people who are called by my name will humble themselves and pray, and seek my face, and turn from their wicked ways, then I will hear from heaven and will forgive their sin and heal their land.

Psalm 122:6

Pray for the peace of Jerusalem; they shall prosper who love thee.

Words for Comfort of the Soul

Ephesians 4:29 Let no corrupt word proceed out of your mouth, but what is good for necessary edification, that it may impart grace to the hearers.

Ephesians 4:30 Do not grieve the Holy Spirit of God, by whom you were sealed for the day of redemption.

Ephesians 4:31 Let all bitterness, wrath, anger, clamor, and evil speaking be put away from you, with all malice.

Ephesians 4:32 Be kind to another, tenderhearted, forgiving one another, even as God in Christ forgave you.

Lesson Plan 85

The Book of 2 Corinthians

Chapters 3, 4, & 5

Objective: To give us insight and discernment concerning examples of accountability, image-consciousness, and a code of ethics for Christian witness.

Objective Breakdown:

1. Introduction

2. Paul's Best Defense: The Corinthians Themselves   Chapter 3:1-6

3. The New Testament Ministry   Chapter 3:7-18

4. Christ Is the Message   Chapter 4:1-6

5. Natural Messengers, Supernatural Powers   Chapter 4:7-17

6. We Are Headed for Eternity with God   Chapter 5:1-11

7. A New Creation for Christ   Chapter 5:12-20

Introduction: Epistles of Commendation. This expression was probably suggested by the fact that the Judaizing teachers carried Letters of Introduction from Jerusalem. They were always edging in on Paul's work, and were among his chief troublemakers, and availed themselves of every possible excuse or opportunity to fight him. They were now asking, Who is Paul? Can he show Letters from anybody standing in Jerusalem? Which on the face of it was absurd. Letters commending Paul to a Church he founded. The Church itself was Paul's letter.

This led to a contrast of his ministry with theirs: The Gospel with the Law. One written on Stone, the other on Hearts. One of the Letter, the other of the Spirit. One unto Condemnation, the other unto Righteousness. One Passes, the other Remains. Beholding Christ, we are Changed, from Glory to Glory, into His Image.

In Chapter 4 (also in chapters 6 & 11), Paul speaks much of his sufferings. At his conversion, the Lord said, "I will show him how many things he must suffer for my name's sake (Acts 9:16)." The sufferings began immediately and continued in unbroken succession for over thirty years. They plotted to kill him in Damascus (Acts9:24). And in Jerusalem (Acts 9:29). Drove him out of Antioch (Acts 13:50). Attempted to Stone him in Iconium (Acts 14:5). Did Stone him, leave him for Dead, in Lystra (Acts 14:19). In Philippi, they beat him with rods and put him in stocks (Acts16:23,24). In Thessalonica, the Jews and rabble tried to mob him (Acts 17:5). They drove him out of Berea (Acts 17:13,14). Plotted against him in Corinth Acts 18:12). In Ephesus, they almost killed him (Acts 19:29); II Corinthians 1:8,9). In Corinth again, shortly after he had written this Epistle, they plotted his death (Acts 20:3). In Jerusalem again they would have made a quick end of him, except for Roman soldiers (Acts 22). Then he was imprisoned in Caesarea for two years, and two more years in Rome.

And besides all this, there were beatings, imprisonments, shipwrecks, and unceasing privations of every kind (II Corinthians 11:23-27). Then finally he was taken to Rome to be executed as a criminal (II Timothy 2:9). He must have had amazing endurance, for he sang as he suffered (Acts 16:25). Paul's mind was on the future world.

II Chronicles 7:14

If my people, which are called by my name, shall humble themselves, and pray, and seek my face, and turn from their wicked ways; then will I hear from heaven, and will forgive their sin, and will heal their land.

Psalm 122:6

Pray for the peace of Jerusalem; they will prosper that love thee.

259

Lesson Plan 86

The Book of 2 Corinthians

Chapters 6, 7, & 8

Objective: To give us insight and discernment concerning Paul's vindication of his Apostleship, the glory of his ministry, and the long martyrdom of his life.

Objective Breakdown:

Introduction: For many people in the world today, tension, conflict, weariness, and suffering have become commonplace. Nevertheless, some offer the vain hope that life's troubles can be done away with, that we can somehow get to the point where things will always be great. They suggest faith in Christ will deliver us into a state of serenity and ease and bring prosperity, health, and constant pleasure.

However, that was neither the experience nor the teaching of early Christians such as Paul, James, or Peter, and certainly not of their Lord Jesus. Paul described the life of a servant of God in terms of tribulation, distress, tumult, and sleeplessness (2 Corinthians 6:4-5). But, he also linked these stress producers with rich treasures that money cannot buy purity, kindness, sincere love, honor, good report, joy, and possessions of all things (2 Corinthians 6:6-10).

So as long as we live as God's people on earth, we can expect a connection between trouble and hope. That connection is never pleasant, but our troubles can about lasting benefits: Jesus told us that if we want to follow Him, we must deny ourselves and take up a cross. If we try to save our lives, we will only lose them. But if we lose our lives for His sake, we will find them (Matthew 16:24-25).

We can count on feeling stress if we're going to obey Christ. But we can take comfort that stress is preparing us for riches we will enjoy for eternity.

II Chronicles 7:14

If my people, which are called by my name, shall humble themselves, and pray, and seek my face, and turn from their wicked ways; then will I hear from heaven, and will forgive their sin, and will heal their land.

Psalm 122:6

Pray for the peace of Jerusalem; they will prosper that love thee.

Lesson Plan 87

The Book of 2 Corinthians

Chapters 9, 10, 11, 12, & 13

Objective: To give us insight and discernment concerning Paul's vindication of his Apostleship,the glory of his ministry, and the long martyrdom of his life.

Objective Breakdown:

1. Introduction

2. Readiness in Giving   Chapter 9:1-5

3. Principles in Giving   Chapter 9:6-7

4. Promises from Living   Chapter 9:8-15

5. A Charge of Cowardice Is Answered   Chapter 10:1-2

6. A Charge of Walking in the Flesh Is Answered   Chapter 10:3-9

7. A Charge of Personal Weakness Is Answered   Chapter 10:10-19

8. Paul's Declaration of His Apostleship   Chapter 11:1-15

9. Paul's Sufferings Support His Apostleship   Chapter 11:16-33

10. Vision of Paradise   Chapter 12:1-6

11. Thorn in the Flesh   Chapter 12:7-10

12. Paul's Signs Support His Apostleship   Chapter 12:11-13

13. Paul's Concern Not to Be a Financial Burden   Chapter 12:14-18

14. Paul's Concern Not to Find Them Carnal   Chapter 12:19- 21

15. Paul's Warning to Examine Yourselves   Chapter 13:1-10

16. Conclusion   Chapter 13:11-14

Introduction: There is no better indicator of growth in the new life than in the area of giving. This passage (2 Corinthians 9-15) deals with the area of giving. The passage (2 Corinthians 9: 6-8) deals with the attitude one should have in his giving—it should be cheerful.

When giving is cheerful, it will also be generous. The important rule of thumb is not how much is given, but how much is left after given. God is not primarily occupied with the amount of the gift, but with the motive that lies behind it. All the money in the world belongs to God. My gift to Him will not make Him any richer; it makes you richer spiritually, because of the realization that everything we have belongs to Him. We are giving because we love Him.

A key to Second Corinthians is Paul's defense of his ministry. The major theme of Second Corinthians is his defense of his apostolic credentials and authority. This is evident in the portion directed to still the rebellious minority (2 Corinthians 10–13), but the theme of vindication is also in chapters 1–9. Certain false prophets had mounted an effective campaign against Paul in the Church of Corinth, and Paul was forced to take steps to overcome the opposition.

This epistle expresses the apostle's joy over the triumph of the true gospel in Corinth (2 COrinthians 1-7), and it acknowledges the godly sorrow and repentance of the bulk of the believers. It also urges the Corinthians to fulfill the promise of making a liberal contribution for the poor among the Christians in Judea (2 Corinthians 8–9). This collection would not only assist the poor, but it would also demonstrate the concern of gentile Christians in Macedonia and Achaia for Jewish Christians in Judea, thus displaying the unity of Jews and Christians in the body of Christ.

II Chronicles 7:14

If my people, which are called by my name, shall humble themselves, and pray, and seek my face, and turn from their wicked ways; then will I hear from heaven, and will forgive their sin, and will heal their land.

Psalm 122:6

Pray for the peace of Jerusalem; they will prosper that love thee.

Overcoming Negative Thoughts

Read:

Galatians 6:7   Ephesians 2:2

Proverbs 23:7   Psalm 23:1-6

Galatians 5:23   Romans 12:19

2 Corinthians 5:17   Deuteronomy 6:5

Romans 10:9   Philippians 4:13

John 8:44   Galatians 6:15

Psalm 19:14   Romans 12:21

2 Corinthians 10:5   Isaiah 26:3

The Book of Galatians

Scripture Focus Chapters 1 - 6

Objective: To gain an understanding of the Epistle to the Galatians which has been called the Magna Carta of Christian Liberty.

Objective Breakdown:

1. Salutation: The Ground of Grace	Chapter 1:1-5
2. Situation: The Departure from Grace	Chapter 1:6-9
3. The Gospel of Grace Is Given by Divine Revelation	Chapter 1:10- 24
4. Gospel of Grace Is Approved by Jerusalem Leadership	Chapter 2:1-10
5. Gospel of Grace Is Vindicated by Rebuking Peter	Chapter 2:11-21
6. Holy Spirit Is Given by Faith Not by Works	Chapter 3:1-5
7. Abraham Was Justified by Faith, Not by Works	Chapter 3:6-9
8. Christ Redeems Us from the Curse of the Law	Chapter 3:10-14
9. Abrahamic Covenant Is Not Voided by the Law	Chapter 3:15-18
10. Law Given to Drive Us to Faith	Chapter 3:19-22
11. Believers Are Free the Law	Chapter 3:23-29
12. Believers Are Free the Law (cont.)	Chapter 4:1-11
13. Galatians Receive Blessings by Faith Not by the Law	Chapter 4:12-20
14. Law and Grace Cannot Coexist	Chapter 4:21-31
15. Position of Liberty	Chapter 5:1-12
16. Practice of Liberty: Love One Another	Chapter 5:13-15

Lesson Plan 88

The Book of Galatians

Chapters 1 & 2

Objective: To give us insight and discernment concerning Paul's continued challenges with the converts to Christianity.

Objective Breakdown:

1. Introduction

2. To the Churches of Galatia   Chapter 1:1-5

3. Don't Turn Away from the True Gospel   Chapter 1:6-9

4. The Gospel Was Revealed by God   Chapter 1:10-24

5. The Apostles Approved Paul's Message   Chapter 2:1-10

6. A Rebuke for Compromising the Gospel   Chapter 2:11-21

Introduction: Galatia's borders varied. It included the cities of Iconium, Lystra, Derbe, and probably Pisidian Antioch. Galatians was a branch of Gauls, originally from north of the Black sea, split off from the main migration westward to France, and settled in Asia Minor, 3rd Century B.C.

The Occasion of this Epistle: Paul's work in Galatia had been extremely successful. Great multitudes, mostly Gentiles, had enthusiastically accepted Christ. Sometime after Paul had left Galatia, certain Jewish teachers came along insisting that Gentiles could not become Christians without keeping the law of Moses. And the Galatians gave heed to their teaching with the same wholeheartedness with which they had at first received Paul's message; as a result, there was a general epidemic of circumcision among these Gentile Christians. Circumcision is the name of the Initiatory Rite into Judaism.

Paul wrote this Epistle to explain to Galatians that Circumcision, while it had been a necessary part of Jewish National Life, was not a part of the Gospel of Christ and had nothing whatever to do with Salvation.

Paul had founded these Galatian Churches about A.D. 45-48. He had re-visited them, as he was setting out on his Second Journey about A.D. 50 (Acts 16:1-6); and again, as he was starting on his Third Journey about A.D. 54 (Acts 18:23).

The commonly accepted traditional date of the writing of this Epistle is about A.D. 57, at the close of his Third Missionary Journey, in Ephesus, or Macedonia, or Corinth, and shortly before he wrote the Epistle to the Romans.

II Chronicles 7:14

If my people who are called by my name will humble themselves and pray, and seek my face, and turn from their wicked ways, then I will hear from heaven and will forgive their sin and heal their land.

Psalm 122:6

Pray for the peace of Jerusalem; they shall prosper who love thee.

God's Blessing on Israel   (Numbers 6:24-27)

Jabez's Prayer to the Lord   (I Chronicles 4:10)

Words for Comfort of the Soul

Ephesians 4:29 Let no corrupt word proceed out of your mouth, but what is good for necessary edification, that it may impart grace to the hearers.

Ephesians 4:30 Do not grieve the Holy Spirit of God, by whom you were sealed for the day of redemption.

Ephesians 4:31 Let all bitterness, wrath, anger, clamor, and evil speaking be put away from you, with all malice.

Ephesians 4:32 Be kind to another, tenderhearted, forgiving one another, even as God in Christ forgave you.

Romans Road to Salvation

Romans 3:23 For all have sinned and fall short of the glory of God.

Romans 6:23 For the wages of sin is death, but the free gift of God is eternal life in Christ Jesus our Lord.

Romans 5:8 But God demonstrates His own love toward us, in that while we were yet sinners, Christ died for us.

Romans 10:9 That if you confess with your mouth Jesus as Lord and believe in your heart that God raised Him from the dead, you shall be saved.

Romans 10:13 For "Whoever will call upon the Name of the Lord will be saved."

Lesson Plan 89

The Book of Galatians

Chapter 3

Objective: To give us insight and discernment concerning Paul's continued challenges with the converts to Christianity.

Objective Breakdown:

1. Introduction

2. Abraham Was Justified by Faith   Chapter 3:1-25

3. Believers Are Children of God by Faith   Chapter 3:26-29

Introduction: The Gentiles Galatians had swallowed the Judaizers' message so completely that they had instituted Jewish Festival days and Ceremonies (Chapter 4:8-11), evidently trying to combine the Gospel with Mosaic Law. But Paul tells them that the two systems do not combine. Did the Judaizers work any miracles among them? Abraham figures largely in this chapter because the Jewish message which they had accepted was largely on the promise to Abraham. They were misinterpreting the promise, as was shown plainly in Abraham's narrative itself (Chapter 4:21-31). Their early love for Paul was in sad contrast with their present coolness (Chapter 4:12-20).

Who Was Paul?

Paul was a Hellenist, a Greek-speaking Jew. He was born in Tarsus, the capital city of Cilicia (Acts 21:39. He was of the tribe of Benjamin (Philippians 3:5). He was a Pharisee and the son of a Pharisee (Acts 23:6). He was born a Roman citizen. He was sent to Jerusalem at an early age and went to school there under one of the most learned and distinguished teachers Gamaliel. He was taught according to the strict manner of the law of the fathers (Acts 22:3). He grew up an ardent Pharisee who believed in the resurrection, angels, and other fundamentals of the faith. The Pharisees made changes and added to what Moses had written and the changes became "tradition" which our Lord rebuked (Matthew 15:1-7)

Abraham was Justified by Faith   Chapter 3:1-25

II Chronicles 7:14

If my people who are called by my name will humble themselves and pray, and seek my face, and turn from their wicked ways, then I will hear from heaven and will forgive their sin and heal their land.

Psalm 122:6

Pray for the peace of Jerusalem; they shall prosper who love thee.

Key Points of Galatians to Remember

1. Galatians 1:9 As we have said before, so now I say again, if anyone preaches any other gospel to you that what you have received, let him be accursed.

2. Galatians 3:24, 25 Therefore the law was our tutor to bring us to Christ, that we might be justified by faith. But after faith has come, we are no longer under a tutor.

3. Galatians 3:28, 29 There is neither Jew nor Greek, neither slave nor free, there is neither male nor female; for you are all one in Christ Jesus. And if you are Christ's, then you are Abraham's seed, and heirs according to the promise.

Words for Comfort of the Soul

I Peter 2:9 But ye are a chosen generation, a royal priesthood, an holy nation, a peculiar people; that ye should shew forth the praises of him who hath called you out of darkness into his marvelous light.

Ephesians 4:29 Let no corrupt word proceed out of your mouth, but what is good for necessary edification, that it may impart grace to the hearers.

Ephesians 4:30 Do not grieve the Holy Spirit of God, by whom you were sealed for the day of redemption.

Ephesians 4:31 Let all bitterness, wrath, anger, clamor, and evil speaking be put away from you, with all malice.

Ephesians 4:32 Be kind to another, tenderhearted, forgiving one another, even as God in Christ forgave you.

Philippians 4:6 Be anxious for nothing, but in everything by prayer and supplication, with thanksgiving, let your requests be made known to God; and the peace of God, which surpasses all understanding, will guard your hearts and minds through Christ Jesus.

Romans Road to Salvation

1. Romans 3:23 For all have sinned and fall short of the glory of God.

2. Romans 6:23 For the wages of sin is death, but the free gift of God is eternal life in Christ Jesus our Lord.

3. Romans 5:8 But God demonstrates His own love toward us, in that while we were yet sinners, Christ died for us.

4. Romans 10:9 That if you confess with your mouth Jesus as Lord and believe in your heart that God raised Him from the dead, you shall be saved.

5. Romans 10:13 For "Whoever will call upon the Name of the Lord will be saved."

II Chronicles 7:14

If my people who are called by my name will humble themselves and pray, and seek my face, and turn from their wicked ways, then I will hear from heaven and will forgive their sin and heal their land.

Psalm 122:6

Pray for the peace of Jerusalem; they shall prosper who love thee.

God's Blessing on Israel   (Numbers 6:24-27)

Jabez's Prayer to the Lord   (I Chronicles 4:10)

Lesson Plan 90

The Book of Galatians

Chapter 4

Objective: To give us insight and discernment concerning Paul's continued challenges with the converts to Christianity.

Objective Breakdown:

1. Introduction

2. No Longer Slaves But Heirs   Chapter 4:1-11

3. Whose Message Is to Believed   Chapter 4:12-20

4. Two Alternatives - Freedom or Slavery   Chapter 4:21-31

Introduction: Key Points of Galatians to Remember:

Galatians 1: 9 As we have said before, so now I say again, if anyone preaches any other gospel to you that what you have received, let him be accursed.

Galatians 3:24, 25 Therefore the law was our tutor to bring us to Christ, that we might bejustified by faith. But after faith has come, we are no longer under a tutor.

Galatians 3:28, 29 There is neither Jew nor Greek, neither slave nor free, there is neither male nor female; for you are all one in Christ Jesus. And if you are Christ's, then you are Abraham's seed, and heirs according to the promise.

<u>Words for Comfort of the Soul</u>

I Peter 2:9 But ye are a chosen generation, a royal priesthood, a holy nation, a peculiar people; that ye should shew forth the praises of him who hath called you out of darkness into his marvelous light.

Ephesians 4:29 Let no corrupt word proceed out of your mouth, but what is good for necessary edification, that it may impart grace to the hearers.

Ephesians 4:30 Do not grieve the Holy Spirit of God, by whom you were sealed for the day of redemption.

Ephesians 4:31 Let all bitterness, wrath, anger, clamor, and evil speaking be put away from you, with all malice.

Ephesians 4:32 Be kind to another, tenderhearted, forgiving one another, even as God in Christ forgave you.

Philippians 4:6 Be anxious for nothing, but in everything by prayer and supplication, with thanksgiving, let your requests be made known to God; and the peace of God, which surpasses all understanding, will guard your hearts and minds through Christ Jesus.

II Chronicles 7:14

If my people who are called by my name will humble themselves and pray, and seek my face, and turn from their wicked ways, then I will hear from heaven and will forgive their sin and heal their land.

Psalm 122:6

Pray for the peace of Jerusalem; they shall prosper who love thee.

Lesson Plan 91

The Book of Galatians

Chapters 5 & 6

Objective: To give us insight and discernment concerning Paul's continued challenges with the converts to Christianity.

Objective Breakdown:

1. Introduction

2. Live in The Liberty of The Gospel   Declaration of Christian Freedom

3. Liberty Means Living in Love   Example of Christian Freedom

4. Liberty Means Living by The Spirit   Confusion over Christian Freedom

5. Liberty Means a Concern for Purity   Calling for Spiritual Alertness

6. Liberty Means Caring About All Believers   Concern over Spiritual Deception

7. A Handwritten Conclusion   Giving a Summary

Introduction: Paul spent his life teaching Gentiles that they could be Christians without becoming Jewish Proselytes. This was very displeasing to Jews generally, for they thought of the Mosaic Law as binding upon All, and were bitterly prejudiced against uncircumcised Gentiles who presumed to call themselves disciples of the Jewish Messiah. While Paul taught Gentile Christians to stand like a rock for their Liberty in Christ, as he did in this Book of Galatians and in the Book of Romans, yet he did not want them to be prejudiced against their Jewish fellow-Christians but regard them as brothers in Christ.

He (Paul) did not want to see two churches; a Jewish church and a Gentile church; but One Church: Jews and Gentiles, one in Christ. His gesture on behalf of Unity to the Jewish elements in the Church was the great love offering of money which he took from Gentile churches at the close of his third missionary journey; to the poor in the Mother-Church at Jerusalem (Acts 21). He hoped that this demonstration of Christian love might bring Jewish Christians to feel more kindly toward Gentile Christians.

Key Points in Galatians to Remember

1. Galatians 1:9 As we have said before, so now I say again, if anyone preaches any other gospel to you that what you have received, let him be accursed.

2. Galatians 3:24-25 Therefore the law was our tutor to bring us to Christ, that we might be justified by faith. But after faith has come, we are no longer under a tutor.

3. Galatians 3:28-29 There is neither Jew nor Greek, neither slave nor free, there is neither male nor female; for you are all one in Christ Jesus. And if you are Christ's, then you are Abraham's seed, and heirs according to the promise.

4. Galatians 4:16 Have I become your enemy because I tell you the Truth?

5. Galatians 5:16 "Walk in the Spirit and you shall not fulfill the lusts of the Flesh."

6. Galatians 5:22-23 "But the fruit of the Spirit is love, joy, peace, long suffering, kindness, goodness, faithfulness, gentleness, self-control."

7. Galatians 6:7 "Do not be deceived, God is not mocked; for whatever a man sows, he will also reap."

8. Galatians 6:10 "Let us do good to all, especially to those who are of the household of faith."

II Chronicles 7:14

If my people who are called by my name will humble themselves and pray, and seek my face, and turn from their wicked ways, then I will hear from heaven and will forgive their sin and heal their land.

Psalm 122:6

Pray for the peace of Jerusalem; they shall prosper who love thee.

God's Blessing on Israel   (Numbers 6:22-27)

Jabez's Prayer to the Lord   (I Chronicles 4:10)

Words for Comfort of the Soul

Ephesians 4:29 Let no corrupt word proceed out of your mouth, but what is good for necessary edification, that it may impart grace to the hearers.

Ephesians 4:30 Do not grieve the Holy Spirit of God, by whom you were sealed for the day of redemption.

Ephesians 4:31 Let all bitterness, wrath, anger, clamor, and evil speaking be put away from you, with all malice.

Ephesians 4:32 Be kind to another, tenderhearted, forgiving one another, even as God in Christ forgave you.

Romans Road to Salvation

1. Romans 3:23 For all have sinned and fall short of the glory of God.

2. Romans 6:23 For the wages of sin is death, but the free gift of God is eternal life in Christ Jesus our Lord.

3. Romans 5:8 But God demonstrates His own love toward us, in that while we were yet sinners, Christ died for us.

4. Romans 10:9 That if you confess with your mouth Jesus as Lord and believe in your heart that God raised Him from the dead, you shall be saved.

5. Romans 10:13 For "Whoever will call upon the Name of the Lord will be saved."

The Book of Ephesians

Scripture Focus Chapters 1- 6

Objective: To gain an understanding of the Epistle to the Ephesians which focuses on the believers' responsibility to walk in accordance with their heavenly calling in Christ Jesus.

Objective Breakdown:

1.	Salutation from Paul	Chapter 1:1-2
2.	Chosen by the Father	Chapter 1:3-6
3.	Redeemed by the Son	Chapter 1:7-12
4.	Sealed by the Spirit	Chapter 1:13-14
5.	Prayer for Revelation	Chapter 1:15-23
6.	Old Condition: Dead to God	Chapter 2:1-3
7.	New Condition: Alive to God	Chapter 2:4-10
8.	Reconciliation of Jews and Gentiles	Chapter 2:11-22
9.	Revelation of the Mystery of the Church	Chapter 3:1-13
10.	Prayer for Realization	Chapter 3:14-21
11.	Exhortation to Unity	Chapter 4:1-3
12.	Explanation of Unity	Chapter 4:4-6
13.	Means for Unity: The Gifts	Chapter 4:7-11
14.	Purpose of the Gifts	Chapter 4:12-16
15.	Put Off the Old Man	Chapter 4:17-22
16.	Put on the New Man	Chapter 4:23-29
17.	Grieve Not the Holy Spirit	Chapter 4:30-32
18.	Walk in Love	Chapter 5:1-12

Lesson Plan 92

The Book of Ephesians

Chapters 1 & 2

Objective: To give us insight and discernment concerning Paul's continued challenges with the converts to Christianity.

Objective Breakdown:

1. Introduction

2. Greetings & Blessed Beyond Measure   Chapter 1:1-14

3. A Prayer for Eye Opening   Chapter 1:15-23

4. Christ Has Overcome Sin   Chapter 2:1-10

5. Christ Has Abolished the Law's Enmity   Chapter 2:11-22

Introduction: Paul spent life teaching Gentiles that they could be Christians without becoming Jewish Proselytes. This was very displeasing to Jews generally, for they thought of the Mosaic Law as binding upon All, and were bitterly prejudiced against Uncircumcised Gentiles who presumed to call themselves disciples of the Jewish Messiah. While Paul taught Gentile Christians like a rock for their Liberty in Christ, as he did in Galatians and Romans, yet he did not want them to be prejudiced against their Jewish fellow Christians, but to regard them as brothers in Christ.

Paul did not want to see Two Churches: a Jewish Church and a Gentile Church; but One Church. His gesture, on behalf of Unity, to Jewish elements in the church was the great offering of money he took from the Gentile Churches at the close of his third missionary journey to the poor Mother Church in Jerusalem (Acts 21). He hoped that this demonstration of Christian love might bring Jewish Christians to feel more kindly toward Gentiles.

Paul's gesture on behalf of Unity to Gentile elements in the church, this Epistle (Ephesians) written to the leading center of his own Gentile converts, exalting the ONENESS, UNIVERSALITY and UNSPEAKABLE GRANDEUR of the body of Christ.

To Paul, Christ was a Great Big Something in whom there was room not only for people of different races, viewpoints and prejudices, but he has the power to solve all the problems of mankind and bring into unity and harmony with God all earthly social and family life (Ephesians 5:22-6:9), and even the myriads of Beings in the infinite unseen universe (Ephesians 3:10).

This is one of the four "Prison Epistles," written from Paul's Roman imprisonment, A.D. 61-63, the others being Philippians, Colossians, Philemon.

II Chronicles 7:14

If my people who are called by my name will humble themselves and pray, and seek my face, and turn from their wicked ways, then I will hear from heaven and will forgive their sin and heal their land.

Psalm 122:6

Pray for the peace of Jerusalem; they shall prosper who love thee.

Lesson Plan 93

The Book of Ephesians

Chapters 3 & 4

Objective: To give us insight and discernment concerning Paul's continued challenges with the converts to Christianity.

Objective Breakdown:

1. Introduction

2. The Mystery of the Church   Chapter 3:1-13

3. A Prayer to Experience Christ's Love   Chapter 3:14-21

4. Walk Worthy of Your Calling   Chapter 4:1-16

5. Walk Differently Than Unbelievers   Chapter 4:17-32

Introduction: The Time of Ephesians. At the end of his second journey, Paul visited Ephesus where he left Priscilla and Aquila (Acts 18:18-21). This strategic city was the commercial center of Asia Minor, but the heavy silting required a special canal to be maintained so that ships could reach the harbor. Ephesus was a religious center as well, famous especially for its magnificent temple of Diana (Roman name) or Artemis (Greek name, a structure considered to be one of the seven wonders of the ancient world) (Acts 19:35). The practice of magic and the local economy were clearly related to this temple. Paul remained in Ephesus for nearly three years on his third missionary journey (Acts 18:23–19:41); the Word of God was spread throughout the providence of Asia. Paul's effective ministry began to seriously hurt the traffic in magic and images, leading up to an uproar in the huge Ephesians theater. Paul then left for Macedonia but met with the Ephesians elders while on his way to Jerusalem (Acts 20:17-38).

Paul the "Prison Epistles" (Ephesians, Philippians, Colossians, and Philemon) during his first Roman imprisonment in A.D. 60-62. These epistles all refer to his imprisonment (Ephesians 3:1; 4:1; 6:20; Philippians 1:7,13, 14; Colossians 4:3, 10, 18; Philemon 9, 10, 13, 23), and fit well against the background in Acts 28:16–31. This especially true of Paul's reference to the palace guard (governors official residential guard Philippians 1:13) and "Caesar's household"

(Philippians 4:22).

Ephesians focuses on the believers' responsibility to walk in accordance with his heavenly calling in Christ Jesus (Ephesians 4:1). Ephesians was not written to correct specific errors in a local church, but to prevent problems in the church by encouraging the body of Christ to mature in Him. It was also written to make believers more aware of their position in Christ because this is the basis for their practice on every level of life.

II Chronicles 7:14

If my people who are called by my name will humble themselves and pray, and seek my face, and turn from their wicked ways, then I will hear from heaven and will forgive their sin and heal their land.

Psalm 122:6

Pray for the peace of Jerusalem; they shall prosper who love thee.

Lesson Plan 94

The Book of Ephesians

Chapters 5 & 6

Objective: To give us insight and discernment concerning Paul's continued challenges with the converts to Christianity.

Objective Breakdown:

1. Introduction

2. Walk in Love   Chapter 5:1-7

3. Walk as Children of Light   Chapter 5:8-21

4. Instructions to Husbands and Wives   Chapter 5:22-33

5. Instructions to Children and Fathers   Chapter 6:1-4

6. Instructions to Servants and Masters   Chapter 6:5-9

7. Spiritual Warfare   Chapter 6:10-20

8. Concluding Matters   Chapter 6:21-24

Introduction: All Believers Are Ministers. A simple way to define "ministry" is that it is the work of God for the people of God (Ephesians 4:12). It is the work of serving others using the gifts, resources, and power that God gives us.

This is important for the church today to understand because many Christians assume that "ministry" belongs only to professional ministers or clergy. But ministry belongs to everyone in the body of Christ. All believers are "ministers." All have been gifted to carry out the work of God (Romans 12:4-8; 1 Corinthians 12).

What, then, is the role of the clergy? To equip, or prepare, the ministers to do their work of ministry (Ephesians 4:11-12). This involves teaching the truth of God's Word, helping believers overcome the problems that hinder them, giving them a vision for reaching out to others with the love of Christ and helping them develop and use the practical skills required to carry out their God-given tasks.

Ministry is the calling, privilege, and responsibility of every member of the body of Christ. It has been said that when believers are baptized, they are ordained into the ministry. Perhaps it would help to recover this perspective. It could free pastors and other church leaders to focus on the crucial role of equipping the saints for the work of the ministry. It might help to redistribute the load.

Martin Luther stated, "There is nothing which will more surely earn Hell for a man than the improper training of his children...it is highly necessary that every person regard the soul of his child with great concern; that he considers the child nothing less than a precious, eternal treasure, entrusted to his protection by God so that the devil, the world and the flesh do not steal and destroy it." (Deuteronomy 6:5-9).

II Chronicles 7:14

If my people who are called by my name will humble themselves and pray, and seek my face, and turn from their wicked ways, then I will hear from heaven and will forgive their sin and heal their land.

Psalm 122:6

Pray for the peace of Jerusalem; they shall prosper who love thee.

The Book of Philippians

Objective: To gain an understanding of the Epistle to the Philippians which focuses on the concept of "to Live is Christ and to die is gain" (Philippians 1:21) and in Chapter 2, Christ is the model of Humility. Chapter 3 presents Christ as the one who will transform our lowly body that it may be transformed to His glorious body and in chapter 4, He is the source of Paul's power over circumstances ("I can do all things through Christ who strengthens me" (Philippians 4:13). Paul wrote this Book from Rome about A.D. 62.

Objective Breakdown:

1. Paul's Prayer of Thanksgiving	Chapter 1:1-11
2. Paul's Afflictions Promotes the Gospel	Chapter 1:12-18
3. Paul's Afflictions Exalt the Lord	Chapter 1:19-26
4. Paul's Exhortation to the Afflicted	Chapter 1:27-30
5. Paul's Exhortation to Humility	Chapter 2:1-4
6. Christ's Example of Humility	Chapter 2:5-16
7. Paul's Example of Humility	Chapter 2:17-18
8. Timothy's Example of Humility	Chapter 2:19-24
9. Epaphroditus's Example of Humility	Chapter 2:25-30
10. Warning Against Confidence in the Flesh	Chapter 3:1-9
11. Exhortation to Know Christ	Chapter 3:10-16
12. Warning Against Living for the Flesh	Chapter 3:17-21
13. Peace with the Brethren	Chapter 4:1-3
14. Peace with the Lord	Chapter 4:4-9
15. Peace in all Circumstances	Chapter 4:10-19
16. Conclusion	Chapter 4:20-23

Lesson Plan 95

The Book of Philippians

Chapters 1 & 2

Objective: To give us insight and discernment concerning Paul's continued challenges with the converts to Christianity.

Objective Breakdown:

Introduction/Background

Grace & Peace	Chapter 1:1-2
Thanks for the Philippians' Gift	Chapter 1:3-11
In Prison for the Gospel	Chapter 1:12-26
A Call to Stand Firm	Chapter 1:27-30
The Humble Example of Christ	Chapter 2:1-11
Shine as Lights in the World	Chapter 2:12-18
Paul Hopes to Send Timothy and to Come Himself	Chapter 2:19-24
Epaphroditus Is on His Way	Chapter 2:25-30

Introduction/Background: The Church was founded as a result of a supernatural vision experienced by Paul while at Troas during his second missionary trip (see Acts 16:8-10). It was Paul's favorite church. During his brief stay there, Paul and Silas saw God work marvelously in the lives of at least three individuals:

a. An Asian woman named Lydia whom God saved from Judaism (Acts 16:13-15).

b. A Greek soothsayer from whom God saved from demonism (Acts 16:16-18).

c. A Roman jailer whom God saved from Emperiorism (the worship of Caesar) (Acts 16:19-20).

The city of Philippi was founded by Philip of Macedonia (father of Alexander the Great) in 357 B.C. and named after him. It was some 700 miles from Rome and enjoyed full Roman citizenship privileges.

Rome in its conquest of the Middle East had been engaged in a war against Macedonia. History tells us the Roman Army ran out of salt, and it was with salt that Roman soldiers were paid. (From this we get our expression that a man is not worth his salt.) The Roman Legions threatened to defect and return home from the battle, which meant that Macedonia would remain unconquered. The people of Philippi preferred to be ruled by the Romans rather than by the Macedonians, so they collected salt and turned it over to the Roman army, thus the soldiers were paid. The Romans continued their conquest and defeated the Macedonians, incorporating Macedonia into the Roman empire. As a reward, the citizens of Philippi were given the status of a colony by the Roman emperor. This meant that they had the same rights and privileges as a Roman citizen of the city of Rome.

Thus, the city of Philippi became the first European city to receive the Gospel. In AD 57, at the end of his third missionary journey (some five years after his first visit)), Paul seems to have paid two brief visits to Philippi (see 2 Corinthians 1:16; Acts 19:21; Acts 20:1-3).

II Chronicles 7:14

If my people who are called by my name will humble themselves and pray, and seek my face, and turn from their wicked ways, then I will hear from heaven and will forgive their sin and heal their land.

Psalm 122:6

Pray for the peace of Jerusalem; they shall prosper who love thee.

Lesson Plan 96

The Book of Philippians

Chapters 3 & 4

Objective: To give us insight and discernment concerning Paul's continued challenges with the converts to Christianity.

Objective Breakdown:

1. Background/Introduction

2. A Warning About Judaizers   Chapter 3:1-6

3. What Really Matters   Chapter 3:7-14

4. Paul Says to Follow His Example   Chapter 3:15-21

5. A Word to Euodia and Syntyche   Chapter 4:1-3

6. How to Have the Peace of God   Chapter 4:4-9

7. Praise for the Philippians's Gift   Chapter 4:10-20

8. Greetings for Everyone   Chapter 4:21-23

Background/Introduction: In 356 B.C., King Philip of Macedonia (the father of Alexander the Great) took this town and expanded it, renaming it Philippi. The Romans captured it in 168 B.C.; and 42 B.C. the defeat of the forces of Brutus and Cassius by those of Anthony and Octavian (later Augustus) took place outside the city. Octavian turned Philippi into a Roman colony (Acts 16:12) and a military outpost. The citizens of this colony were regarded as citizens of Rome and given a number of special privileges. Because Philippi was a military city and not a commercial center, there were not enough Jews for a synagogue when Paul came (Acts 16:3).

Paul's "Macedonian Call" in Troas during his second missionary journey led his ministry in Philippi with the conversion of Lydia and others. Paul and Silas were beaten and imprisoned, but this resulted in the conversion of the Philippian jailer and his family. The magistrates were placed in a dangerous position by beating a Roman citizen without a trial (Acts 16:37-

40), and that embarrassment may have prevented future reprisals against the new Christians in Phillipi. Paul visited the Philippians again on his third missionary journey (Acts 20:1,6). When they heard of his Roman imprisonment, the Philippian church sent Epaphroditus with financial help (Philippians 4:18); they had helped Paul in this manner on two other occasions (Philippians 4:16). Epaphroditus almost died of an illness, yet remained with Paul long enough for the Philippians to receive word of his malady. Paul sent this letter back with him to Philippi (Philippians 2:25-30).

Silas, Timothy, Luke, and Paul first came to Philippi in A.D. 51, eleven years before Paul wrote this letter.

II Chronicles 7:14

If my people, which are called by my name, shall humble themselves, and pray, and seek my face, and turn from their wicked ways; then will I hear from heaven, and will forgive their sin, and will heal their land.

Psalm 122:6

Pray for the peace of Jerusalem; they will prosper that love thee.

The Book of Colossians

Scripture Focus Chapters 1 - 24

Objective: To gain the understanding that the Book of Colossians is perhaps the most Christ-centered book in the Bible. It was written in Rome about A.D. 60-61.

Objective Breakdown:

1.	Paul's Greeting to the Colossians	Chapter 1:1-2
2.	Paul's Thanksgiving for the Colossians	Chapter 1:3-8
3.	Paul's Prayer for the Colossians	Chapter 1:9-14
4.	Christ Is Preeminent in Creation	Chapter 1:15-18
5.	Christ Is Preeminent in Redemption	Chapter 1:19-23
6.	Christ Is Preeminent in the Church	Chapter 1:24-29
7.	Christ Is Preeminent in the Church (cont.)	Chapter 2:1-3
8.	Freedom from Enticing Words	Chapter 2:4-7
9.	Freedom from Vain Philosophy	Chapter 2:8-10
10.	Freedom from the Judgment of Men	Chapter 2:11-17
11.	Freedom from Improper Worship	Chapter 2:18-19
12.	Freedom from the Doctrine of Men	Chapter 2:20-23
13.	The Position of the Believer	Chapter 3:1-4
14.	Put Off the Old Man	Chapter 3:5-11
15.	Put on the New Man	Chapter 3:12-17
16.	Holiness in Family Life	Chapter 3:18-21
17.	Holiness in Work Life	Chapter 3:22-25
18.	Holiness in Work Life (cont.)	Chapter 4:1-1

Lesson Plan 97

The Book of Colossians

Chapters 1 & 2

Objective: To gain an understanding of who Christ is and the problems of the early church which Paul had to contend with.

Objective Breakdown:

1. Background/Introduction:

2. Greetings   Colossians 1:1-2

3. Praise for Faith, Hope, and Love   Colossians 1:3-14

4. The Pre-eminence of Christ   Colossians 1:15-29

5. Paul's Burden for the Colossians   Colossians 2:1-5

6. Continue in Christ   Colossians 2:6-7

7. Beware of False Teaching   Colossians 2:8-23

Background/Introduction: Colosse was a Roman city of Asia Minor located at the base of 8,000-foot-high Mount Cadmus in the Lycus River Valley, east of Ephesus. A prosperous industrial center especially famous for its textiles, but clearly in decline at the time of Christ, squeezed by its competitive neighbor, Laodicea. It survived a devastating earthquake in A.D. 61, but later its population moved 3 miles south to Chonai (modern Honaz).

Judaism, Platonism, and mystery cults from surrounding mountain people blended into strange, often contradictory religious practices. Cultic worship of angels persisted, with Michael as the favorite. He was credited with sparing the town in times of disaster. Colosse was home of Archippus and Epaphras, associates of Paul who helped spread the gospel throughout Asia, up and down the Lycus Valley. The region was also the home to Onesimus, a runaway slave who became a believer (see Book of Philemon).

First-century Colosse was an ideological swamp into which three main cultural streams drained. The first was Hellenism, the vestiges of Greek civilization that dominated the world before the Romans. Hellenism brought a "dualistic" view of the world, the idea that things are either material or spiritual. A second stream was a form of Judaism that tended to be rigid and puritanical, leading to outright withdrawal from and condemnation of the world. A third influence was the local pagan culture. This included superstitious occultism and primitive mystical rites. These three streams blended into a pseudo-philosophical swamp that mired the Colossians church into debates, division, and depravity. The problem was one of syncretism. Syncretism involves the confusion of various ideas, beliefs, and practices.

Syncretist has a mind like a blender. The person throws in notions from any number of systems of thought–even notions that contradict each other. Then they are ground into a single philosophical stew to generate a system that satisfies one's intellectual demands and preferences. Result: a custom-made world view that invariably leads away from biblical truth. Syncretism flourishes in times of rapid change and cultural upheaval.

Back to Colossians: The Letter to the Colossians is believed to have been written about the same time as Ephesians (A.D. 60-61) by the Apostle Paul (Colossians 1:1). Paul had not visited Colosse (Colossians 2:1), but for two years he had lived in Ephesus, which is about 100 miles to the West. Paul established a thriving church in Ephesus, and it was probably through the outreach of this congregation that the gospel was carried to Colosse (Acts 19:10), probably by Epaphras (Colossians 4:12). Paul wrote Colossians while in prison about A.D. 61. Apparently, he intended the letter to be circulated among other congregations (Colossians 4:16) and told the Colossians to read an "epistle from Laodicea," possibly a reference to Ephesians.

II Chronicles 7:14

If my people who are called by my name will humble themselves and pray, and seek my face, and turn from their wicked ways, then I will hear from heaven and will forgive their sin and heal their land.

Psalm 122:6

Pray for the peace of Jerusalem; they shall prosper who love thee.

Lesson Plan 98

The Book of Colossians

Chapters 3 & 4

Objective: To gain an understanding of who Christ is and the problems of the early church that Paul had to contend with.

Objective Breakdown:

1. Background/Introduction

2. Christ the Focus of Life   Chapter 3:1-4

3. A Christlike Lifestyle   Chapter 3:5-17

4. Instructions for Families   Chapter 3:18-21

5. Instructions to Servants and Masters   Chapter 3:22-25

6. Instructions and Requests   Chapter 4:1-6

7. News, Greetings, and Final Words   Chapter 4:7-18

Background/Introduction: The city of Colosse included people from a wide variety of ethnic and cultural backgrounds. Greeks, whose cultural heritage dominated the Roman world; Jews, who prided themselves as "God's chosen people;" Barbarians, who spoke no Greek and therefore lacked social standing; Scythians, a crude, cruel warlike people from the north; and slaves, menial workers at the bottom of the society.

Members from all these groups came to faith and joined the community of believers at Colosse. But their ethnic prejudices created problems, which Paul listed (Colossians 3:8-9). He pulled no punches, calling the problems by their ugly names: anger, wrath, malice, blasphemy, filthy language, and lying.

Paul challenged his culturally mixed group of readers to shed such behaviors like an old set of clothes and put on Christ instead, who is "is all and in all." He was possibly reminding them of a first-century baptismal creed that as new converts, they were joining a new family in Christ as Galatians 3:26-29 reflects. "For ye are all the children of God by faith in Christ

Jesus. For as many of you as have been baptized into Christ, have put on Christ. There is neither Jew nor Greek, there is neither bond nor free, there is neither male nor female: for ye are all one in Christ Jesus. And if ye be Christ's, then are ye Abraham's seed, and heirs according to the promise."

God's family has no place for prejudices. Radically new ways of relating to others are called for; see Colossians 3:12-17 which reads: "Put on therefore, as the elect of God, holy and beloved, bowels of mercies, kindness, humbleness of mind, meekness, longsuffering; Forbearing one another, and forgiving one another, if any man have a quarrel against any: even as Christ forgave you, so also do ye. And above all these things put on charity, which is the bond of perfectness. And let the peace of God rule in your hearts, to the which also ye are called in one body; and be ye thankful. Let the word of Christ dwell in you richly in all wisdom; teaching and admonishing one another in psalms and hymns and spiritual songs, singing with grace in your hearts to the Lord. And whatsoever ye do in word or deed, do all in the name of the Lord Jesus, giving thanks to God and the Father by him. If believers today lived out these ideals, we would see God change our churches and begin to transform our culture.

II Chronicles 7:14

If my people who are called by my name will humble themselves and pray, and seek my face, and turn from their wicked ways, then I will hear from heaven and will forgive their sin and heal their land.

Psalm 122:6

Pray for the peace of Jerusalem; they shall prosper who love thee.

The Book of 1 Thessalonians

Scripture Focus Chapters 1 - 5

Objective: To help us understand what the Book of 1 Thessalonians, teaches: that Jesus Christ's will return, for we HIS children, to take us home to Heaven in what we refer to as the Rapture. The Book of 1 Thessalonians was written in Corinth in A. D. 51.

Objective Breakdown:

1. Paul's Commendation for Their Growth   Chapter 1:1-10

2. Paul's Founding of the Church   Chapter 2:1-16

3. Satan Hinders Paul   Chapter 2:17-20

4. Paul Sends Timothy   Chapter 3:1-5

5. Timothy's Encouraging Reports   Chapter 3:6-13

6. Directions for Growth   Chapter 4:1-12

7. Revelation Concerning the Dead in Christ   Chapter 4:13-18

8. Description of the Day of the Lord   Chapter 5:1-11

9. Instruction for Holy Living   Chapter 5:12-22

Lesson Plan 99

The Book of 1 Thessalonians

Chapters 1, 2, & 3

Objective: To gain insight into the ministry of Paul, Silas' (Silvanus), and Timothy in Macedonia, specifically in Thessalonica and Berea.

Objective Breakdown:

1. Introduction.

2. The Thessalonians Act as Believers   1 Thessalonians 1:1-10

3. Fond Memories of Paul's First Visit   1 Thessalonians 2:1-12

4. A Model Church   1 Thessalonians 2:13-16

5. Paul Has Been Hindered from Visiting   1 Thessalonians 2:17-20

6. Timothy Was Sent to Thessalonica   1 Thessalonians 3:1-5

7. Timothy's Encouraging Report   1 Thessalonians 3:6-10

8. Paul's Prayer for the Thessalonians   1 Thessalonians 3:11-13

Introduction: Paul felt great love for the Thessalonian believers, and he drew upon a touching image to communicate his affection, that of a woman nursing an infant (1 Thessalonians 2:7).

Most mothers in the first-century world nursed their own infants. However, some wealthy women employed wet nurses. In that case, the child lived in the home of the wet nurse, who agreed to certain conditions such as not nursing other children and avoiding alcohol. The wet nurse took the responsibility not only for feeding the child but also raising it until it was weaned, often up to three years of age. Many contracts specified that the wet nurse's fee had to be returned if the child died. Paul clearly intended to convey a sense of tender affection and responsible, loving care for his spiritual children, the Thessalonians. In doing so, he showed a side of spiritual leadership and nurture that Christian leaders do well to emulate today.

Paul mentions two dangers that he avoided so as not to compromise his credibility (1Thessalonians 2:5); the use of "flattering words," which amounts to telling people what they want to hear; and a cloak for covetousness, which involves hidden motives. To use either of these approaches is to deceive people. That is unacceptable for someone who presents himself as a representative of Christ.

The key to Paul's integrity was his realization that God Himself had entrusted him with the message (1 Thessalonians 2:4). The task of taking the message to the Gentiles was not something that Paul had thought up by himself but was a calling from God (Galatians 1:11-17). Thus, his aim was not to please people, but God.

As we consider ways in which to communicate Christ to people around us, what obstacles to our credibility might there be? Are there things about our methods or motives that conflict with the message with which we've been entrusted?

Zechariah 2:8 For thus saith the Lord of hosts; After the glory hath he sent me unto the nations which spoiled you: for he that toucheth you toucheth the apple of his eye.

Zechariah 8:22-23: 22. Yea, many people and strong nations shall come to seek the Lord of hosts in Jerusalem, and to pray before the Lord. 23. Thus saith the Lord of hosts; In those days it shall come to pass, that ten men from every language of the nations shall grasp the sleeve of a Jewish man, saying, "Let us go with you for we have heard that God is with you."

II Chronicles 7:14

If my people who are called by my name will humble themselves and pray, and seek my face, and turn from their wicked ways, then I will hear from heaven and will forgive their sin and heal their land.

Psalm 122:6

Pray for the peace of Jerusalem; they shall prosper who love thee.

Lesson Plan 100

The Book of 1 Thessalonians

Chapters 4 & 5

Objective: To gain insight into the ministry of Paul, Silas (Silvanus), and Timothy in Macedonia, specifically in Thessalonica and Berea.

Objective Breakdown:

1. Introduction

2. Maintain Sexual Purity   Chapter 4:1-8

3. Contribute to Society   Chapter 4:9-12

4. Concerning Believers Who Have Died   Chapter 4:13-18

5. Concerning the Times   Chapter 5:1-11

6. The Community Life of Believers   Chapter 5:12-22

7. Blessings and Greetings   Chapter 5:23-28

Introduction: The Dead Will Live! The resurrection of the dead is an Old Testament concept. Job writes, "For I know that my Redeemer lives, and He shall stand at last on the earth; And after my skin is destroyed, this I know, that in my flesh I shall see God" (Job 19:25, 26). Job was confident there would be resurrection day through the Redeemer who would come in the last days.

Isaiah writes, "Your dead shall live; Together with my dead body they shall arise. Awake and sing, you who dwell in dust; For your dew is like the dew of herbs, And the earth shall cast out the dead" (Isaiah 26:19).

Daniel writes, "And many of those who sleep in the dust of the earth shall awake, Some to everlasting life, Some to shame and everlasting contempt" (Daniel 12:2). Daniel is saying there are two resurrections–the resurrection of the just, and that of the unjust. Jesus taught the same truth saying, "Do not marvel at this: for the hour is coming in which all who are in graves will hear His voice and come forth–those who have done good to the resurrection of life, and those who have done evil, to the resurrection of condemnation (John 5:28, 29).

The resurrection of the just is in three waves. The first wave was at Calvary when the dead rose from their graves when Jesus was crucified. The second wave will be the Rapture of the church just prior to the Tribulation. The third wave will be in the Tribulation and will consist of those who were saved during the Tribulation and beheaded by the Antichrist.

The resurrection of the unjust occurs at the Great White Throne judgment at the end of time.

Paul felt great love for the Thessalonian believers, and he drew upon a touching image to communicate his affection, that of a woman nursing an infant (1 Thessalonians 2:7).

Most mothers in the first-century world nursed their own infants. However, some wealthy women employed wet nurses. In that case, the child lived in the home of the wet nurse, who agreed to certain conditions such as not nursing other children and avoiding alcohol. The wet nurse took the responsibility not only for feeding the child but also raising it until it was weaned, often up to three years of age. Many contracts specified that the wet nurse's fee had to be returned if the child died. Paul clearly intended to convey a sense of tender affection and responsible, loving care for his spiritual children, the Thessalonians. In doing so, he showed a side of spiritual leadership and nurture that Christian leaders do well to emulate today.

Paul mentions two dangers that he avoided so as not to compromise his credibility (1Thessalonians 2:5); the use of "flattering words," which amounts to telling people what they want to hear., and a cloak for covetousness, which involves hidden motives. To use either of these approaches is to deceive people. That is unacceptable for someone who presents himself as a representative of Christ.

The key to Paul's integrity was his realization that God Himself had entrusted him with the message (1 Thessalonians 2:4). The task of taking the message to the Gentiles was not something that Paul had thought up by himself but was a calling from God (Galatians 1:11-17). Thus, his aim was not to please people, but God.

As we consider ways in which to communicate Christ to people around us, what obstacles to our credibility might there be? Are there things about our methods or motives that conflict with the message with which we've been entrusted?

The Book of 2 Thessalonians

Scripture Focus Chapters 1 - 3

Objective: To help us understand what the Book of 2 Thessalonians teaches: That the Day of the Lord has not already come upon the Thessalonian Church. Paul makes it clear that certain identifiable events will precede that Day and those events have not yet occurred. 2 Thessalonians was written in Corinth in A.D. 51.

Objective Breakdown:

1. Thanksgiving for Their Growth   Chapter 1:1-4

2. Encouragement in Their Persecution   Chapter 1:5-10

3. Prayer for God's Blessing   Chapter 1:11-12

4. Events Preceding the Day of the Lord   Chapter 2:1-12

5. The Comfort of the Believer on the Day of the Lord   Chapter 2:13-17

6. Wait Patiently for Christ   Chapter 3:1-5

7. Withdraw from the Disorderly   Chapter 3:6-15

8. Conclusion   Chapter 3:16-18

Lesson Plan 101

The Book of 2 Thessalonians

Chapters 1, 2, & 3

Objective: To gain insight into the ministry of Paul, Silas (Silvanus), and Timothy in Macedonia, specifically in Thessalonica and Berea.

Objective Breakdown:

1. Introduction

2. Greetings   Chapter 1:1-2

3. Praise for Withstanding Persecution   Chapter 1:3-12

4. Discerning of Times   Chapter 2:1-12

5. Thanksgiving, Exhortation, and a Prayer   Chapter 2:13-17

6. Paul Requests Prayer   Chapter 3:1-5

7. Every Believer Has Work to Do   Chapter 3:6-15

8. Peace & Grace from The Lord   Chapter 3:16-18

Introduction: When Paul wrote to the believers in Thessalonica, they were in the midst of intense suffering (2 Thessalonians 1:4-5). But Paul encouraged them to look beyond their immediate troubles to return of Christ and the affirmation they would receive from Him at that time

(2 Thessalonians 1:6-7). Their enemies, who were really enemies of the Lord, would be judged and dealt with (2 Thessalonians 1:8-9). By contrast, they would join with their Savior in joy and praise (2 Thessalonians 2:10). Paul went on in the next chapter (2 Thessalonians chapter 2) to expand on this theme and its impact on the Thessalonians' current difficulties (2 Thessalonians 2:1-12).

God calls us as His people to finish our lives well by holding onto the truths that last

(2 Thessalonians 2:15). He challenges us to maintain life-long faithfulness and not to be entirely caught up in the here and now, whether good or bad.

A Command to Work. God wants Christians to take responsibility to provide for their material needs and those of their families. In fact, 2 Thessalonians 3:10 states this is a command.

God has created a world of resources for this purpose. He gives us authority, along with strength and skills, to use those resources to earn a living. Work is His gift to us, a means of supplying what we need.

Obviously, there are times when grown children must care for their parents or grandparents (Mark 7:9–13; 1 Timothy 5:4). Likewise, the church community sometimes must assume responsibility for those in need. But responsibility always starts with the individual, as this passage (1 Timothy 5:4) makes plain.

Earlier, in 1 Thessalonians 4:12, Paul explained why: (1) Because of the testimony that Christians have among unbelievers. Believers who beg, borrow unnecessarily or steal, discredit Christ and the Church. (2) Because God doesn't want His children to "lack" what they need. He hasn't called us to poverty, but to adequacy.

The Dangers of Preoccupation: Are you anxious about the future of the world? Do dire predictions about coming disasters trouble you? Or do dramatic solutions to the world's many problems hold your curiosity?

Like many people today, the believers in Thessalonica were vulnerable to urgent warnings and announcements related to the future (2 Thessalonians 2:1–2). In fact, certain false teachers of the day pandered to people's interest in such things, playing to the greatest hopes and worst fears about the return of Christ (2 Thessalonians 2:3; 1 Thessalonians 5:2–5). In response, Paul appealed for reason and critical thinking based on clear instructions he had given

(2 Thessalonians 2:3–12,15).

As you consider the long-term direction of your life, what memories are you creating in others about your values and reputation? What will people choose to remember about you?

What would be an appropriate epitaph on your tombstone? What statement would describe your overall rather than whatever current circumstances you are temporarily facing right now?

II Chronicles 7:14

If my people who are called by my name will humble themselves and pray, and seek my face, and turn from their wicked ways, then I will hear from heaven and will forgive their sin and heal their land.

Psalm 122:6

Pray for the peace of Jerusalem; they shall prosper who love thee.

What Can I Do?

U. S. House of Representatives Switchboard   (202) 225- 3121

U. S. Senatorial Switchboard   (202) 224-3121

You can provide your views to your U. S. Senator and Congressperson on:

Abortion

Prayer in School

Support for Israel

Our Immoral Debt

Any Other Issue Important to You as a Christian

The Book of 1 Timothy

Scripture Focus Chapters 1 - 6

Objective: To help us understand what the Book of 1 Timothy teaches: that Christ is the "One Mediator" between God and men and that God was manifested in the flesh, justified in the 'Spirit seen by Angels and preached among the Gentiles. 1 Timothy was written in Macedonia in A.D. 62-63.

Objective Breakdown:

1. Paul's Past Charge to Timothy   Chapter 1:1-11

2. Christ's Past Charge to Paul   Chapter 1:12-17

3. First Charge: "Wage a Good Warfare"   Chapter 1:18-20

4. Prayer in Public Worship   Chapter 2:1-8

5. Women in Public Worship   Chapter 2:9-15

6. Qualifications of Bishops   Chapter 3:1-13

7. Second Charge: "Conduct Yourself in the House of God"   Chapter 3:14-16

8. Descriptions of False Teachers   Chapter 4:1-5

9. Instruction for the True Teachers   Chapter 4:6-16

10. How to Treat All People   Chapter 5:1-2

11. How to Treat Widows   Chapter 5:3-16

12. How to Treat Elders   Chapter 5:17-20

13. Fourth Charge: "Observe These Things Without Prejudice" Chapter 5:21-25

14. Exhortation to Servants   Chapter 6:1-2

15. Exhortation to Godliness with Contentment   Chapter 6:3-16

16. Exhortation to the Rich   Chapter 6:17-19

Lesson Plan 102

The Book of 1 Timothy

Chapters 1, 2, & 3

Objective: To give us continued insight and discernment concerning Paul's continued challenges with the converts to Christianity.

Objective Breakdown:

Background/Introduction

Counter False Teaching	Chapter 1:1-11
Paul's Testimony	Chapter 1:12-17
A Charge to Timothy	Chapter 1:18-20
Instructions for Men & Women	Chapter 2:1-15
Standards for Leaders	Chapter 3:1-13
Paul's Reason for Writing	Chapter 3:14-16

Background/Introduction: This letter is one of three New Testament books written especially to pastors of local churches. The other two are 2 Timothy and Titus. Also, this letter was written about AD 62-63 between Paul's first and second imprisonment.

It is the first New Testament book to discuss in detail the conditions which should prevail in a local church. The letter was written by Paul to Timothy, who was pastoring the local church in Ephesus.

The Church was attracting teachers who were contradicting the gospel of Timothy and Paul, so it needed a clear statement of faith that would be regularly defended. The worship service needed order.

Early Church tradition holds that Paul did go to Spain. Before the end of the first century, Clement of Rome said Paul reached the limits of the West (1 Clement 5:7 which is an extra Biblical reference). Clement writes that Paul traveled "west" of Rome and that Paul made it to the furthest reach of the west, i.e., Spain) evidently had Spain in mind. Paul may have been in Spain from AD 64 to AD 66. He then returned to Greece and Asia–to Corinth, Miletus, and Troas (2Timothy 4:13, 20), – and may have been arrested in Troas where he left his valuable books and parchments (2 Timothy 4:13,15).

Now that Christianity had become an illegal religion in the Empire (the burning of Rome took place in A.D.64). Paul's enemies were able to successfully accuse him. He was imprisoned in A.D. 67 and wrote his Second Timothy Epistle from his Roman cell after his first defense before the Imperial Court (2 Timothy 1:8, 17; 2:9; 4:16, 17). He was delivered from condemnation, but he held no hope of release and expected to be executed (2 Timothy 4:6-8, 18). He urged Timothy to come before that happened (2 Timothy 4:9, 21); and, according to tradition, the Apostle Paul was beheaded west of Rome on the Ostian Way.

II Chronicles 7:14

If my people who are called by my name will humble themselves and pray, and seek my face, and turn from their wicked ways, then I will hear from heaven and will forgive their sin and heal their land.

Psalm 122:6

Pray for the peace of Jerusalem; they shall prosper who love thee.

Lesson Plan 103

The Book of 1 Timothy

Chapters 4, 5, & 6

Objective: To give us continued insight and discernment concerning Paul's continued challenges with the converts to Christianity.

Objective Breakdown:

Background/Introduction: Truth and Error have battled since the first days of the Christian Faith. Paul urged Timothy to counter those who taught strange doctrines at Ephesus (1 Timothy 1:3-4). Today, Christianity has become a major world religion with well-established beliefs. Nevertheless, believers must contend with doctrinal error and misconceptions about the faith.

Unfortunately, many believers have accepted a number of myths about Christianity with the result that they never respond to Jesus as He really is. They reject the gospel on the basis of half-truths and lies rather than on clear understanding of Christ's message or its consequences.

Abandon the myths and go for the truth. Oh, for the truth about God. There are many things in the world that point to the truth about God...the kind of God that the Bible talks about, the God who loves us, and communicates Himself to us.

Go for the Truth about Jesus. Jesus claimed to be the Truth and the Way and the Life (John 14:6). Everything in His life, His teachings, death, and resurrection validates that astonishing claim. So feel free to take a good look at Jesus, He won't disappoint you.

Finally, go for the truth about yourself. Each of us is something of an enigma. At times we can be kind and thoughtful, generous and unselfish. Yet we can also be self-centered and vindictive, lustful and treacherous. What a contradiction. Paul wrote: "The good that **I will to do, I do not do**, but the evil, **I will not to do, that I do** (Romans 7:19).

II Chronicles 7:14

If my people who are called by my name will humble themselves and pray, and seek my face, and turn from their wicked ways, then I will hear from heaven and will forgive their sin and heal their land.

Psalm 122:6

Pray for the peace of Jerusalem; they shall prosper who love thee.

The Book of 2 Timothy

Scripture Focus Chapters 1 - 4

Objective: To help us understand what the Book of 2 Timothy teaches: the keys to an enduring and successful and reproducing ministry, a studying ministry, and a Holy ministry. This Epistle was written in a Roman prison in A.D. 67.

Objective Breakdown:

1.	Thanksgiving for Timothy's Faith	Chapter 1:1
2.	To Timothy My Beloved Son	Chapter 1:2-5
3.	Reminder of Timothy's Responsibility	Chapter 1:6-18
4.	Discipling Teacher	Chapter 2:1-2
5.	Single-Minded Soldier	Chapter 2:3-5
6.	Enduring Farmer	Chapter 2:6-13
7.	Diligent Woman	Chapter 2:14-19
8.	Sanctified Vessel	Chapter 2:20-23
9.	Gentle Servant	Chapter 2:24-26
10.	Coming Apostasy	Chapter 3:1-9
11.	Confronting Apostasy	Chapter 3:10-17
12.	Charge to Preach the Word	Chapter 4:1-5
13.	Paul's hope in Death	Chapter 4:6-8
14.	Paul's Situation in Prison	Chapter 4:9-18
15.	Paul's Closing Greetings	Chapter 4:19-22

Lesson Plan 104

The Book of 2 Timothy

Chapters 1, 2, 3, & 4

Objective: To give us continued insight and discernment concerning Paul's continued challenges with the converts to Christianity.

Objective Breakdown:

1. Introduction/Background

2. A Beloved Son & Valuable Heritage   Chapter 1:1-12

3. The Faithful & Faithless   Chapter 1:13-18

4. Pass on the Teaching   Chapter 2:1-7

5. A Sure Foundation   Chapter 2:8-19

6. Character and Conduct   Chapter 2:20-26

7. Perilous Times Will Come   Chapter 3:1-9

8. Consistency is Needed in Hard Times   Chapter 3:10-17

9. A Charge to Timothy   Chapter 4:1-5

10. Paul's Example and Reward   Chapter 4:6-8

11. Personal News and Requests   Chapter 4:9-22

Introduction/Background: The name Timothy means "Honored of God." Originally Timothy was from Lystra in Asia Minor. Later, as an associate of Paul, he traveled widely and worked among the believers in Macedonia, especially Thessalonica, and in Corinth and Ephesus. His father was Greek; his mother Eunice and his grandmother were Jewish. His "spiritual father" was Paul

Timothy is known as a traveling teacher and short-term pastor; tradition holds that he became bishop of Ephesus. He also helped in the sending of 6 epistles: 2 Corinthians, Philippians,

Colossians, 1 & 2 Thessalonians, and Philemon and is best known today for being the recipient of two New Testament letters.

Wherever people accept the truth of God and begin practicing it, counterfeits soon surface. That is what Paul found at Ephesus, and what Paul warns Timothy about (2 Timothy 3:8-9). Paul mentions two characters, Jannes and Jambres, whose names mean "he who seduces" and "he who is rebellious." Neither name is in the Old Testament, but Jewish legend held that these were the names of two Egyptian magicians who opposed Moses's demands of Pharaoh to free the Israelites. They tried to duplicate the miracles of Moses in an attempt to discredit him. But God showed that Moses's authority was more powerful (Exodus 7:11-12, 22).

Paul faced a similar experience at Ephesus. For two years he taught the message of Christ there, in a culture heavily steeped in pagan idolatry and occultism. God confirmed His teaching through powerful miracles and the release of many from evil spirits. But local exorcists attempted to duplicate the miracles. Their schemes backfired, however, to the benefit of the gospel (Acts 19:8-20). Counterfeits to the truth of Christ abound today, as Paul predicted they would.

II Chronicles 7:14

If my people, which are called by my name, shall humble themselves, and pray, and seek my face, and turn from their wicked ways; then will I hear from heaven, and will forgive their sin, and will heal their land.

Psalm 122:6

Pray for the peace of Jerusalem; they will prosper that love thee.

The Book of Titus

Scripture Focus Chapters 1 - 3

Objective: To Learn about the role and the responsibility of Titus in the organization and supervision of the church in Crete. This Epistle was probably written Corinth in A.D. 63.

Objective Breakdown:

1. Introduction   Chapter 1:1-4

2. Ordain Qualified Elders   Chapter 1:5-9

3. Rebuke False Teachers   Chapter 1:10-16

4. Speak Sound Doctrine   Chapter 2:1-15

5. Maintain Good Works   Chapter 3:1-11

6. Conclusion   Chapter 3:12-15

Lesson Plan 105

The Book of Titus

Chapters 1, 2, & 3

Objective: To give us continued insight and discernment concerning Paul's continued challenges with the converts to Christianity, and his guidance to Titus his fellow servant in the Lord.

Objective Breakdown:

1. God Cannot Lie	Chapter 1:1-4
2. Titus to Establish New Leaders	Chapter 1:5-9
3. Counter False Teachers	Chapter 1:10-16
4. Develop Human Resources	Chapter 2:1-10
5. Build on What God Has Done	Chapter 2:11-15
6. Believers Conduct in the Community	Chapter 3:1-8
7. Unprofitable Disputes	Chapter 3:9-11
8. Plans and Greetings	Chapter 3:12-15

Introduction: Some people say that it doesn't really matter what you believe, as long as you do the right thing. However, Paul's letter to Titus contradicts that sort of thinking. He knew people become what they think, and that everything they do is shaped by what they believe.

Crete had an ancient culture that was notorious for its corruption. In the face of this moral wasteland, Christians needed to live counter-culturally. They needed to speak the truth and live the truth.

Just as 1 and 2 Timothy were meant to provide continuity for the church at Ephesus, Titus was meant to provide continuity for the Church at Crete. What did believers there need? In a word, Authenticity.

That is why he urged Titus, his valued associate who was Pastoring a church on the island of Crete, to "speak the things which are proper for sound doctrine" (Titus 2:1). He knew that correct living is a product of correct belief. Error can never lead to godliness. Only truth produces genuine Christlikeness.

In our world today, many streams of thought lay claim to being "true." Yet they produce nothing that even approaches the character, integrity, and humility of Christ. That is why believers need to pay attention to the teaching they receive. Does it square with scripture? Does it honor Christ? Does it acknowledge what Paul calls "the truth which accords with godliness" (Titus 1:1)?

Has our own walk with Christ produced any visible fruit in front of our coworkers and or neighbors, such as patience, staying power, compassion, loyalty, better management, hard work, faithful service, or just being a good neighbor and setting good examples in our language and conduct? This is the kind of evidence that shows that faith in Christ has impact and power.

II Chronicles 7:14

If my people who are called by my name will humble themselves and pray, and seek my face, and turn from their wicked ways, then I will hear from heaven and will forgive their sin and heal their land.

Psalm 122:6

Pray for the peace of Jerusalem; they shall prosper who love thee.

The Book of Philemon

Objective: To Learn that Christian love really works even in situations of extraordinary tensions and difficulty. This Book (Letter) was written in Rome in A.D. 61.

Objective Breakdown:

1. The Prayer of Thanksgiving for Philemon   Chapter 1:1-7

2. The Petition of Paul for Onesimus   Chapter 1:8-16

3. The Promise of Paul to Philemon   Chapter 1:17-25

Lesson Plan 106

The Book of Philemon

Chapter 1

Objective: To give us continued insight and discernment concerning Paul's continued challenges with the converts to Christianity.

Objective Breakdown:

Introduction/Background

Paul's Praise for Philemon	Chapter 1:1-7
Paul's Appeal for Onesimus	Chapter 1:8-25

Introduction/Background: Philemon was a Christian of Colossae, a convert of Paul's, apparently a very well-to-do man. A church met in his house. He and Paul, it seems, were intimate friends. The occasion for the writing of the epistle is the story of Onesimus, a slave of Philemon, who had run away, having evidently robbed his master (Philemon verse 18).

His travels brought him to Rome where, in the providence of God, he came in contact with Paul. Through this contact, Paul led Onesimus to know the Savior. Then, Onesimus in some way became useful to Paul (verses 12-13), But Paul realized that Onesimus had a responsibility to Philemon and should make restitution for his thievery.

Thus, Paul deemed it right to return Onesimus to Philemon. Tychicus was given the responsibility of carrying Paul's letter from Rome to Colossae, and Onesimus must evidently have traveled back with him (Colossians 4:7-9).

"All my state shall Tychicus declare unto you, who is a beloved brother, and a faithful minister and fellow servant in the Lord, which I have sent unto you for the same purpose, that he might know your estate, and comfort your hearts; With Onesimus, a faithful and beloved brother, who is one of you. They shall make known unto you all things which are done here."

II Chronicles 7:14

If my people who are called by my name will humble themselves and pray, and seek my face, and turn from their wicked ways, then I will hear from heaven and will forgive their sin and heal their land.

Psalm 122:6

Pray for the peace of Jerusalem; they shall prosper who love thee.

The Book of Hebrews

Scripture Focus Chapters 1 - 13

Objective: To gain an understanding of the theology being imparted to the Hebrew and Gentile believers.

Objective Breakdown:

A. Better Than the Prophets	Hebrews 1:1-5,10
1. Creator of All Things	Hebrews 1:1-3
2. Upholder of All Things	Hebrews 1:1-3
3. Heir of All Things	Hebrews 1:1-3
4. Expression of God's Person & Glory	Hebrews 1:1-3
5. Purger of Sins	Hebrews 1:1-3
6. Intercessor for Sins	Hebrews 1:1-3
B. Better Than the Angels	Hebrews 1:4; 2:8
1. Because of His Rank	Hebrews 1:4, 9,13,14
2. Because of His Relationship	Hebrews 1:5
3. Because of His Reign	Hebrews 1:8
4. Because of His Righteousness	Hebrews 1;8
5. Because of His Redemptive Ministry	Hebrews 2:5-18
C. Why Did Jesus Become Man?	
1. To Recapture Our (Man's) Lost Destiny	Hebrews 2:5-9
2. To Recover Our Lost Destiny	Hebrews 2:10-13
3. To Reassure Our Lost Confidence	Hebrews 2:14-18
D. Better Than Moses	Hebrews 3:1-4, 7

1. Moses Was a Servant in God's House1   Hebrews 3:3, 5

2. Christ Is the Only Son in God's House   Hebrews 3:3, 4, 6

3. Moses Was Unsuccessful in Providing Rest for His People   Hebrews 3:7-11, 15-19, 4:1-7

4. Christ Was Successful in Providing a Rest for His People   Hebrews 3:6,14

E. Better Than Joshua   Hebrews 4: 8-16

1. Jesus Is the Rest of God   Hebrews 4: 8-11

2. Jesus Is the Word of God   Hebrews 4:12-13

3. Jesus Is the Priest of God   Hebrews 4:14-16

F. Better Than Aaron   Hebrews 5:1-10

1. Like Aaron He Was Taken Among Men   Hebrews 5:5:1

2. Like Aaron He Was Chosen by God   Hebrews 5:5:4

3. Like Aaron He Learned Obedience   Hebrews 5:8

4. Like Aaron He Prayed   Hebrews 2:7

5. Like Aaron He Suffered   Hebrews 2:8

6. Unlike Aaron He Is God's Son   Hebrews 5:5

7. Unlike Aaron He Is a Priest Like Melchizedek   Hebrews 5:6

8. Unlike Aaron He Is the Author of Eternal Salvation   Hebrews 5:9

G. Perfection the Superior Purpose   Hebrews 5:11, 6:20

The Perfection here is Spiritual Maturity and the Foes of this Perfection

1. Apathy   Hebrews 5:11

2. Ignorance   Hebrews 6:1-3, 8-12

3. Falling Away	Hebrews 6:4-6

Friends of this Perfection

1. The Believers Performance	Hebrews 6:1-3
2. The Father's Promises	Hebrews 6:13-18
3. The Saviors Priestly Work	Hebrews 6:19-20
4. Melechizedek the Superior Priesthood	Hebrews 7:1, 10:28
5. Faith the Superior Faith	Hebrews 11:1, 13:25

We Also Learned of The First of 5 Warnings or Dangers of Neglect:

1. Don't Disregard His Word (First Warning)	Hebrews 2:1-4
2. Don't Doubt His Word (Second Warning)	Hebrews 3:12,13, 4:11
3. Don't Depart from His Word (Third Warning)	Hebrews 6:4-6
4. Don't Despise His Word (Fourth Warning)	Hebrews 10:26-29
5. Don't Disagree with His Word (Fifth Warning)	Hebrews 12:25

H. The Superior Priesthood

His Priesthood had a 10-Fold Advantage over Aaron's Priesthood	Hebrews 7:1-28
1. It Was Royal	Hebrews 7:1-2
2. It Was Timeless	Hebrews 7:3
3. It Was Authoritative	Hebrews 7:4-10
4. It was Independent	Hebrews 7:14
5. It Was Everlasting	Hebrews 7:16,17
6. It Was Perfecting	Hebrews 7:11,19:25
7. It Was Guaranteed	Hebrews 7:21
8. It Was Changeless	Hebrews 7:23,24

9. It Was Holy	Hebrews 7:26
10. It Was All Inclusive	Hebrews 7:28

Note: The Priesthood of Melchizedek is a Heavenly priesthood because no earthly priesthood qualifies under Hebrews Chapter 7:3, which says: "without father, without mother, without genealogy, having neither the beginning of days nor end of life, but made like the Son of God, remains a priest continually."

This occurrence in scripture reflects all the signatures of an epiphany. An epiphany is the manifestation of a divine or supernatural being (not an angel because angels had a beginning at creation). I believe it had to be a foreshadowing of our Lord.

I. The Melchizedek Priesthood offers a better script from The Old Covenant to the New Covenant.

The Old Covenant dealt with Israel's right to occupy the Promised land:

1. Was Mediated by Moses	Hebrews 8:5
2. It Was Unconditional	Hebrews 8:7,9
3. It Was Unable to Produce Righteousness	Hebrews 8:8
4. It Was Written on Dead Stones	Exodus 32:15

The New Covenant dealt with Israel's right to occupy the Promised Land

1. Mediated by Christ	Hebrews 8:6 9:15
2. Unconditional	Hebrews 8:9
3. Able to Produce Righteousness	Hebrews 8:11
4. Written on Living Hearts	Hebrews 8:10

J. The Superior Priesthood Also offered a better Sanctuary from the Earthly to the Heavenly.

The Earthly Tabernacle:

1. Of This World	Hebrews 9:1
2. Temporary	Hebrews 9:8

3. A Shadow of the Real	Hebrews 9:9
4. Inaccessible	Hebrews 9:7
5. Associated with Creation	Hebrews 9:11
6. Made with Human Hand	Hebrews 9:24
7. Featured Animal Blood	Hebrews 9:13
8. Could Not Purge Sin	Hebrews 9: 9
9. Had No Abiding Hope	Hebrews 9: 10

The Heavenly Tabernacle:

1. Of Heaven	Hebrews 9:11, 24
2. Permanent	Hebrews 9:12
3. The Real Thing	Hebrews 9:24
4. Accessible to All	Hebrews 4:16, 10:19
5. Associated with Redemption	Hebrews 9:26
6. Made without Human Hands	Hebrews 9:24
7. Featured Christ's Blood	Hebrews 9:12
8. Able to Purge sin	Hebrews 9:12
9. Has an Abiding Hope	Hebrews 9:28

K. It Offers a Better Sacrifice

From Animal Lambs to Gods Lamb	Hebrews 10:4
1. The Necessity for God's Lamb	Hebrews 10:4
2. The Obedience of God's Lamb	Hebrews 10:5-7
3. Accomplishments of God's Lamb	Hebrews 10:10
4. He Laid Down His Life	Hebrews 10:10

5. He Sat Down (Upon God's Right Hand)   Hebrews 10:12

6. He Wrote Down Upon Human Hearts (His Word)   Hebrews 10:16

The Exhortation from God's Lamb:

1. Concerning Supplications   Be Bold   Hebrews 10:19

2. Concerning Past Sins   Be Assured   Hebrews 10:22

3. Concerning Service   Be Steadfast   Hebrews 10:23,25

4. Concerning Other Saints   Be Helpful   Hebrews 10:24

5. Concerning the Second Coming   Be Patient   Hebrews 10:35-39

6. The Warning from God's Lamb   Hebrews 10:26-34

L. People of Faith   Hebrews 11:1-40

Who Were They?

1. Abel   Hebrews 11:4

2. Enoch   Hebrews 11:5

3. Noah   Hebrews 11:7

4. Abraham   Hebrews 11:8-10,17-19

5. Sarah   Hebrews 11:11-12

6. Isaac   Hebrews 11:20

7. Jacob   Hebrews 11:21

8. Joseph   Hebrews 11:22

9. Moses' Parents   Hebrews 11:23

10. Moses   Hebrews 11:24-29

11. Joshua   Hebrews 11:30

12. Rahab   Hebrews 11:31

13. Gideon   Hebrews 11:32

14. Barak	Hebrews 11:32
15. Samson	Hebrews 11:32
16. Jephthah	Hebrews 11:32
17. David	Hebrews 11:32
18. Samuel	Hebrews 11:32

What they Did

1. Offered Proper Sacrifices	Hebrews 11:4
2. Left Earth Without Dying	Hebrews 11:5
3. Surviving the Flood	Hebrews 11:7
4. Inherited a land	Hebrews 11:8
5. Bore Children in Old Age	Hebrews 11:11
6. Gave Up Their Own Children	Hebrews 11:17
7. Predicted the Future	Hebrews 11:20
8. Defied Kings	Hebrews 11:23
9. Forsook the Pleasures of Sin	Hebrews 11:25
10. Left Egypt	Hebrews 11:27
11. Kept the Passover	Hebrews 11:28
12. Crossed the Red Sea	Hebrews 11:29
13. Shouted Down a City	Hebrews 11:30
14. Subdued Kingdoms	Hebrews 11:33
15. Stopped the Mouths of Lions	Hebrews 11:33
16. Quenched the Violence of Fire	Hebrews 11:34
17. Won Great Battles When Outnumbered	Hebrews 11:34
18. Saw the Dead Raised	Hebrews 11:35

M. The Pattern of Faith	Hebrews 12:1-29
1. Look to the Son of God	Hebrews 12:1-3
2. Submit to the Discipline of God	Hebrews 12:4-11
3. Prepare for the Kingdom of God	Hebrews 12:12-29
N. The Performance of Faith	Hebrews 13:1-25

By the Saints

1. They Are to Achieve Brotherly Love	Hebrews 13:1
2. They Are to Avoid Ungodly Lusts	Hebrews 13:4-5

By the Leaders

1. They Are to Be Prayed for	Hebrews 13:7,18
2. They Are to Be Obeyed	Hebrews 13:17

By the Savior We Are to Share His Reproach	Hebrews 13:13
1. What He Is -The Same Yesterday, Today & Forever	Hebrews 13:8
2. Who He Is- The Great Shepherd of the Sheep	Hebrews 13:20

By the Father

1. We Are to Sing His Praises	Hebrews 13:15
2. Grace Be to You All. Amen! & Amen!	Hebrews 13:25

Lesson Plan 107

The Book of Hebrews

Chapters 1, 2, & 3

Objective: To Present Jesus Christ as God, and better than all Men and Angels;To prove that Judaism and the law have come to an end;To Confirm Jewish Christians in the faith; To set forth New Covenant Doctrines for all men.

Objective Breakdown:

1. Background/Introduction

2. God Has Spoken Through Jesus   Chapter 1:1-4

3. Jesus is Superior to the Angels   Chapter 1:5-14

4. A Warning   Chapter 2:1-4

5. Jesus Lord Over All the Earth   Chapter 2:5-18

6. Jesus is Superior to Moses   Chapter 3:1-6

7. Listen to Jesus   Chapter 3:7-19

Background/Introduction: The book of Hebrews presents the only full discussion in the New Testament of Christ as the Believer's High Priest. It answers the question, "Whatever happened to Jesus." The book of Hebrews has been called the Fifth Gospel. The first four describe what Christ did on earth and His Deity, while Hebrews describe what He is now doing in Heaven.

There are some suggested authors of the Book of Hebrews: Paul, Barnabas, and Apollos. Yes, some even suggested Luke. However, the thoughts and reasoning are Paul's. Any difference in style is due to his writing to the Jews as a Jew, and not to Gentile Churches as in other Epistles.

Furthermore, the translation of the Book into Greek by Luke may account for some changes in style. The Book of Hebrews is ascribed to Paul, by over 100 ancient writers in both Greek and Latin, from 70 to 730 A.D. It was received as Paul's, by the Council of Laodicea (363 A.D.), by the Council of Carthage (397 A.D.), by the Syrian churches in A.D. 397. In addition,

Eusebius, the father of church history, explains that Paul wrote the epistle in Hebrew, leaving his name off so that it would be read and received more readily by the Jews who hated him and would not listen to anything he had to say. Luke translated it into Greek, hence it is similar to the book of Acts in expression.

Also, Paul was the only writer of the New Testament who requested prayer for himself (Hebrews 13:18; 2 Thessalonians 3:1). Regardless, of any other view, we all know that the Holy Spirit inspired the entire book to His Scribe.

II Chronicles 7:14

If my people, which are called by my name, shall humble themselves, and pray, and seek my face, and turn from their wicked ways; then will I hear from heaven, and will forgive their sin, and will heal their land.

Psalm 122:6

Pray for the peace of Jerusalem; they will prosper that love thee.

Lesson Plan 108

The Book of Hebrews

Chapters 4, 5, & 6

Objective: To present Jesus Christ as God, and as better than all men and angels; to prove that Judaism and the law have come to an end; to confirm Jewish Christians in the faith; to set forth New Covenant doctrines for all men.

1. Background/Introduction

2. A Promise of Rest   Chapter 4:1-13

3. Trials Are Shared by Christ   Chapter 4:14-16

4. Jesus Is a Superior Priest   Chapter 5:1-11

5. Press on to Maturity   Chapter 5:12-14

6. Grow Beyond the Basics   Chapter 6:1-8

7. Great Expectations   Chapter 6:9-20

Background/Introduction: How would you explain the gospel to Jews in the first century? How would you describe what it means to trust in Christ's work on the Cross rather than working to merit by strict observance of the Law? In chapter 4:1-13 of Hebrews, there is useful information concerning the Sabbath.

When God completed His work of creation, He rested. He stopped. It wasn't that He was tired and needed a break. He no longer needed to work because His work was finished. Creation was complete (Hebrews 4:4; Genesis 2:1-2). In the same way, people don't need to work for salvation because in Christ, salvation is finished. The way to God is open.

We can rest from slavish adherence to the Law in an attempt to make ourselves acceptable to God. We need only trust in Christ's finished work on our behalf (Hebrews 4:3; Romans 10:4). Every seven days the Jews ceased their work. They just didn't take the day off to catch up on chores or go to the lake, as many modern people do on Saturdays. They put an emphatic pause in their life for an entire day. Society came to a screeching halt to remind everyone of what God had done (Exodus 20:8-11). So when Hebrews equates rest in Christ with Sabbath rest, it draws on the heart of Jewish culture. Jesus is God's Sabbath rest when it comes to the work of Salvation.

God "rested" or ceased from His created labors on that seventh day of creation. Christians today have a degree of latitude in how we fulfill God's intentions for the Sabbath. But the spirit of "keeping the Sabbath holy" still means to honor God, to focus on the needs of others rather than ourselves, and to pursue fellowship, unity, and concern for other believers.

II Chronicles 7:14

If my people, which are called by my name, shall humble themselves, and pray, and seek my face, and turn from their wicked ways; then will I hear from heaven, and will forgive their sin, and will heal their land.

Psalm 122:6

Pray for the peace of Jerusalem; they will prosper that love thee.

Lesson Plan 109

The Book of Hebrews

Chapters 7, 8, & 9

Objective: To present Jesus Christ as God, and as better than all men and angels; to prove that Judaism and the law have come to an end; to confirm Jewish Christians in the faith; to set forth New Covenant doctrines for all men.

Objective Breakdown:

1. Introduction

2. Melchizedek   Chapter 7:1-13

3. Jesus Is Our High Priest   Chapter 7:14-28

4. A New Covenant   Chapter 8:1-6

5. They Shall Be My People   Chapter 8:7-13

6. The Old Covenant   Chapter 9:1-10

7. Eternal Redemption–Once for All   Chapter 9:11-28

Introduction: One of the most mysterious figures in the Old Testament serves as an illustration for Christ. Melchizedek (Hebrews 7:1; Genesis 14:18) suddenly appears in the Book of Genesis to bless Abraham after his defeat of Chedorlaomer, King of Elam, and his three allies (Genesis 14:18-20). Then, just as suddenly, Melchizedek disappears from the biblical record, until hundreds of years later, when David refers to him in Psalm 110.

Melchizedek (King of Righteousness) was a real man, Genesis reports that he was the king of Salem (Jerusalem) and a priest of God Most High. It was apparently in this priestly role that he first met Abraham returning from the rescue of his nephew Lot from Chedorlaomer. Melchizedek presented bread and wine, which was probably a demonstration of friendship and religious kinship. Some theologians suggest that this was a foreshadow of the Lord's supper and some Bible students suggest that Melchizedek was a theophany, an appearance of the pre-incarnate Christ.

The Book of Hebrews issues at least 5 warnings:

1. The Danger of Neglect (Hebrews 2:1-4)

2. Danger of Unbelief (Hebrews 3:17 to 4:1-13)

    a. Hardening of the Heart (Hebrews 3:7-19

    b. Challenge to Enter His Rest (Hebrews 4:1-13)

3. Danger of Not Maturing (Hebrews 5:11-6:20)

    c. Dullness of Hearing (Hebrews 5:11-14)

    d. Need for Maturity (Hebrews 6:1-8)

    e. Exhortation to Maturity (Hebrews 6:9-20)

4. Danger of Drawing Back (Hebrews10:26-29)

5. Danger of Refusing God (Hebrews 12:25-29)

II Chronicles 7:14

If my people, which are called by my name, shall humble themselves, and pray, and seek my face, and turn from their wicked ways; then will I hear from heaven, and will forgive their sin, and will heal their land.

Psalm 122:6

Pray for the peace of Jerusalem; they will prosper that love thee.

Lesson Plan 110

The Book of Hebrews

Chapters 10 & 11

Objective: To give us insight on the New Covenant and a closer look at the Christian's Walk of Faith.

Objective Breakdown:

Introduction

Introduction: Toughening Timid Faith. For some followers of Christ, faith is not merely a private matter, but a timid one as well. It is as if faith is such a delicate thing that unless one carefully protects it, the world will surely destroy it. However, Hebrews challenges believers to a different way of living. Yes, we live in a world of roaring lions (1 Peter 5:8) and therefore we must be on guard. The safest way to live in a world of spiritual dangers is to build up our strength, and not to hide our faith in secrecy. The Book of Hebrews offers some suggestions:

1. We can take confidence by freely entering into God's presence through Christ (Hebrews 10:19, 22).

2. Our faith can rest in full assurance that because of Christ's work on our behalf, our sins have been forgiven (Hebrews 10:21-22).

3. We can keep a firm grip on the basics of our faith, which rest on the integrity of Christ (Hebrews 10:23).

4. As believers we can stir each other up to loving, active faith (Hebrews 10:24).

5. We can meet with other believers regularly for encouragement, accountability, worship, and prayer (Hebrews 10:25).

6. We can leave judgment and repayment up to God, who is the ultimate Judge of people (Hebrews 10:29-31).

7. We can keep a loose grip on privilege, comfort, and possessions and instead show compassion toward those in need, such as prisoners (Hebrews 10:32-33).

8. We can condition ourselves for the long haul to finish well (Hebrews 10:35-39).

Spiritual strength and health means integrating our faith with every area of our life. Faith is not just one more thing on a list of hundred things, but rather the foundation of who we are. If our walk with Christ is real, it should become evident to others (James 2:14, 26; 3:13). Faith that is alive and growing is faith unleashed.

II Chronicles 7:14

If my people who are called by my name will humble themselves and pray, and seek my face, and turn from their wicked ways, then I will hear from heaven and will forgive their sin and heal their land.

Psalm 122:6

Pray for the peace of Jerusalem; they shall prosper who love thee.

Lesson Plan 111

The Book of Hebrews

Chapters 12 & 13

Objective: To present Jesus Christ as God, and as better than all men and angels; to prove that Judaism and the law have come to an end; to confirm Jewish Christians in the faith; to set forth New Covenant doctrines for all men.

Objective Breakdown:

1. Introduction

2. Let Us Run the Race   Chapter 12:1-2

3. God's loving Discipline   Chapter 12:3-13

4. New Life Means New Relationships   Chapter 12:14-28

5. A Lifestyle of Love   Chapter 13:1-6

6. Obey Leaders   Chapter 13:7-17

7. Greetings & Blessings   Chapter 13:18-25

Introduction: A time-worn adage that makes a lot of sense in the world of business and industry is: "If it ain't broke, don't fix it! However, that doesn't apply when it comes to people's health. In fact, health experts report that preventive care can not only lead to better health and risk from disease but vastly reduce medical costs. People are unwise to neglect their physical condition.

This truth has its parallel in the spiritual realm, as the Book of Hebrew reflects. Twice the book warns us to pay attention to their spiritual condition (Hebrews 6:1-20;12:14-29). Notice the strong language used in Hebrews 12 to describe what can happen to us if we fail to walk with Christ:

1. We can fall short of the Grace of God (Hebrews 12:15)

2. Bitterness can take root and sprout up, causing trouble (Hebrews 12:15)

3. Many people can become defiled (Hebrews 12:15)

4. We may make a foolish or even catastrophic mistake like Esau did (Hebrews 12:16-17; Genesis 25:27-34; 27:1-45)

5. We may refuse to listen when God speaks to us (Hebrews 12:25)

6. God's judgment may consume us (Hebrews 12:29).

Those are dire consequences! Fortunately, the Book of Hebrews offers some ways to check our spirituality and make corrections when we detect trouble:

Are we pursuing peace with others (Hebrews 12:14)? For example, how do we respond to conflicts at home, work, or school?

Are we pursuing holiness (Hebrews 12:14)? For example, is our thought life focused on that which purifies (see Philippians 2:1-13; 4:8-9; 1 Thessalonians 4:1-8)?

Are we listening to God (Hebrews 12:25)? For example, do we regularly wrestle with scripture, allowing it to challenge us and keep us accountable?

Do we live in grace, serving God in an acceptable way with reverence and respect

(Hebrews12:18)? For example, are we growing in our appreciation for God and His salvation, and for, other believers? Do we express that clearly and regularly? Would others describe us as "thankful?" (See 1 Timothy 4:4; Colossians 3:17).

II Chronicles 7:14

If my people, which are called by my name, shall humble themselves, and pray, and seek my face, and turn from their wicked ways; then will I hear from heaven, and will forgive their sin, and will heal their land.

Psalm 122:6

Pray for the peace of Jerusalem; they will prosper that love thee.

The Book of James

Scripture Focus Chapters 1 - 5

Objective: To gain a better understanding of faith. Jewish believers were beset with problems that were testing their faith, and James was concerned that they were succumbing to impatience, bitterness, materialism, disunity, and spiritual apathy. James, therefore, felt a responsibility to exhort and encourage the believers in their struggles of faith.

Objective Breakdown:

1. The Purpose of Tests	Chapter 1:1-12
2. The Source of Temptations	Chapter 1:13-18
3. Faith Obeys the Word	Chapter 1:19-27
4. Faith Removes Discrimination	Chapter 2:1-13
5. Faith Proves Itself by Works	Chapter 2:14-26
6. Faith Controls the Tongue	Chapter 3:1-12
7. Faith Produces Wisdom	Chapter 3:13-18
8. Faith Produces Humility	Chapter 4:1-12
9. Faith Produces Dependence on God	Chapter 4:13-17
10. Faith Produces Dependence on God (continued)	Chapter 5:1-6
11. Faith Endures Awaiting Christ's Return	Chapter 5:7-12
12. Faith Prays for the Afflicted	Chapter 5:13-18
13. Faith Confronts the Erring Brother	Chapter 5:19-20

Lesson Plan 112

The Book of James

Chapters 1, 2, & 3

Objective: To gain spiritual insight and understanding from the Book of James.

Objective Breakdown:

Background/Introduction

True Faith Involves Practical Obedience	Chapter 1:19-27
True Faith Does Not Play Favorites	Chapter 2:1-7
The Royal Law	Chapter 2:8-13
Faith Without Works is Dead	Chapter 2:14-26
The Test of Self-Control	Chapter 3:1-12
True Wisdom	Chapter 3:13-18

Background/Introduction: James means "supplanter" the same as Jacob. James is the English equivalent for the Hebrew name Jacob. The name appears approximately 40 times in the New Testament and refers to four different men. Two of the Apostles were named James: one the brother of John, sons of Zebedee (Matthew10:2) the other the son of Alphaeus (Matthew10:3) possibly known as James the Less (Mark 15:40). Also, James the father of Judas (not Iscariot) in Luke 6:16). The New Testament also teaches that Jesus grew up among the family of Joseph (a carpenter) and the Virgin Mary with four brothers named James, Joses, Juda, and Simon; and several sisters (naturally these were half brothers and sisters in the flesh.)

James was known as an unusually good man. He was surnamed "The Just" by his countrymen. He was very influential both among the Jews and in the Church. Peter reported to him on his release from prison (Acts 12:17), Paul acted on his advice (Acts 21:18-26). He was a very strict Jew himself but was the author of the tolerant letter to Gentile Christians (Acts 15: 13-29). He endorsed Paul's Gentile work but was himself mainly concerned with Jews. His life work was to win Jews, and "smooth their passage to Christianity."

According to Josephus; and Hegesippus, a Christian historian of the second century, whose narrative Eusebius accepts: Shortly before Jerusalem was destroyed by the Roman Army.' A.D. 70, when Jews were in large numbers embracing Christianity, Ananus, the High-Priest, and the Scribes and Pharisees, about or between the years A.D. 62-A.D. 66 assembled the Sanhedrin and commanded James, "the brother of Jesus, who was called Christ," to proclaim from one of the galleries of the Temple that Jesus Was Not the Messiah. But, instead, James cried out that Jesus, Was the Son of God and Judge of the World. Then his enraged enemies hurled him to the ground and stoned him. A fuller ended his suffering with a club while he was on his knees "praying, forgive them, they know not what they do."

Golden Nuggets in God's Word

James 1:2 "Count it all joy when you fall into various trials."

James 1:5 "If any of you lack wisdom, let him ask of God, who gives to all liberally and without reproach."

James 1:17 "Every good gift and every perfect gift is from above, and comes down from the Father of lights, with whom there is no variation or shadow of turning."

James 1:19-20 "Let every man be swift to hear, slow to speak, slow to wrath, for the wrath of man does not produce the righteousness of God."

James 1:22 "Be doers of the word, and not hearers only."

James 2:20 "Faith without works is dead."

1. Galatians 1:9 As we have said before, so now I say again, If anyone preaches any other gospel to you than what you have received, let him be accursed.

2. Galatians 3:24-25 Therefore the law was our tutor to bring us to Christ, that we might be justified by faith. But after faith has come, we are no longer under a tutor.

3. Galatians 3:28-29 There is neither Jew nor Greek, neither slave nor free, there is neither male nor female; for you are all one in Christ Jesus. And if you are Christ's, then you are Abraham's seed, and heirs according to the promise.

4. Galatians 4:16 Have I become your enemy because I tell you the Truth?

5. Galatians 5:16 "Walk in the Spirit and you shall not fulfill the lusts of the Flesh."

6. Galatians 5:22-23 "But the fruit of the Spirit is love, joy, peace, longsuffering, kindness, goodness, faithfulness, gentleness, self-control."

7. Galatians 6:7 "Do not be deceived, God is not mocked; for whatever a man sows, he will also reap."

8. Galatians 6:10 "Let us do good to all, especially to those who are of the household of faith."

II Chronicles 7:14

If my people who are called by my name will humble themselves and pray, and seek my face, and turn from their wicked ways, then I will hear from heaven and will forgive their sin and heal their land.

Psalm 122:6

Pray for the peace of Jerusalem; they shall prosper who love thee.

God's Blessing on Israel   (Numbers 6:22-27)

Jabez's Prayer to the Lord   (I Chronicles 4: 10)

Words for Comfort of the Soul

Ephesians 4:29 Let no corrupt word proceed out of your mouth, but what is good for necessary edification, that it may impart grace to the hearers.

Ephesians 4:30 Do not grieve the Holy Spirit of God, by whom you were sealed for the day of redemption.

Ephesians 4:31 Let all bitterness, wrath, anger, clamor, and evil speaking be put away from you, with all malice.

Ephesians 4:32 Be kind to another, tenderhearted, forgiving one another, even as God in Christ forgave you.

I Peter 2: 9 You are a chosen generation, a royal priesthood, a holy nation, His own special people.

Romans Road to Salvation

1. Romans 3:23 For all have sinned and fall short of the glory of God.

2. Romans 6:23 For the wages of sin is death, but the free gift of God is eternal life in Christ Jesus our Lord.

3. Romans 5:8 But God demonstrates His own love toward us, in that while we were yet sinners, Christ died for us.

4. Romans 10:9 That if you confess with your mouth Jesus as Lord and believe in your heart that God raised Him from the dead, you shall be saved.

5. Romans 10:13 For "Whoever will call upon the Name of the Lord will be saved."

II Chronicles 7:14

If my people who are called by my name will humble themselves and pray, and seek my face, and turn from their wicked ways, then I will hear from heaven and will forgive their sin and heal their land.

Psalm 122:6

Pray for the peace of Jerusalem; they shall prosper who love thee.

Lesson Plan 113

The Book of James

Chapter 4

Objective: To gain spiritual insight and understanding from the Book of James.

Objective Breakdown:

Introduction

Introduction: The Origins of Wars: covetousness (James 4:1-2). The desire to get that which belongs to others. This has been the cause of most wars.

Reasons for Unanswered Prayer: (James 4:4-10). Because they are for the gratification of our worldly pleasures (James 4:3).

Double-Mindedness (James 4-10). An expansion of Jesus's statement that a person cannot serve God and Mammon (Matthew 6:24), and similar to John's warning against Love of the World (I John 2:15-17). Such passages suggest the need for unceasing self-examination; for having to live in the world, and things being needful to our daily subsistence, it requires a great watchfulness to keep our affections above the borderline. We need constantly to draw nigh to God, to cleanse our hands, to purify our hearts, and to humble ourselves.

The tongue, again (James 4:11-12). This time on the utter absurdity of one sinner setting himself up as the judge of another sinner.

If Lord Will (James 4:13-17). One of the most amazing doctrines of scriptures that God, with the infinite universe on His hands, yet has a definite plan for each of His people (Acts 18:21; Romans1:10;15:32; I Corinthians 4:19; I Peter 3:17).

II Chronicles 7:14

If my people who are called by my name will humble themselves and pray, and seek my face, and turn from their wicked ways, then I will hear from heaven and will forgive their sin and heal their land.

Psalm 122:6

Pray for the peace of Jerusalem; they shall prosper who love thee.

Golden Nuggets in God's Word

James 1:2 "Count it all joy when you fall into various trials."

James 1:5 "If any of you lack wisdom, let him ask of God, who gives to all liberally and without reproach."

James 1:17 "Every good gift and every perfect gift is from above, and comes down from the Father of lights, with whom there is no variation or shadow of turning."

James 1: 19-20 "Let every man be swift to hear, slow to speak, slow to wrath, for the wrath ofman does not produce the righteousness of God."

James 1:22 "Be doers of the Word, and not hearers only."

James 2:20 "Faith without works is dead."

James 4:2-3 "Yet you do not have because you do not ask. You ask and do not receive, because you ask amiss, that you may spend it on your pleasures."

James 4:6 "God resists the proud, but gives grace to the humble."

James 4:7 "Resist the devil and he will flee from you. Draw near to God and He will draw near to you."

James 4:17 "To him who knows to do good and does not do it, to him it is sin."

James 5:16 "The effective, fervent prayer of a righteous man avails much."

I Peter 2:9 "You are a chosen generation, a royal priesthood, a holy nation, His own special people."

1. Galatians 1:9 As we have said before, so now I say again, If anyone preaches any other gospel to you than what you have received, let him be accursed.

2. Galatians 3:24,25 Therefore the law was our tutor to bring us to Christ, that we might be

345

justified by faith. But after faith has come, we are no longer under a tutor.

3. Galatians 3:28,29 There is neither Jew nor Greek, neither slave nor free, there is neither male nor female; for you are all one in Christ Jesus. And if you are Christ's, then you are Abraham's seed, and heirs according to the promise.

4. Galatians 4:16 Have I become your enemy because I tell you the Truth?

5. Galatians 5:16 "Walk in the Spirit and you shall not fulfill the lusts of the Flesh."

6. Galatians 5:22-23 "But the fruit of the Spirit is love, joy, peace, longsuffering, kindness, goodness, faithfulness, gentleness, self-control."

7. Galatians 6:7 "Do not be deceived, God is not mocked; for whatever a man sows, he will also reap."

8. Galatians 6:10 "Let us do good to all, especially to those who are of the household of faith."

II Chronicles 7:14

If my people who are called by my name will humble themselves and pray, and seek my face, and turn from their wicked ways, then I will hear from heaven and will forgive their sin and heal their land.

Psalm 122:6

Pray for the peace of Jerusalem; they shall prosper who love thee.

God's Blessing on Israel   (Numbers 6:22-27)

Jabez's Prayer to the Lord   (I Chronicles 4:10)

Words for Comfort of the Soul

Ephesians 4:29 Let no corrupt word proceed out of your mouth, but what is good for necessary edification, that it may impart grace to the hearers.

Ephesians 4:30 Do not grieve the Holy Spirit of God, by whom you were sealed for the day of redemption.

Ephesians 4:31 Let all bitterness, wrath, anger, clamor, and evil speaking be put away from you, with all malice.

Ephesians 4:32 Be kind to another, tenderhearted, forgiving one another, even as God in Christ forgave you.

I Peter 2: 9 You are a chosen generation, a royal priesthood, a holy nation, His own special people.

Lesson Plan 114

The Book of James

Chapter 5

Objective: To gain spiritual insight and understanding from the Book of James.

Objective Breakdown:

Introduction

True Faith Reacts to Injustice	Chapter 5:1-6
Patience & Perseverance	Chapter 5:7-12
The Power of Prayer	Chapter 5:13-20

Introduction: The Rich (James 5:1-6). James's fourth and strongest blast at them, the others being James 1:9-11; 2:1-13; 4:1-10. There must have been a good many rich men in the Judean Church who were thoroughly Un-Christian bent on Worldly Pleasure. Rare Christian souls are to be found among the rich; but, quite largely, James's picture of them still holds; and his warning to them of coming retribution is frightful.

Patience under Suffering (James 5:7-11). One day the Lord will Come on That Glad Day. The greater the Suffering here the greater will be the Glory there.

The Tongue, again (James 5:12). Our Sinful Tongue. The cause of so much trouble. This time, swearing. A very serious Sin, very displeasing to God. Yet how many professed Christians, in their ordinary conversation, profane God's Name? Better use of the tongue is to sing (James 5:13).

Prayer, again (James 5:13-18). Believing prayer will surely be answered. Elijah's closing and opening of the heavens.

II Chronicles 7:14

If my people who are called by my name will humble themselves and pray, and seek my face, and turn from their wicked ways, then I will hear from heaven and will forgive their sin and heal their land.

Psalm 122:6

Pray for the peace of Jerusalem; they shall prosper who love thee.

The Book of 1 Peter

Scripture Focus Chapters 1 - 5

Objective: To gain an understanding of the Book of Peter which is written to pilgrims of the world that are growing increasingly hostile to Christians. The Book is believed to be written in Rome in A.D. 63-64.

Objective Breakdown:

1. Salutation	Chapter 1:1-2
2. Hope for the Future	Chapter 1:3-4
3. Trials for the Present	Chapter 1:5-9
4. Anticipation in the Past	Chapter 1:10-12
5. Be Holy	Chapter 1:13-21
6. Love One Another	Chapter 1:22-25
7. Desire the Pure Mild of the Word	Chapter 2:1-3
8. Offer Up Spiritual Sacrifices	Chapter 2:4-10
9. Abstain from Fleshly Lusts	Chapter 2:11-12
10. Submission to the Government	Chapter 2:13-17
11. Submission in Business	Chapter 2:18-25
12. Submission in Marriage	Chapter 3:1-8
13. Submission in All of Life	Chapter 3:9-12
14. Conduct in Suffering	Chapter 3:13-17
15. Christ's Example of Suffering	Chapter 3:18-22
16. Christ's Example of Suffering (cont.)	Chapter 4:1-6
17. Commands in Suffering	Chapter 5:7-19

Lesson Plan 115

The Book 1 Peter

Chapters 1 & 2

Objective: To Gain Spiritual Insight and Understanding from the Book of 1 Peter.

Objective Breakdown:

Introduction

Greetings to the Pilgrim Believers	Chapter 1:1-2
Put Your Hope in Christ	Chapter 1:3-12
An Encouragement to Holiness and Love	Chapter 1:13-25
The Way to Spiritual Growth	Chapter 2:1-3
God's New People	Chapter 2:4-10
Living in the Community	Chapter 2:11-17
The Challenge of Work Relationships	Chapter 2:18-25

Introduction: First Peter offers unique hope to people grieved by various trials (1 Peter 1:6), a hope rooted in the power of Jesus Christ triumphs over death (1 Peter 1:3, 21) and the certainty of His return (1 Peter 1:13). What practical difference does that hope make? It dramatically affects one's behavior. Instead of caving in under the stress and pressure of adversity, the person of hope responds with Christlike dignity and moral integrity.

Second Peter shifts the emphasis from a hope by which we can live to a hope on which we can count. We can rely on God to provide us with "all (2 Peter 1:3). We can trust things that pertain to life and godliness" to guide us in the way of truth (2 Peter 1:16-21) and help us avoid error (2 Peter 2:1–3:7). We can also count on Jesus to return just as He said He would (2 Peter 3:8–18).

One of the great comforts of these letters is that we are not alone when we encounter disappointment, pain, or persecution. Jesus suffered the same kind of "fiery trial" and stands with us in our troubles. Best of all, He gave us an example of how to face the fires of adversity. Now 1 & 2 Peter invites us to "follow His steps" (1 Peter 2:21).

II Chronicles 7:14

If my people, which are called by my name, shall humble themselves, and pray, and seek my face, and turn from their wicked ways; then will I hear from heaven, and will forgive their sin, and will heal their land.

Psalm 122:6

Pray for the peace of Jerusalem; they will prosper that love thee.

Lesson Plan 116

The Book 1 Peter

Chapters 3, 4, & 5

Objective: To gain spiritual insight and understanding from the Book of Peter.

Objective Breakdown:

Introduction

Christ-Like Families	Chapter 3:1-7
Relating to Other Believers	Chapter 3:8-12
If You Should Suffer	Chapter 3:13-22
A Radically Different Lifestyle	Chapter 4:1-6
Commitment to Other Believers	Chapter 4:7-11
Rejoice in Suffering	Chapter 4:12-19
Leaders and Followers	Chapter 5:1-7
Watch Out for the Enemy	Chapter 5:8-11
Final Greetings	Chapter 5:12-14

Introduction: In our culture, Christians enjoy privileges and freedoms that first-century believers could have only imagined to be sure. Christians today may disapprove of many things that our increasingly secular society permits or encourages, and there we find believers discriminated against for their faith. Nevertheless, the system remains open to us. In fact, believers occupy positions of influence at all levels of society.

Things were far different for followers of Christ in the first century. As the gospel spread throughout the Roman Empire, it ran into a lot of hostility at the local level and eventually Rome itself. Christians were harassed, threatened, arrested, jailed, beaten, and even killed for their unwavering commitment to Christ. During Domitian's reign as emperor (A.D. 81-96), official persecution intensified, turning many believers into migrants and driving them to live underground in the catacombs.

First Peter speaks to believers enduring "fiery trials" (I Peter 4:12), people who had been rejected by the system. Likewise, 2 Peter speaks to Christians whose faith may have been wavering as they endured long years of struggle, waiting for the return of the Lord and deliverance from their oppressors.

The letters highlight a number of themes for Christians living under these conditions:

1. The need for clarity as to position. The early Christians were enemies of Rome because the system defines them as enemies. The writer urged believers to submit to authorities, to persevere in face of injustice, and to love their enemies rather than retaliate (1 Peter 2:13-20, 3:13-170, 4:12-16).

2. The need to affirm identity and worth.

Some in the first century regarded believers as evildoers (1 Peter 2:12, 3:16, 4:4). By contrast, Peter gave the believers names and titles that affirmed their value to God—chosen generation, a royal priesthood, a holy nation, God's own special people (1 Peter 2:9).

3. The value of community. People under trial need each other. That is why Peter urged suffering saints to hold on to each other, to take care of each other, and to identify with other believers who are facing tough times (1 Peter 3:8-9).

4. The crucial importance of character. When squeezed by opposition to their beliefs and morality, many people find it easy to compromise their ethical standards. Peter challenged his readers not to use persecution as an excuse to fail to grow in grace, but to stand firm in their faith and let suffering establish Christlike virtues within them (1 Peter 1:13-16, 2:1-2,11-12, 2 Peter 1:5-9; 3:17-18).

II Chronicles 7:14

If my people who are called by my name will humble themselves and pray, and seek my face, and turn from their wicked ways, then I will hear from heaven and will forgive their sin and heal their land.

Psalm 122:6

Pray for the peace of Jerusalem; they shall prosper who love thee.

The Book of 2 Peter

Scripture Focus Chapters 1 - 3

Objective: To gain an understanding of Book 2 Peter which is written to expose the dangerous and seductive work of false teachers, and to warn believers to be on their guard so that they will not be led away with the error of the wicked. The Book is believed to be written in Rome in A.D. 64-66.

Objective Breakdown:

1.	Salutation	Chapter 1:1-2
2.	Growth in Christ	Chapter 1:3-14
3.	Experience of the Transfiguration	Chapter 1:15-18
4.	Certainty of the Scriptures	Chapter 1:19-21
5.	Danger of False Teachers	Chapter 2:1-3
6.	Destruction of False Teachers	Chapter 2:4-9
7.	Description of False Teachers	Chapter 2:10-22
8.	Mockery in the Last Days	Chapter 3:1-7
9.	Manifestation of the Day of the Lord	Chapter 3:8-10
10.	Maturity in View of the Day of the Lord	Chapter 3:11-18

Lesson Plan 117

The Book 2 Peter

Chapters 1, 2, & 3

Objective: To gain spiritual insight and understanding from the Book of 2 Peter.

Objective Breakdown:

Introduction

Called, Equipped, and Growing	Chapter 1:1-11
Peter's Intent in Writing	Chapter 1:12:21
Beware of False Teachers	Chapter 2:1-3
God Will Protect	Chapter 2:4-11
Interpersonal Relations	Chapter 2:12-22
Scoffers Will Come	Chapter 3:1-7
A New View of Time	Chapter 3:8-9
Pursue Holiness and Maturity	Chapter 3:10-18

Introduction: Do You Have What It Takes? Do you think you have what it takes to "make it" in life? According to 2 Peter 1:3 you do. Peter says that God's power gives us what we need to experience real life in a way that pleases Him. God wants to affect every area of our lives–work, marriage and family, relationships, church, and community.

How can you make God's power operational in your experience? Peter says that it comes "through the knowledge of Him who called us." In other words, we must grow closer to Christ. The real power comes from having an understanding of our place in God's purposes and relying on His provisions. Where were you ten years ago? Does it seem like a distant memory, or as if it were only yesterday? Does the "here and now" totally consume you, dominating your perspective? Where do you expect to be ten years from now?

As Peter neared the end of his life, he wrote a letter in which he offers some insight into the nature of time and eternity. He beckons us to view time in both thousand years units and as mere days (2 Peter 3:8), recalling the beginning of creation (2 Peter 3:4-6). He also projects into the future, when judgment will be rendered and a new heaven and earth will be home to us who fear God (2 Peter 3:10-13). Peter reminds us that God values a day as much as a thousand years, affirming the importance of the here and now (2 Peter 3:8). But He also affirms God's activity long before we came on the scene (2 Peter 3:9).

Peter's perspective challenges us to live with a view toward eternity and values that last–purity, holiness, and righteousness (2 Peter 3:11,14). We need to avoid getting caught up in the here and now and losing sight of our eternal destiny. Neither the joys of today nor the problems of this week can quite compare with what God has prepared for us in eternity.

A special day of prayer has been called for our nation (II Chronicles 7:14) starting this 20 September through 30 October 2010. So remember that this is a Conditional Covenant (II Chronicles 7:14) which God has offered us and pray for each other. Also, pray for the peace of Jerusalem (Psalms 122:6).

II Chronicles 7:14

If my people who are called by my name will humble themselves and pray, and seek my face, and turn from their wicked ways, then I will hear from heaven and will forgive their sin and heal their land.

Psalm 122:6

Pray for the peace of Jerusalem; they shall prosper who love thee.

The Book of 1 John

Scripture Focus Chapters 1 - 5

Objective: To gain an understanding of the Book of 1 John and its theme: Fellowship with God. 1 John was written in Ephesus in A.D. 90.

Objective Breakdown:

1. Introduction	Chapter 1:1-4
2. Walk in the Light	Chapter 1:5-7
3. Confession of Sin	Chapter 1:8-10
4. Confession of Sin (cont.)	Chapter 2:1-2
5. Obedience to His Commandments	Chapter 2:3-6
6. Love for One Another	Chapter 2:7-14
7. Love of the World	Chapter 2:15-17
8. Spirit of the Antichrist	Chapter 2:18-27
9. Purity of Life	Chapter 2:28-29
10. Purity of Life (cont.)	Chapter 3:1-3
11. Practice of Righteousness	Chapter 3:4-12
12. Love in Deed and Truth	Chapter 3:13-24
13. Testing the Spirits	Chapter 4:1-6
14. Love as Christ Loved	Chapter 4:7-23
15. Love as Christ Loved (cont.)	Chapter 5:1-3
16. Victory Over the World	Chapter 5:4-5
17. Assurance of Salvation	Chapter 5:6-13
18. Guidance in Prayer	Chapter 5:14-17
19. Freedom from Habitual Sin	Chapter 5:18-21

Lesson Plan 118

The Book of 1 John

Chapters 1 & 2

Objective: To gain spiritual insight and understanding from the Book of 1 John.

Objective Breakdown:

Introduction

With Our Own Eyes	Chapter 1:1-4
God's Offer and Our Response	Chapter 1:5-10
Dealing with Sin	Chapter 2:1-2
Loving God and One Another	Chapter 2:3-11
Three Stages of Faith	Chapter 2:12-14
Do Not Love the World	Chapter 2:15-29

Introduction: John is often described as the "apostle of love" and 1, 2, and 3 John as the "love letters" of the New Testament. But these writings are far from mere sentimentalism. They're about "tough love," love that shoots straight, even if it hurts because it cares for others and wishes them the best.

The tone of the letters has the feeling of an older believer pleading with a younger. Nine times in 1 John, John addresses his readers as "little children" and nine times among the three letters as "beloved."

How does one discern genuine Christianity? John claims there is a core truth to believe–that Jesus has come in the flesh –and that the practice of love and righteousness is the best test of whether one truly believes in and follows Jesus. His message is similar to Paul's word to the 'Ephesians that true spirituality involves "speaking the truth in love" (Ephesians 4:15).

Toward the end of the first century, some Christians began drifting away from the truth about Christ. As the founders of the Church began to die off many lost touch with those who had known Jesus in the flesh. They were being seduced by competing doctrines, especially early forms of Gnosticism (see I John 5:20). As a result, second and third generations believers began to grow cold in their love for each other and also lukewarm in their commitment to the truth. They had, as the Lord put it to the Ephesians, "left their first Love" (Revelations 2:4).

Christianity had been in the world for some 60 or 70 years, and in many parts of the Roman Empire had become an important religion and a powerful influence. Naturally, there came to be all sorts of efforts to amalgamate the Gospel with prevailing philosophies and systems of thought.

One such cult was a form of Gnosticism which was disrupting the Churches in John's day, taught that there is in human nature an irreconcilable principle of Dualism: that the Spirit and the Body are two separate entities; that sin resided in the flesh only; that the Spirit could have its raptures, and the Body do as it pleased; that the lofty mental mystical Piety was entirely consistent with voluptuous sensual life. They denied the Incarnation, that God had in Christ actually become flesh, and they maintained that Christ was a Phantom, a Man in appearance only. The leader of this cult, located in Ephesus, was a man named Cerinthus. He claimed for himself inner mystic experiences and exalted knowledge of God, but was a voluptuary (one whose chief interest is luxury and in the gratification of sensual appetites).

The response to this trend was the writing of 1, 2, and 3 John. These letters call Christians back to the basics...the truth about Christ, and the love of Christ. These Epistles are crucial for Christians today.

II Chronicles 7:14

If my people, which are called by my name, shall humble themselves, and pray, and seek my face, and turn from their wicked ways; then will I hear from heaven, and will forgive their sin, and will heal their land.

Psalm 122:6

Pray for the peace of Jerusalem; they will prosper that love thee.

Lesson Plan 119

The Book of 1 John

Chapters 3, 4, & 5

Objective: To gain spiritual insight and understanding from the Book of 1 John.

Objective Breakdown:

Introduction

The Children of God	Chapter 3:1-12
Love Cares for Other Needs	Chapter 3:13-24
Discernment	Chapter 4:1-6
Love Serves Others	Chapter 4:7-21
If You Love God, Obey Him	Chapter 5:1-5
Certainty About Eternal Life	Chapter 5:6-15
Avoiding Sin	Chapter 5:16-20

Introduction: One reason John was so concerned that his readers exercise discernment (1 John 4:1, 2 John 1–2, 4, 3 John 3-4) was that a system of false teachings known as Gnosticism was becoming popular.

The name Gnosticism comes from the Greek word for knowledge, gnosis. The gnostics believed that a special knowledge about the nature of the world was the way to salvation. For that reason, several writers of the New Testament condemned early manifestations of the philosophy as false. Paul for example emphasized wisdom and knowledge that comes from God as opposed to idle speculation and fables (Colossians 2:8-23, 1 Timothy 1:4, 2 Timothy 2:16-19, Titus 1:10-16). Likewise, John, both in his Gospel and epistles, countered heretical teaching which in a broad sense could be considered gnostic.

The Gnostic teachers accepted the Greek idea of radical dualism between God (spirit) and the world (matter). According to their worldview, the created order was evil, inferior, and opposed to good. They believed that we are surrounded by a number of cosmic spheres which separate humans from God. These spheres are ruled by archons (spiritual powers) who guard their spheres by barring the souls of those who are seeking to ascend from the realm of darkness and captivity which is below to the realm of light which is above.

The gnostics taught that humans are composed of body, soul, and spirit. Since the body and soul are part of people's earthly existence, they were held to be evil; enclosed in the soul they said is the spirit, the divine substance of man. According to gnostic teaching, the spirit is asleep and ignorant and needs to be awakened and liberated by knowledge. Thus, the aim of salvation in Gnosticism is to release the inner man from his earthly dungeon so that he can return to the realm of light where the soul is reunited with God.

II Chronicles 7:14

If my people, which are called by my name, shall humble themselves, and pray, and seek my face, and turn from their wicked ways; then will I hear from heaven, and will forgive their sin, and will heal their land.

Psalm 122:6

Pray for the peace of Jerusalem; they will prosper that love thee.

The Book of 2 John

Scripture Focus Chapter 1

Objective: To gain an understanding of the Book of 2 John and its theme: Abide in God's Commandments and abide not with false teachers who deny the incarnation of Jesus Christ. 2 John was written in Ephesus in A.D. 90.

Objective Breakdown:

1. Salutation	Chapter 1:1-3
2. Walk in Truth	Chapter 1:4
3. Walk in Love	Chapter 1:5-6
4. Doctrine of False Teachers	Chapter 1:7-9
5. Avoid False Teachers	Chapter 1:10-11
6. Benediction	Chapter 1:12-13

The Book of 3 John

Objective: To gain an understanding of the Book of 2 John and its theme: Beloved do not imitate what is evil, but what is good. He who does good is of God, but he who does evil has not seen God. 3 John is the shortest Book in the Bible and was written in Ephesus in A.D. 90.

Objective Breakdown:

1.	Salutation	Chapter 1:1
2.	Godliness of Gaius	Chapter 1:2-4
3.	Generosity of Gaius	Chapter 1:5-8
4.	Pride of Diotrephes	Chapter 1:9-11
5.	Praise for Demetrius	Chapter 1:12
6.	Benediction	Chapter 1:13-14

Lesson Plan 120

The Books of 2 & 3 John

Objective: To give us insight and discernment regarding genuine Christian love.

Objective Breakdown:

Background/Introduction

The Elect Lady	II John 1:1-3
Joy Over Truth & Love	II John 1:4-6
Watch Out for False Teachers	II John 1:7-11
John Plans to Visit in Person	II John 1:12-13
Encouragement for Gaius	III John 1:8
Disappointing Diotrephes	III John 1:9-11
The Testimony of Demetrius	III John 1:12

Background/Introduction: The identity of the "elect lady" (2 John 1) is unknown. Some believe that she was an individual woman and that John chose to use this title instead of her personal name in order to protect her from persecution. Others believe that the term is symbolic, referring to a group of believers, perhaps the church at Ephesus.

If indeed she was writing to a particular woman, she must have been a wise and loving mother as John's praise for her children attests (verses 4-6). He warned her not to welcome those who spread false teachings (verses 9-10). His closing remarks also hint that the "elect lady" and John shared a close friendship (verses 12-13). Though the name of this woman (if she was an individual woman) is lost to us today, this description of her reveals a person whose faith in Christ was influential in the lives of her family and others around her.

John was concerned to help this "elect woman" to become more discerning and not lend the reputation of her household to those who would distort the truth about Christ (verses 7,11). He knew that not all who claim Christ are true followers. So believers must develop discernment if they are to remain loyal to the truth.

II Chronicles 7:14

If my people, which are called by my name, shall humble themselves, and pray, and seek my face, and turn from their wicked ways; then will I hear from heaven, and will forgive their sin, and will heal their land.

Psalm 122:6

Pray for the peace of Jerusalem; they will prosper that love thee.

The Book of Jude

Objective: To gain an understanding of the Book of Jude and its theme: Jude addresses his letter to believers who are called "sanctified" and "preserved," and wishes for them a three-fold blessing of mercy, peace, and love. It is not known where the book of Jude was written, but it is estimated that it was written between 66-80 A.D.

Objective Breakdown:

1. Purpose of Jude   Chapter 1:1-4

2. Past Judgment of False Teachers   Chapter 1:5-7

3. Present Characteristics of False Teachers   Chapter 1:8-13

4. Future Judgment of False Teachers   Chapter 1:14-16

5. Defense Against False Teachers   Chapter 1:17-23

6. Doxology of Jude   Chapter 1:24-25

Lesson Plan 121

The Book of Jude

Objective: To gain an understanding of what was happening to the Church in the first century.

Objective Breakdown:

1. Introduction

2. A Bond Servant of Jesus   Jude 1:1-2

3. Contend for the Faith   Jude 1:3-4

4. Examples from History   Jude 1:1:5-7

5. False Teachers Are Described and Condemned   Jude 1:8-15

6. Stay in the Love of God   Jude 1:16-23

7. A Doxology   Jude 1:24-25

Introduction: Jude is an English form of the name Judas—an infamous name among believers both then and now, because of Judas Iscariot, whom the New Testament never mentions without reminding us that it was he who betrayed Jesus to the Jewish leaders (Matthew10:4, Mark 3:19, John 12:4).

In contrast to Judas Iscariot, the author Jude was a devoted defender of the Lord and the faith. We know little about the man, except that he called himself "a bondservant of Jesus Christ and brother of James" (Jude 1). If that James was James the apostle, the half-brother of Jesus (Matthew 13:55, Galatians 1:19), then Jude must also have been a half-brother of Jesus.

Jude's Letter has the character of a tract or brief essay written for a general audience of Christians (Jude 1). Its date cannot be determined with precision, but it appears to have been written in the second half of the first century, possibly after the fall of Jerusalem to the Romans in A.D. 70.

Jude tells his readers: "Remember the words which were spoken by the apostles of our Lord Jesus Christ" (Jude 17). By the time he wrote, faith had become the faith, once for all delivered to the saints (Jude 3), suggesting a formal and even codified body of beliefs and practice. That spiritual treasure was under attack, so Jude, urged believers to contend earnestly for the faith (Jude 3).

However, the battle was not with outsiders, such as the Jewish council, the Roman government, or with many esoteric philosophies and mystery religions of the day. Instead, the danger came from within. Curiously, Jude never mentions names, except the Old Testament: sinful Israel (Jude 5; Numbers 14:22-23), rebellious angels (Jude 6), Sodom and Gomorrah (Jude 7); Genesis 19:24-25), Cain (Jude 11; Genesis 43-8), Balaam (Jude 11; Numbers 22-24), and Korah (Jude 11; Numbers 16:19-35).

Little has changed in the two thousand years since Jude was written. Believers still need to be on their guard against doctrinal error and persuasive teachers who lead people away from the truth of Jesus. In reading Jude, we are reminded that Christianity is no game. The Old Testament rebels mentioned in Jude came to very bad ends. So will today's false teachers and those who follow them.

II Chronicles 7:14

If my people, which are called by my name, shall humble themselves, and pray, and seek my face, and turn from their wicked ways; then will I hear from heaven, and will forgive their sin, and will heal their land.

Psalm 122:6

Pray for the peace of Jerusalem; they will prosper that love thee.

The Book of Revelation

Scripture Focus Chapters 1 - 22

Objective: To gain an understanding of the Book of Revelation and its theme. We need to consider just as the Book of Genesis is the book of beginnings, Revelation is the book of consummation. In it, the divine program of redemption is brought to fruition, and the Holy name of God is vindicated before all creation. The Book of Revelation was written by the Apostle John while he was on the Island of Patmos in A.D. 55-96.

Objective Breakdown:

1. Introduction   Chapter 1:1-8

2. Revelation of Christ   Chapter 1:9-20

3. Message to Ephesus   Chapter 2:1-7

4. Message to Smyrna   Chapter 2:8-11

5. Message to Pergamos   Chapter 2:12-17

6. Message to Thyatira   Chapter 2:18-29

7. Message to Sardis   Chapter 3:1-6

8. Message to Philadelphia   Chapter 3:7-13

9. Message to Laodicea   Chapter 3:14-22

10. The Throne of God   Chapter 4:1-11

11. The Sealed Book   Chapter 5:1-14

12. First Seal   Chapter 6:1-2

13. Second Seal   Chapter 6:3-4

14. Third Seal   Chapter 6:5-6

15. Fourth Seal   Chapter 6:7-8

16. Fifth Seal   Chapter 6:9-11

Lesson Plan 122

The Book of Revelation

Chapter 1

Objective: To gain insight into the exciting events that God has planned for his people and the secular world.

Objective Breakdown:

Introduction/Background

Revelation of Jesus to John	Chapter 1:1-3
John's Greeting to the Seven Churches	Chapter 1:4-8
John's Encounter with the Glorified Jesus	Chapter 1:9-18
John's Commission to Write	Chapter 1:19-20

Truths Learned from This Lesson

Introduction/Background: These visions were given, and the book written, in the lurid light of burning martyrs. The Church was 66 years old. It had made enormous growth. It had suffered, and was suffering, terrific persecutions.

The First Imperial Persecutions of Christians, 30 years before this book was written, was that of Nero, A.D. 64-67. In that persecution, multitudes of Christians were crucified, or thrown to wild beasts, or wrapped in combustible garments and burned to death while Nero laughed at the pitiful shrieks of burning men and women. In Nero's persecution, Paul and Peter suffered martyrdom.

The Second Imperial Persecution was instituted by Emperor Domitian (A.D. 95). It was short but extremely severe. Over 40,000 Christians were tortured or slain. This was the persecution in which John was banished to the Isle of Patmos (1:9).

The revelation of Jesus to John (1:1-3): The Book of Revelation has much to say about all three persons of the Godhead, but it is especially clear in its presentation of the awesome resurrected Christ who has received all authority to judge the earth. He is called Jesus Christ

(1:1) the faithful witness, the firstborn from the dead, the ruler over kings of the earth (1:5), the First and Last (1:17), He who lives (1:18), the Son of God (2:18), Holy and True (3:7), The Amen, The Faithful and True Witness, the beginning of the creation of God (3:14), the Lion of the Tribe of Judea, the Root of David (5:5)), the Lamb (5:6), Faithful and True (19:11), The Word of God (19:13), King of Kings, and Lord of Lords (19:16), Alpha and Omega (22:13), the Bright and Morning Star (22:16), and the Lord Jesus Christ (22:21).

This book is indeed "The Revelation of Jesus Christ" (1:1) since it comes from Him and centers on Him. It begins with a vision of His glory, wisdom, and power (Chapter 1) and portrays His authority over the entire church (2:3). He is the Lamb who was slain and declared worthy to open the book of judgment (Chapter 5). His righteous wrath is poured out upon the whole earth (Chapters 6-18) and He returns in power to judge His enemies and to reign as Lord over all (19:20). He will rule forever over the heavenly city in the presence of all who know Him (21:22).

John's Greeting to the Seven Churches (1:4-8): Ephesus, Smyrna, Pergamum, Thyatira, Sardis, Philadelphia, Laodicea. These Seven Cities, connected by great triangular highway, are named in their geographic order, beginning with Ephesus, thence north about 100 miles to Pergamum, and thence southeast to Laodicea which is about 100 miles east of Ephesus. There were many churches in Asia. These, called the Seven Churches, must have been the main centers in their respective districts, key cities in John's pastoral care of the region.

John's Encounter with the Glorified Jesus (a Vision of Christ 1:9-18): "Patmos (1:9), the Island to which John was banished in the Persecution orchestrated by Domitian, and in which these visions were given, is in the Aegean Sea, about 60 miles southwest of Ephesus, and about 150 miles east of Athens. It is 10 miles long, 6 miles wide, treeless, and rocky.

John's Commission to "Write" or a call to Service (1:19-20): "Write" commands the voice from Heaven. "What thou seest, Write in a book" (1:11). "Write the things which thou hast seen" (1:19). "To Ephesus...Write." "To Smyrna...Write." "To Pergamum... Write." "To Thyatira... Write." "To Sardis...Write." "To Philadelphia... Write." "To Laodicea... Write." "Write, Blessed are the dead in the Lord" (14:15). "Write, Blessed are those bidden to the Marriage Supper" (19:9).

Thus, it is emphasized, again and again, in the strongest possible manner, that God Himself commanded that the Book be written and that He Himself told John exactly what to write.

Truths Learned from This Lesson:

a. We may be certain that the Lord wants to Bless us through the study of the Book of Revelation.

b. We are wise to follow John's example of worshiping Jesus on the Lord's Day.

c. We can cultivate an attitude of worship by meditating on the vision of Christ described in Revelation 1.

d. We need to remain alert to Jesus's call to service.

II Chronicles 7:14

If my people, which are called by my name, shall humble themselves, and pray, and seek my face, and turn from their wicked ways; then will I hear from heaven, and will forgive their sin, and will heal their land.

Psalm 122:6

Pray for the peace of Jerusalem; they will prosper that love thee.

Lesson Plan 123

The Book of Revelation

Chapter 2

Objective: Our study today will cover the first four of the seven churches.

Objective Breakdown:

Introduction and Background

Ephesus Has Left Her First Love	Chapter 2:1-7
Symrna Is Suffering	Chapter 2:8-11
Pergamos Is Confused	Chapter 2:12-17
Thyatira Is Too Tolerant	Chapter 2:18-29

Introduction and Background: Our study today will cover the first four of the seven churches which are the Voice from Heaven (Jesus), the Alpha and Omega, the First, and the Last, who gave John the following instruction: "What thou seest, Write in a book and send it to the seven churches which are in Asia: to Ephesus, to Smyrna, to Pergamos, to Thyatira, to Sardis, to Philadelphia, and to Laodicea."

The first-century church believers faced stiff opposition from political authorities determined to stop the spread of their message. Nevertheless, despite increasingly harsh treatment, they were able to go a long way toward fulfilling the Lord's mandate to take the Gospel "to the ends of the earth" (Acts 1:8). In fact, within about thirty years they had won converts throughout the Roman Empire, including the capital of Rome itself.

One reason for these spectacular results was a concentration on reaching cities (see "Paul's Urban Strategy" at Acts 16:4). In Ephesus, for example, Christian leaders influenced strategic groups of workers who not only turned the city upside down with their new faith but took the gospel inland so that "all who dwelt in Asia heard the word of the Lord" (Acts 19:10; see "The Ephesus approach" at Acts 19:8-41).

In Revelation, John writes letters from the Lord to some of the churches that were probably established through the Ephesus initiative. The seven churches mentioned were in provincial capitals what is now called Turkey. A courier would have taken a circular route to deliver the epistles to the seven cities, which in turn serve as distribution points to other churches in the region.

By the time John wrote to these churches, Christians were facing intense persecution under Emperor Domitian (A.D. 81-96 A.D.). He extended the practice of emperor worship to demand that all citizens in the empire refer to him as "Lord and God." He also used political, economic, and social measures to suppress what he perceived to be resistance, including the burgeoning Christian movement. It is probably during this period that believers in Rome began seeking refuge in the catacombs, deep underground tunnels intended as burial chambers for the dead.

Internally, many of the churches struggled with poverty, heresy, and dissension. In Revelation, heretical teachers are variously referred to as teachers of Balaam (Rev 2:14), Jezebel (Rev 2:20), the Nicolaitans Rev 2:6, 15), and the Synagogue of Satan (Rev 2:9; 3:9). We don't know exactly what the nature of these heresies was, though one possibility is Gnosticism (see 1 John 5:20). But we do know that problems of syncretism and worldliness were common.

Our study today will cover the first four of the seven churches which the Voice from Heaven, (Jesus) the Alpha and Omega, the First and the Last, who gave John the following instruction: "What thou seest, Write in a book and send it to the seven churches which are in Asia: to Ephesus, to Smyrna, to Pergamos, to Thyatira, to Sardis, to Philadelphia, and to Laodicea."

Background on Ephesus, Symrna, Pergamos, and Thyatira Ephesus, (30-100 A.D. – its name means desirable)

A city of 225,000 population, the mother of Asian churches, was a metropolis and commercial center of Asia. Its Temple Diana was one of the Seven Wonders of the World.

There, 40 years before, Paul had done his most successful work (A.D. 54-57); such a multitude of converts to Christ that almost overnight, the Church became one of the most powerful influences in the city and soon one of the most famous churches in the world.

After the death of Paul, Timothy, it is said, spent most of his time in Ephesus, and there suffered martyrdom under Domitian, the same persecution that sent John to Patmos.

In Ephesus, John spent his old age; and if not as an active pastor, (due to his age), then as the last surviving Apostle of Christ. He must have been a dominating influence among pastors.

Smyrna (100-313 A.D. – its name means myrrh)

Although smaller than Ephesus, Smyrna was still prosperous because it sat on the coast at the end of a major trade route to the east. Unlike Ephesus, it continues to be a thriving city to this day–the second largest in Asiatic Turkey. In John's time, it had been solidly loyal to Rome for centuries and contained a temple to the goddess of Rome and another to the emperor. It also boasted a stadium, a library, and the largest public theater in Asia.

The real danger to Smyrnan Christians was not the Roman patriots but the large population of Jews who detested Christians as heretics and inflamed the Romans to persecute them. One of the most famous martyrs of the second century was Polycarp, the bishop of Smyrna. The contemporary record of his death states that he was "the twelfth to meet a martyr's death in Smyrna. Polycarp was burned to death on a Saturday in 155 A.D., and the Jews of Smyrna broke the Sabbath to gather wood for the fire. They abhorred the idea that a man executed for blasphemy was the Messiah and that a person became pleasing to God not by obeying the Law of Moses but by putting faith in this Messiah.

Smyrna means "bitter" or "myrrh," a tree resin with a bitter taste that was crushed and used in perfume, in incense, and as a preservative in burial.

Pergamum (314-590 A.D. – its name means marriage)

Pergamum was the political capital of Asia, even though Ephesus was larger. It was the center of the imperial cult in the province. In addition to its temple to Caesar and Rome, Pergamum's most popular tourist attraction was the temple of Asclepios, the god of healing. People flocked to the shrine in hopes of miraculous cures. (The myth of Asclepios had its roots in Babylon. His symbol was the serpent; doctors still use it today) Three other major temples also loomed over Pergamum atop its mountain citadel. In particular, "an enormous altar of Zeus...stood on a platform on the hill overlooking the city."

The governor of Asia, who resided in Pergamum, was the official champion of both justice and the imperial cult. He held the "right of the sword" to execute anyone he willed.

Pergamum means something like "additional marriage." (Per is "elevation" and gamum is marriage.")

Thyatira (590-1517 A.D. its name means continuing sacrifice)

Thyatira was not a remarkable city; it was simply a thriving center of manufacturing and marketing. Practically everyone in town belonged to one of the dozens of trade and craft gilds. Membership in these was crucial since they were the focus of business and social life. But each was dedicated to a patron god, and meetings included a common meal in its honor. The meat for the meal came from an animal sacrificed to the god. In addition, drunkenness, carousing, and even orgies were not rare. What should a Christian do? Evidently, many in Thyatira who were otherwise full of love and faith were willing to listen to a woman teaching (Jezebel) that it was okay to tolerate–even participate in–pagan practices.

II Chronicles 7:14

If my people who are called by my name will humble themselves and pray, and seek my face, and turn from their wicked ways, then I will hear from heaven and will forgive their sin and heal their land.

Psalm 122:6

Pray for the peace of Jerusalem; they shall prosper who love thee.

Synopsis: Epistles to the Churches in Asia, with warnings and encouragements, to the Church at Ephesus; (1-7) at Smyrna; (8-11) at Pergamos; (12-17) and at Thyatira. (18-29)

Text: Verses 1-7 - These churches were in such different states as to the purity of doctrine and the power of godliness, that the words of Christ to them will always suit the cases of other churches, and professors. Christ knows and observes their state; though in heaven, yet he walks in the midst of his churches on earth, observing what is wrong in them, and what they want. The church of Ephesus is commended for diligence in duty. Christ keeps an account of every hour's work his servants do for him, and their labour shall not be in vain in the Lord. But it is not enough that we are diligent; there must be bearing patience, and there must be waiting patience. And though we must show all meekness to all men, yet we must show just zeal against their sins. The sin Christ charged this church with, is, not the having left and forsaken the object of love, but having lost the fervent degree of it that at first appeared. Christ is displeased with his people, when he sees them grow remiss and cold toward him. Surely this mention in scripture, of Christians forsaking their first love, reproves those who speak of it with carelessness, and thus try to excuse indifference and sloth in themselves and others; our Saviour considers this indifference as sinful. They must repent: they must be grieved and ashamed for their sinful declining, and humbly confess it in the sight of God. They must endeavour to recover their first zeal, tenderness, and seriousness, and must pray as earnestly, and watch as diligently, as when they first set out in the ways of God. If the presence of Christ's grace and Spirit is slighted, we may expect the presence of his displeasure. Encouraging mention is made of what was good among them. Indifference as to truth and error, good and evil, may be called charity and meekness, but it is not so; and it is displeasing to Christ. The Christian life is a warfare against sin, Satan, the world, and the flesh. We must never yield to our spiritual enemies, and then we shall have a glorious triumph and reward. All who persevere, shall derive from Christ, as the Tree of life, perfection and confirmation in holiness and happiness, not in the earthly paradise, but in the heavenly. This is a figurative expression, taken from the account of the garden of Eden, denoting the pure, satisfactory, and eternal joys of heaven; and the looking forward to them in this world, by faith, communion with Christ, and the consolations of the Holy Spirit. Believers, take your wrestling life here, and expect and look for a quiet life hereafter; but not till then: the word of God never promises quietness and complete freedom from conflict here.

8-11 Our Lord Jesus is the First, for by him were all things made; he was before all things, with God, and is God himself. He is the Last, for he will be the Judge of all. As this First and Last, who was dead and is alive, is the believer's Brother and Friend, he must be rich in the deepest poverty, honourable amidst the lowest abasement, and happy under the heaviest tribulation, like the church of Smyrna. Many who are rich as to this world, are poor as to the next; and some who are poor outwardly, are inwardly rich; rich in faith, in good works, rich in privileges, rich in gifts, rich in hope. Where there is spiritual plenty, outward poverty may be well borne; and when God's people are made poor as to this life, for the sake of Christ and a good conscience, he makes all up to them in spiritual riches. Christ arms against coming troubles. Fear none of these things; not only forbid slavish fear, but subdue it, furnishing the soul with strength and courage. It should be to try them, not to destroy them. Observe, the sureness of the reward; "I will give thee:" they shall have the reward from Christ's own hand. Also, how suitable it is; "a crown of life:" the life worn out in his service, or laid down in his cause, shall be rewarded with a much better life, which shall be eternal. The second death is unspeakably worse than the first death, both in the agonies of it, and as it is eternal death: it is indeed awful to die, and to be always dying. If a man is kept from the second death and wrath to come, he may patiently endure whatever he meets with in this world.

12-17 The word of God is a sword, able to slay both sin and sinners. It turns and cuts every way; but the believer need not fear this sword; yet this confidence cannot be supported without steady obedience. As our Lord notices all the advantages and opportunities we have for duty

381

in the places where we dwell, so he notices our temptations and discouragements from the same causes. In a situation of trials, the church of Pergamos had not denied the faith, either by open apostacy, or by giving way so as to avoid the cross. Christ commends their steadfastness, but reproves their sinful failures. A wrong view of gospel doctrine and Christian liberty was a root of bitterness from which evil practices grew. Repentance is the duty of churches and bodies of men, as well as of particular persons; those who sin together, should repent together. Here is the promise of favour to those that overcome. The influences and comforts of the Spirit of Christ come down from heaven into the soul, for its support. This is hidden from the rest of the world. The new name is the name of adoption; when the Holy Spirit shows his own work in the believer's soul, this new name and its real import are understood by him.

18-29 Even when the Lord knows the works of his people to be wrought in love, faith, zeal, and patience; yet if his eyes, which are as a flame of fire, observe them committing or allowing what is evil, he will rebuke, correct, or punish them. Here is praise of the ministry and people of Thyatira, by One who knew the principles from which they acted. They grew wiser and better. All Christians should earnestly desire that their last works may be their best works. Yet this church connived at some wicked seducers. God is known by the judgments he executes; and by this upon seducers, he shows his certain knowledge of the hearts of men, of their principles, designs, frame, and temper. Encouragement is given to those who kept themselves pure and undefiled. It is dangerous to despise the mystery of God, and as dangerous to receive the mysteries of Satan. Let us beware of the depths of Satan, of which those who know the least are the most happy. How tender Christ is of his faithful servants! He lays nothing upon his servants but what is for their good. There is promise of an ample reward to the persevering, victorious believer; also knowledge and wisdom, suitable to their power and dominion. Christ brings day with him into the soul, the light of grace and of glory, in the presence and enjoyment of him their Lord and Saviour. After every victory let us follow up our advantage against the enemy, that we may overcome and keep the works of Christ to the end.

Lesson Plan 124

The Book of Revelation

Chapter 3

Objective: Our study today will cover the last three of the seven churches which are the Voice from Heaven, (Jesus), the Alpha and Omega, the First and the Last who gave John the following instruction: "What thou seest, Write in a book and send it to the seven churches which are in Asia: to Ephesus, to Smyrna, to Pergamos, to Thyatira, to Sardis, to Philadelphia, and to Laodicea."

Objective Breakdown:

Background/Introduction

Sardis is Sleeping

Philadelphia Is Working

Laodicea Is Lukewarm

Background/Introduction of Sardis, Philadelphia, and Laodicea:

Sardis (1517 - 1700 A.D. – its name means remnant)

Sardis was located 30 miles south of Thyatira and the capital of Lydia. The city was thought to be impregnable, but Cyrus the great captured it by following a secret path up the cliff. Coins were first minted here. The city was noted for its great wealth, and the chief industry was its flourishing carpet industry.

Philadelphia (1700 - 1900 A.D. – its name means brotherly love)

It was built as a center of Greek culture around 200 B.C.

It is located some thirty miles southeast of Sardis. Philadelphia is celebrated for its excellent wine. The city had a heavily Jewish population. It was destroyed by an earthquake in A.D. 17, but soon rebuilt by Tiberius Caesar.

Laodicea (1900 A.D. – Rapture – its name means people's rights)

This city was ninety miles due east of Ephesus and 45 miles southeast of Philadelphia. The name of the town means "judgment of the people." This city was founded by Antiochus II and named after his wife. It was a very common name for women. It was a banking center and possessed immense wealth. It was graced with resplendent temples and theaters. An excellent and well-known medical school was built there. The city was famous for its eye salve called collyrium for its manufacture of rich garments of black glossy wool.

Sardis is Sleeping	Chapter 3:1-6
Philadelphia Is Working	Chapter 3:7-13
Laodicea Is Lukewarm	Chapter 3:14-22

II Chronicles 7:14

If my people, which are called by my name, shall humble themselves, and pray, and seek my face, and turn from their wicked ways; then will I hear from heaven, and will forgive their sin, and will heal their land.

Psalm 122:6

Pray for the peace of Jerusalem; they will prosper that love thee.

Lesson Plan 125

The Book of Revelation

Chapters 4 & 5

Objective: To learn and gain insight concerning future events which God has in store for both the faithful and the unfaithful; e. g. the Rapture of the Church, the Great Tribulation, the Antichrist, the Millennium, and other related events.

Objective Breakdown:

Introduction

Worship in Heaven   Revelation 4:1-11

A Sealed Book   Revelation 5:1-14

Introduction: John is told to do three things in Revelation (Revelation 1:19).

1. John was told to write what he had seen (Revelation Chapter 1:1-20) the past

    a. Jesus as the heavenly High Priest

    b. Jesus as the head of the church

2. Write the things which are (Revelation Chapters 2 and 3) the Present

    a. The seven churches that existed in John's day

    b. The seven church dispensations

Note: This present time is called the "dispensation of grace," according to Ephesians 3:2.

3. Write the things that must be hereafter (Revelation Chapters 4-22) the future

Here begins the Predictive part of the Book of Revelation. Things that will take place.

"Things which must be Hereafter" (4-1), is the theme from here on relating to the History and Destiny of the Church. Some think that at this point, the rapture of the Church takes place. It may, but the Book of Revelation does not say so. It is only an opinion and should be stated as an opinion, and not as unequivocal teaching of scripture.

The Throne of God - Verses 4:2-3

The first thing in lifting the veil of the future is this vision of God, to assure the Church that no matter how disheartening some of the revelations may be, God is still on the throne. God's form is not described except that He had the appearance of Jasper and Sardis in a Rainbow of Emerald. Jasper is thought to have been a diamond. Sardis is red and Emerald is green. Thus, God shows Himself to earthly eyes as One enswathed in a halo of clear dazzling white, shaded with red and Green.

The Twenty-Four Elders - Verses 4:4-5

Seated on 24 thrones around the Throne of God, clothed in white with crowns of gold, they are thought by some to represent the Glorified Church: a union of the 12 Old Testament Tribes and the 12 New Testament Apostles: basically a symbol of God's People. It is also possible that they may represent a distinct class of heavenly intelligence, princes of heaven, or various classes of Angels. Lightning and thunder (verse 5) represent the majesty and power and awesomeness of God. The seven burning lamps are the Holy Spirit in His complete and full majesty. The Sea of Glass represents the calmness of God's rule.

The Four Living Creatures - Verses 4:6-11

"Beasts" (verse 6) is more properly translated as "Living Creatures." These are Heavenly Beings. It is a different word from that which is translated "Beast" in Chapter 13:1; which is the Horrible Monster that figures so largely in the latter part of the book of Revelation. These Living Creatures are thought to be Cherubims spoken of in Genesis 3:24 and Ezekiel 1:10, 10:14. Here they join in songs of Praise for man's Redemption.

Here are several important points to consider:

a. Revelation chapters 4 through 22 have not yet occurred.

b. Chapters 4 through 22 are a summary of the prophet's end-time predictions.

c. Revelation 4 begins the final seven years of time.

1. Daniel 9:27 called it "Daniel's last week."

2. This time period has several names: the "time of Jacob's trouble" (Jeremiah 30:7), or the time of "great tribulation" (Matthew 24:21). Both Daniel and John give references to this final tribulation in their prophecies.

Worship in Heaven - Chapter 4:1-11

A Sealed Book - Chapter 5:1-14

II Chronicles 7:14

If my people, which are called by my name, shall humble themselves, and pray, and seek my face, and turn from their wicked ways; then will I hear from heaven, and will forgive their sin, and will heal their land.

Psalm 122:6

Pray for the peace of Jerusalem; they will prosper that love thee.

God's Blessing on Israel (Numbers 6:24-27)

Lesson Plan 126

The Book of Revelation

Chapter 6

Objective: To learn and gain insight concerning future events which God has in store for both the Faithful and the Unfaithful; e.g., the Rapture of the Church, the Great Tribulation, the Antichrist, the Millennium, and other related events.

Objective Breakdown:

1. Introduction

2. Seals of Wrath and Chaos or The Seal Judgments   Chapter 6:1-17

c. The First Seal........The White Horse   Chapter 6:1-2

d. The Second Seal....The Red Horse   Chapter 6:3-4

e. The Third Seal........The Black Horse   Chapter 6:5-6

f. The Fourth Seal......The Pale Horse   Chapter 6:7,8

g. The Fifth Seal.........The Souls of the Martyrs   Chapter 6:9-11

h. The Sixth Seal.........The Day of Wrath at Hand   Chapter 6:12-17

Symbols Encountered

The White Horse_____ Cold War

The Red Horse _____ Hot War

The Black Horse _____ Famine

The Pale Horse _____ Widespread Death by War, Starvation, and Wild Beasts

a. The First Seal………. The White Horse   Chapter 6:1-2

This is doubtless a symbolic picture of the antichrist as he subdues to himself the ten nations of the revived Roman Empire. This can be thought of as a "cold war" period. It is noted that he carries no arrows, which may indicate conquest by diplomacy rather than a shooting war.

b. The Second Seal…... The Red Horse   Chapter 6:3-4

The uneasy peace which the rider on the white Horse brings to earth is temporary and counterfeit. The antichrist promises peace but only God can actually produce it.

c. The Third Seal.......... The Black Horse   Chapter 6:5-6

The Third Seal brings famine to the world. The Black Horse forebodes death, and the pair of balances suggests careful rationing of food. Normally, a penny (Roman Denarius) a days' wages in Palestine in Jesus's day (Mt. 20:2) would buy eight measures of wheat or twenty-four measures of barley. Under these famine conditions, the same wage will buy only one measure of wheat or three of barley. In other words, there will be one-eighth of the normal supply of food.

d. The Fourth Seal.......... The Pale Horse   Chapter 6:7-8

The identity of these riders is recorded by John as Death and Hades, possibly referring to physical and spiritual death. Thus, the devil will destroy the bodies and damn the souls of multitudes of unbelievers. The damage done by these riders will involve one-fourth of all humanity perishing during this Fourth Plague. It is said that during WWII, one out of 40 people lost their lives, but this seal of judgment will claim one out of four people–or 2.6 billion people.

e. The Fifth Seal.........The Souls of the Martyrs   Chapter 6:9-11

The Cry of the Martyred. This is religious persecution as never before.

f. The Sixth Seal.........The Day of Wrath at Hand   Chapter 6:12-17

Earth's Greatest Earthquake, Earth's Greatest Cosmic Disturbance, Earth's Greatest Prayer Meeting. The greatest earthquake in history. There have of course been hundreds of severe earthquakes in man's history. The earliest recorded was in July of A.D. 365 in the Middle East. The most destructive was in January 1556 in China when one million people lost their lives.

II Chronicles 7:14

If my people who are called by my name will humble themselves and pray, and seek my face, and turn from their wicked ways, then I will hear from heaven and will forgive their sin and heal their land.

Psalm 122:6

Pray for the peace of Jerusalem; they shall prosper who love thee.

God's Blessing on Israel   (Numbers 6:24-27)

Jabez's Prayer to the Lord   (I Chronicles 4: 10)

Lesson Plan 127

The Book of Revelation

Chapter 7

Objective: To learn and gain insight concerning future events which God has in store for both the Faithful and the Unfaithful; e. g. the Rapture of the Church, the Great Tribulation, the Antichrist, the Millennium, and other related events.

Objective Breakdown:

1. Introduction

2. Representatives from Israel   Chapter 7:1-8

3. A Great Multitude from Every Nation   Chapter 7:9-14

Introduction: There is a short interlude between the sixth and seventh seals and is a parenthetical passage in the book. It comes between the sixth and seventh seals and contains some explanations of events that will transpire after the sixth seal. Things that are not contained in the seals, trumpets, and vials are revealed. We recognized it as parenthetical because it breaks up the natural order of things taking place. The explanation is of two companies of redeemed people, the 144,000 Jewish Evangelists, and the Tribulation Saints.

In Elijah's day, God reserved seven thousand men who would not worship Baal (Romans 11:4). Likewise, God will have 144,000 Jews who will not bow down to the antichrist but will accept Jesus Christ as their personal savior. From each of the twelve tribes will come twelve thousand Jewish Servants. This group of Jews will be here during the Seven Seals and the Seven Trumpets and are saved during the first part of the Tribulation and after the Rapture. They are sealed for the express purpose of being kept through the Trumpet Judgments which also takes place during the first part of the Tribulation.

During this pause, we see the conversion and call of the 144,000 Hebrew Billy Sundays (Chapter 7:1-8) and the conversion of a great multitude (Chapter 7:9-17). Revelation Chapter 7 also declares that not only Jews will be saved, but that a great multitude from every nation, tribe, peoples, and every tongue will be saved. This number of 144,000 Jewish Evangelists is a massive number, particularly when we consider that there are less than 35,000 missionaries of all persuasions in the world today. Our Lord apparently had the 144,000 in mind when he said, "And this gospel of the kingdom shall be preached in all the world for a witness unto all nations; and then shall the end come" (Matthew 24:14).

Judah heads up the list on the Tribes and not Reuben, the firstborn. Both Dan and Ephraim are missing from the 144,000 Evangelists. Both these tribes were guilty of going into idolatry (Judges 18; 1 Kings 11:26; Hosea 4). The tribes of Levi and Manasseh have taken their place. However, both are listed in Ezekiel's millennial temple (Ezekiel Chapter 48), so they simply forfeit their chance to preach during the Tribulation. Some have concluded that on the basis of Genesis 49:17 and Jeremiah 8:16 that the antichrist will come from the tribe of Dan.

Representatives from Israel - Read Revelation Chapter 7:1-8

Genesis 49 (Jacob's Sons or 12 Tribes) (144,000 Jewish Evangelists)

Reuben	Judah
Simeon	Reuben
Levi	Gad
Judah	Asher
Zebulun	Naphtali
Issachar	Manasseh
Dan	Simeon
Gad	Levi
Asher	Issachar
Naphtali	Zebulun
Joseph	Joseph
Benjamin	Benjamin

Genesis 36 - Jacob's Sons

Leah	Zilpah *	Rachel	Bilhah**
Reuben	Gad	Joseph	Dan
Simeonb	Asher	Benjamin	Naphtali
Levi			
Judah			
Issachar			
Zebulun			

* Zilpah was Leah's maidservant.

** Bilhah was Rachel's maidservant

A Great Multitude from Every Nation   Chapter 7:9-14

These verses portray the second and last company of redeemed saints seen in the Book of Revelation. They come after the Rapture and we see a picture of the Church and the Old Testament Saints with God in Heaven. Who are these dressed in white robes? These are the Saints who came out of the Great Tribulation? They are seen as distinct from the Elders, the Living Creatures, Angels, and all other beings. They will come out of the Great Tribulation and will have been martyred for the Word of God and the testimony of Christ as well as their own testimony. From the pre-millennial standpoint, these Saints will be saved after the Church has been Raptured and has gone to be with the Lord.

Of the lukewarm and backslidden Christians who remain on the Earth, many of them will accept Jesus Christ as Lord. There will be many of these whose parents, husbands, wives, or loved ones prayed for them and they didn't respond to Jesus Christ fully. They will later realize and respond during the Great Tribulation.

II Chronicles 7:14

If my people, which are called by my name, shall humble themselves, and pray, and seek my face, and turn from their wicked ways; then will I hear from heaven, and will forgive their sin, and will heal their land.

Psalm 122:6

Pray for the peace of Jerusalem; they will prosper that love thee.

God's Blessing on Israel   (Numbers 6:24-27)

Jabez's Prayer to the Lord   (I Chronicles 4: 10)

Lesson Plan 128

The Book of Revelation

Chapters 8 & 9

Objective: To learn and gain insight concerning future events which God has in store for both the Faithful and the Unfaithful; e.g., the Rapture of the Church, the Great Tribulation, the Antichrist, the Millennium, and other related events.

Objective Breakdown:

1. Introduction

2. One Last Seal   Chapter 8:1-5

3. A Sound of Trumpets   Chapter 8:6-13

4. Two More Trumpets and Woe   Chapter 9:1-20

Introduction: A cascade of dramatic events pours from the Book of Revelation as the book unfolds. John narrates his vision in a torrent of images such as the seal (Revelation 8:1), many of which may seem confusing to some. However, close observation reveals that the action is not random. John's vision is told in a tightly woven structure that offers important clues to understanding the book.

One way to summarize the material in Revelation is based on the three times frames that Jesus told John to write about: "Write the things which you have seen, and the things which are, and the things which will take place after this" (Revelation 1:19). This yields the following outline for the book:

1. "The things you have seen" (1:1-20)

    A. Greetings and praise (1:1-8)

    B. A vision of the risen Christ (1:9-20)

2. "The things which are" (2:1-3:22)

    A. Letter to the church at Ephesus (2:1-7)

B. Letter to the church of Smyrna (2:8-11)

C. Letter to the church at Pergamos (2:12-17)

D. Letter to the church at Thyatira (2:18-29)

E. Letter to the church at Sardis (3:1-6)

F. Letter to the church at Philadelphia (3:7-13)

G. Letter to the church at Laodicea (3:14-22)

3. "The Things which will take place after this" (4:1-22:21)

A. Worship in Heaven (4:1-5:14)

B. Seven seals (6:1-8:5)

C. Seven trumpets (8:6-11:19)

D. Seven signs (12:1-14:20)

E. Seven bowels (15:1-16:21)

F. The final judgment and the triumph of God (17:1-20:15)

G. A new Heaven and a new Earth (21:1-22:5)

H. Conclusion (22:6-21)

In the portion of the book devoted to the seven seals, seven trumpets, seven signs, and seven bowls (6:1-16:21) a common pattern repeats. In each case, six of the seven items play out their action, and then there is a break during which God's people are challenged to perseverance and faithfulness. Then the seventh item unfolds. As an example: the seventh seal contains seven trumpets, the seventh trumpet contains seven signs, the seventh sign contains seven bowls, and the seventh bowl contains the final judgment. This suggests that the apocalyptic events increase in their intensity with each passing event, spiraling toward the final defeat of evil and the triumph of Christ.

Throughout these events, the message to the believer remains clear: God is in control; ultimately His will be done; therefore, stand firm, trust in His power, and wait for deliverance from whatever trials befall them.

One Last Seal: When the seventh seal was opened, the scroll was ready to be unrolled, read, and put into effect. At that moment, Heaven fell silent. Seven angels were given trumpets. The prayers of the Saints went up before God, and in response, fire was cast upon the Earth. The thunder of judgment rumbled. With that warning, the trumpets are blown. We need to read carefully and prayerfully, observing what happens when each trumpet sounds.

A Sound of Trumpets: Trumpets that herald the end of the age are a tradition with roots deep in the history of Israel. Trumpets were used to warn the people of an emergency and to summon them to battle, so it was natural for the prophets to use them as a symbol to warn of the approaching judgment (Ezekiel 33:1-6, Joel 2:1). Joel 2:12-17 uses the trumpet as a call to an assembly of repentance to turn judgment into mercy. Finally, the trumpet on the last day heralds the deliverance of God's people (Zechariah 9:14) and therefore the resurrection (Matthew 24:31, 1 Corinthians 15:52, 1 Thessalonians 4:16).

Judgment, repentance, deliverance, salvation, and a new age heralded by the trumpet sound call to mind the use of the trumpet in ancient Israel to proclaim the accession of a king to the throne (1Kings 1:39; Psalm 47:5, 98:6). Just as trumpets preceded God's self-revelation at Sinai (Exodus 19:11-13), so Jews expected His appearance at the end of the age to be heralded with trumpets. All this and more may be behind God's choice of trumpets to launch this series of Judgments on the Earth's inhabitants.

Symbol/Term Encountered this Chapter

Wormwood: a plant named Artemisia has a stinging poisonous tail. A single ounce diluted in 524 gallons of water will still make the water distasteful. (See Jeremiah 9:15)

II Chronicles 7:14

If my people who are called by my name will humble themselves and pray, and seek my face, and turn from their wicked ways, then I will hear from heaven and will forgive their sin and heal their land.

Psalm 122:6

Pray for the peace of Jerusalem; they shall prosper who love thee.

Lesson Plan 129

The Book of Revelation

Chapters 10 & 11

Objective: To learn and gain insight concerning future events which God has in store for both the Faithful and the Unfaithful, e.g., the Rapture of the Church, the Great Tribulation, the Antichrist, the Millennium, and other related events.

Objective Breakdown:

1. Introduction

2. The Little Book   Chapter 10:1-11

3. Two Witnesses and a Second Woe   Chapter 11:1-14

4. The Seventh Trumpet   Chapter 11:15-19

Introduction: In chapter 5 it was a Sealed Book. Here in chapter 10, it is an Open Book. The Open Book is one of the messages of the Sealed Book, for it appears under the Sixth Trumpet, which came out of the Seventh Seal.

It seems to be an announcement, in a setting of awful majesty, that the End is near (10:7), but that before the End comes, there is yet another prophetic period to cover (10:8-11), as told in the next chapter.

"Time no longer" (10:6) may mean that in eternity, our earthly concept of time will have been abolished; and like Jesus, we can say, "Before Abraham was I am," But "Delay" is thought to be a more accurate translation than "Time;" in which case the meaning would be, The Great Day of God is Come; the Hour of Doom is about to strike.

The particular message of the Open Book seems to be the prophecy about the Temple being Measured and the Two Witnesses (chapter 11); a prophecy that made John sick at Heart (10:10).

The Little Book   Chapter 10:1-11

Two Witnesses and Second Woe   Chapter 11:1-14

II Chronicles 7:14

If my people, which are called by my name, shall humble themselves, and pray, and seek my face, and turn from their wicked ways; then will I hear from heaven, and will forgive their sin, and will heal their land.

Psalm 122:6

Pray for the peace of Jerusalem; they will prosper that love thee.

God's Blessing on Israel   (Numbers 6:24-27)

Synopsis: The Angel of the covenant presents a little open book, which is followed with seven thunders. (1-4)

At the end of the following prophecies, time should be no more. (5-7)

A voice directs the apostle to eat the book; (8-10)

and tells him he must prophesy further. (11)

Text: Verses 1-7 The apostle saw another representation. The person communicating this discovery probably was our Lord and Saviour Jesus Christ, or it was to show his glory. He veils his glory, which is too great for mortal eyes to behold; and throws a veil upon his dispensations. A rainbow was upon his head; our Lord is always mindful of his covenant. His awful voice was echoed by seven thunders, solemn and terrible ways of discovering the mind of God. We know not the subjects of the seven thunders, nor the reasons for suppressing them. There are great events in history, perhaps relating to the Christian church, which are not noticed in open prophecy. The final salvation of the righteous, and the final success of true religion on earth, are engaged for by the unfailing word of the Lord. Though the time may not be yet, it cannot be far distant. Very soon, as to us, time will be no more; but if we are believers, a happy eternity will follow; we shall from heaven behold and rejoice in the triumphs of Christ, and his cause on earth.

8-11 Most men feel pleasure in looking into future events, and all good men like to receive a word from God. But when this book of prophecy was thoroughly digested by the apostle, the contents would be bitter; there were things so awful and terrible, such grievous persecutions of the people of God, such desolations in the earth, that the foresight and foreknowledge of them would be painful to his mind. Let us seek to be taught by Christ, and to obey his orders; daily meditating on his word, that it may nourish our souls; and then declaring it according to our several stations. The sweetness of such contemplations will often be mingled with bitterness, while we compare the scriptures with the state of the world and the church, or even with that of our own hearts.

Citation: Revelation 11

Synopsis: The state of the church is represented under the figure of a temple measured. (1, 2)

Two witnesses prophesy in sackcloth. (3-6) They are slain, after which they arise and ascend to heaven. (7-13) Under the seventh trumpet, all antichristian powers are to be destroyed and there will be a glorious state of Christ's kingdom upon earth. (14-19)

Text: Verses 1, 2 This prophetical passage about measuring the temple seems to refer to Ezekiel's vision. The design of this measuring seems to be the preservation of the church in times of public danger, or for its trial, or for its reformation. The worshippers must be measured, whether they make God's glory their end, and his word their rule, in all their acts of worship. Those in the outer court, worship in a false manner, or with dissembling hearts, and will be found among his enemies. God will have a temple and an altar in the world, till the end of time. He looks strictly to his temple. The holy city, the visible church, is trodden under foot; is filled with idolaters, infidels, and hypocrites. But the desolations of the church are limited, and she shall be delivered out of all her troubles.

3-13 In the time of treading down, God kept his faithful witnesses to attest the truth of his word and worship, and the excellence of his ways, the number of these witnesses is small, yet enough. They prophesy in sackcloth. It shows their afflicted, persecuted state, and deep sorrow for the abominations against which they protested. They are supported during their great and hard work, till it is done. When they had prophesied in sackcloth the greatest part of 1260 years, antichrist, the great instrument of the devil, would war against them, with force and violence for a time. Determined rebels against the light rejoice, as on some happy event, when they can silence, drive to a distance, or destroy the faithful servants of Christ, whose doctrine and conduct torment them. It does not appear that the term is yet expired, and the witnesses are not a present exposed to endure such terrible outward sufferings as in former times; but such things may again happen, and there is abundant cause to prophesy in sackcloth, on account of the state of religion. The depressed state of real Christianity may relate only to the western church. The Spirit of life from God quickens dead souls and shall quicken the dead bodies of his people, and his dying interest in the world. The revival of God's work and witnesses will strike terror into the souls of his enemies. Where there is guilt, there is fear; and a persecuting spirit, though cruel, is a cowardly spirit. It will be no small part of the punishment of persecutors, both in this world and at the great day, that they see the faithful servants of God honoured and advanced. The Lord's witnesses must not be weary of suffering and service, nor hastily grasp at the reward, but must stay till their Master calls them. The consequence of their being thus exalted was a mighty shock and convulsion in the antichristian empire. Events alone can show the meaning of this. But whenever God's work and witnesses revive, the devil's work and witnesses fall before him. And that the slaying of the witnesses in the future appears to be probable.

14-19 Before the sounding of the seventh and last trumpet, there is the usual demand of attention. The saints and angels in heaven know the right of our God and Saviour to rule over all the world. But the nations met God's wrath with their own anger. It was a time in which he was beginning to reward his people's faithful services, and sufferings; and their enemies fretted against God, and so increased their guilt, and hastened their destruction. By the opening the temple of God in heaven may be meant, that there was a freer communication between heaven and earth; prayer and praises more freely and frequently going up, graces and blessings plentifully coming down. But it rather seems to refer to the church of God on earth. In the reign of the antichrist, God's law was laid aside, and made void by traditions and decrees; the scriptures were locked up from the people, but now they are brought to the view of all. This, like the ark, is a token of the presence of God returned to his people, and his favour toward them in Jesus Christ, as the Propitiation for their sins. The great blessing of the Reformation was attended with very awful providence as by terrible things in righteousness God answered the prayers presented in his holy temple now opened.

Lesson Plan 130

The Book of Revelation

Chapter 12

Objective: To learn and gain insight concerning future events which God has in store for both the Faithful and the Unfaithful; e.g., the Rapture of the Church, the Great Tribulation, the Antichrist, the Millennium, and other related events.

Objective Breakdown:

1. Introduction

2. A Woman Gives Birth   Chapter 12:1-6

3. War in Heaven   Chapter 12:7-12

4. War on Earth   Chapter 12:13-17

Introduction: Up to this point in the Seven Seals and Seven Trumpets, the story has been carried forward to the Day of Final Judgment (11:15, 18), dealing largely with the fate of the WORLD.

Here, in chapter 12, the writer returns to the starting place, and, in another series of visions, begins portrayal of things previously omitted, relating largely to the fate of the CHURCH.

The Dragon is identified as the Devil, Satan, the Old Serpent (12:9). He had already been mentioned as Persecuting the Churches in Smyrna and Pergamum (2:10,13); and he, or one of his angels, from the abyss, asking of the army of Demon Locusts (9:11), and murderer of the Two Witnesses (11:7). "Red" (12:3), may symbolize his Murderous Nature.

Seven Crowned Heads and Ten Horns" (12:3), evidently, symbolizes his dominion as Prince of this World, permitted, in the wisdom of God, for some reason beyond human understanding, to make trouble for a while. But he is Not God. There are Not Two Gods. Satan is Not All-Powerful. He is not Everywhere, Nor does he Know Everything. He fears the name of Christ. And his doom is inevitable.

"Stars of Heaven" (12:4), which he cast to the earth, may symbolize his power to marshall hosts of the unseen world against saints, or to influence Church Leaders to Apostasy, or both.

A Woman Gives Birth   Chapter 12:1-6

The Woman, about to give birth to a Child, seems, up to verse 5, to represent Israel; and, from verse 6 onward, to represent the Church.

The Hebrew Nation, nurtured by God through long centuries for the purpose of bringing Christ into the world, is here personified as a Queen, in Heavenly Glory, giving birth to the Child of the Ages.

The Child was Christ, the Messiah. Satan was waiting to devour Him at birth (121:4). This seems like a reference to Herod's effort to kill Christ as a babe. If he could have succeeded, he may thus have thwarted Christ's Redemptive Work; for surely a new-born babe could not die for the sins of the world.

Satan did, however, through Judas (John 13:2,27), succeed in having Jesus as a grown man put to death. But that boomeranged against Satan; for it supplied God's people with the one weapon against which Satan is powerless, the "Blood of the Lamb."

The War in Heaven   Chapter 12:7-12

This may mean that Satan, infuriated at his failure to destroy Christ by crucifying Him, followed Him in His Ascension, and made bold to storm the bulwarks of heaven, where he met a crushing defeat at the hands of Michael and his Angels and lost forever any further power to harm Christ or the souls of the redeemed.

Then Satan, henceforth, gave attention to devising ways and methods of hindering the work of the Church on Earth.

"Michael" (12:7), was the Archangel, Prince of Angels, who had had some previous experience in contending with the Devil (Jude 9). He was Guardian Angel of Israel (Daniel 10:13,21). He will be on hand at the time of the End, in the Great Tribulation (Daniel 8:17, 12:1,9,13); and at the Coming of the Lord (1 Thessalonians 4:16).

Michael and his Angels may, even now, be fighting our battles, here on earth, in a more real sense than we know. Our struggle is not entirely against flesh and blood (Ephesians 6:12). The outcome may depend, far more than we realize, on the armies of the invisible world.

In the "Wilderness" (12:14), the Woman sought refuge from the Dragon. This seems to symbolize the True Church as being Drive Underground by Persecution. It was the "Wilderness" that Babylon, the Harlot Church developed (17:3). But, one day, for the True Church, it will be, Not a "Wilderness," but a Mountain with the Glory of God (Revelation 21:11-12).

"The Flood of Water" (12:15), which the Dragon cast after the Woman, may refer to Persecutions of the Church by the Roman Empire.

"The Earth Helped the Woman" (12:16), may allude to the conversion of Emperor Constantine and the Christianization of the Roman Empire, which put an end to the persecutions. The woman was in the wilderness for 1260 days (12:6). She was in the wilderness "a time, times, and a half a time" (12:14). The two witnesses prophesied in sackcloth 1260 Days (11:13).

While the Holy City was trodden down 42 months (11:2), the beast reigned after death-stroke was healed, 42 Months (13:5).

Forty-two months, 1260 days, and a time, times, and a half (a year, years and a half: 3 ½ years), denote the same period. 3 ½ years is 42 months, which at 30 days to a month is 1260 days.

Thus, four things are represented as being co-eval and co-terminous: Woman in the Wilderness: Holy City Trodden Down by the Nations: The Two Witnesses prophesying in Sackcloth: and the Beast's Reign after his Death-Stroke: all four at the same time.

II Chronicles 7:14

If my people who are called by my name will humble themselves and pray, and seek my face, and turn from their wicked ways, then I will hear from heaven and will forgive their sin and heal their land.

Psalm 122:6

Pray for the peace of Jerusalem; they shall prosper who love thee.

God's Blessing on Israel   (Numbers 6:24-27)

Jabez's Prayer to the Lord   (I Chronicles 4:10)

Lesson Plan 131

The Book of Revelation

Chapter 13

Objective: To learn and gain insight concerning future events which God has in store for both the Faithful and the Unfaithful; e. g. the Rapture of the Church, the Great Tribulation, the Antichrist, the Millennium, and other related events.

Objective Breakdown:

Review:

In Chapter 1, we learned that John had been banished to the Island of Patmos for his witness on behalf of the word of God and the testimony of the Lord Jesus Christ. We also learned that the message and visions John received were from Jesus Christ whom God had given to reveal to His servants. John was told to write what he saw in a book and send it to the seven churches in Asia Ephesus, Smyrna, Pergamos, Thyatira, Sardis, Philadelphia, and Laodicea. We learned that there were seven golden lampstands and seven stars. The lampstands represent the seven churches and the seven stars represent the angels or pastors of these churches.

In Chapters 2 & 3 we learned the Lord's evaluation of the seven churches. Ephesus left her first love; Symrna was suffering; Pergamos is confused; Thyatira is too tolerant; Sardis is sleeping; Philadelphia is working; Laodicea is lukewarm.

The two that were good (Smyrna, Philadelphia); two that were bad (Laodicea, Sardis), and the remaining three churches (Ephesus, Pergamum, and Thyatira) were part good and part bad.

The two that were good were facing persecution and the two that were bad were made up of the very well-to-do class and were permitting paganism to be incorporated into the church. The remaining three churches: Well... Ephesus was leaving its first love; Pergamos was allowing false teachings having to do with immorality and idolatry, and Thyatira allowed Jezebel to teach immorality and idolatry and seduce members.

As a refresher on the churches: Ephesus, Symrna, Pergamos, and Thyatira.

Smyrna

Although smaller than Ephesus, Smyrna was still prosperous because it sat on the coast at the end of a major trade route to the east. Unlike Ephesus, it continues to be a thriving city to this day–the second largest in Asiatic Turkey. In John's time, it had been solidly loyal to Rome for centuries and contained a temple to the goddess of Rome and another to the emperor. It also boasted a stadium, a library, and the largest public theater in Asia.

The real danger to the Smyrna Christians was not from the Roman patriots, but the large population of Jews who detested Christians as heretics and inflamed the Romans to persecute them. One of the most famous martyrs of the second century was Polycarp, the bishop of Smyrna. The contemporary record of his death states that he was "the twelfth to meet a martyr's death in Smyrna. Polycarp was burned to death on a Saturday in 155 A D, and the Jews of Smyrna broke the Sabbath to gather wood for the fire. They abhorred the idea that a man executed for blasphemy was the Messiah and that a person became pleasing to God not by obeying the Law of Moses but by putting faith in this Messiah.

Smyrna means "bitter" or "myrrh," a tree resin with a bitter taste that was crushed and used in perfume, incense, and as a preservative in burial.

Pergamum

Pergamum was the political capital of Asia, even though Ephesus was larger. It was the center of the imperial cult in the province. In addition to its temple to Caesar and Rome, Pergamum's most popular tourist attraction was the temple of Asclepios, the god of healing. People flocked to the shrine in hopes of miraculous cures. (The myth of Asclepios had its roots in Babylon. His symbol was the serpent; doctors still use it today) Three other major temples also loomed over Pergamum atop its mountain citadel. In particular, "an enormous altar of Zeus...stood on a platform on the hill overlooking the city."

The governor of Asia, who resided in Pergamum, was the official champion of both justice and the imperial cult. He held the "right of the sword" to execute anyone he willed.

Pergamum means something like "additional marriage." (Per is "elevation" and gamum is marriage.")

Thyatira

Thyatira was not a remarkable city; it was simply a thriving center of manufacturing and marketing. Practically everyone in town belonged to one of the dozens of trade and craft gilds. Membership in these was crucial since they were the focus of business and social life. But each was dedicated to a patron god, and meetings included a common meal in its honor. The meat for the meal came from an animal sacrificed to the god. In addition, drunkenness, carousing, and even orgies were not rare. What should a Christian do? Evidently, many in Thyatira who were otherwise full of love and faith were willing to listen to a woman teaching (Jezebel) that it was okay to tolerate–even participate in–pagan practices.

Thyatira means "unweary sacrifice."

Ephesus Has Left Her First Love	Chapter 2:1-7
Symrna Is Suffering	Chapter 2:8-11
Pergamos Is Confused	Chapter 2:12-17
Thyatira is Too Tolerant	Chapter 2:18-29

Background on the remaining three churches: Sardis, Philadelphia, and Laodicea:

Sardis

Sardis was located 30 miles south of Thyatira and the capital of Lydia. The city was thought to be impregnable, but Cyrus the great captured it by following a secret path up the cliff. Coins were first minted here. The city was noted for its great wealth, and its chief industry was its flourishing carpet industry.

Philadelphia

It was built as a center of Greek culture around 200 B.C. It is located some thirty miles southeast of Sardis. Philadelphia is celebrated for its excellent wine. The city had a heavily Jewish population. It was destroyed by an earthquake in A.D. 17 but was soon rebuilt by Tiberius Caesar.

Laodicea

This city was ninety miles due east of Ephesus and 45 miles southeast of Philadelphia. The name of the town means "judgment of the people." This city was founded by Antiochus II and named after his wife. It was a very common name for women. It was a banking center and possessed immense wealth. It was graced with resplendent temples and theaters. An excellent and well-known medical school was built there. The city was famous for its eye salve called collyrium for its manufacture of rich garments of black glossy wool.

Sardis is Sleeping	Chapter 3:1-6
Philadelphia Is Working	Chapter 3:7-13
Laodicea Is Lukewarm	Chapter 3:14-22

"Things Which Are" (1:19), were pictured in the Seven Letters dealing with the Church situation as it was then.

Chapter 4:

Here begins the predictive part of the Book of Revelation. Things that will take place.

"Things which must be Hereafter" (4-1), is the theme from here on relating to the history and destiny of the Church. Some think that at this point, the rapture of the Church takes place. It may, but the Book of Revelation does not say so. It is only an opinion and should be stated as an opinion and not as unequivocal teaching of scripture.

The Throne of God   Verses 4:2,3

The first thing in lifting the veil of the future is this vision of God, to assure the Church that no matter how disheartening some of the revelations may be, God is still on the Throne. God's form is not described except that He had the appearance of Jasper and Sardis in a Rainbow of Emerald. Jasper is thought to have been a diamond. Sardis is red. Emerald is green. Thus, God shows Himself to earthly eyes as One enswathed in a halo of clear dazzling white, shaded with red and green.

Chapter 5: A scroll was in the Hand of God and God was ready to give it to anyone who could be found worthy to open it. The scroll was sealed with seven separate seals. A strong angel proclaimed with a loud voice, "Who is worthy to open the book and to loose the seal thereof?" This is the first mention of an angel in the book of Revelation. The angels mentioned in chapters two and three are really pastors. The cherubim that are seen in chapters four and five are living creatures. No man in heaven or on the earth or under the earth was qualified to open the book. As John was looking at the situation, which was to be a future event, the Bible says he wept much. It must have been a time of tremendous suspense and anxiety for him.

For Example:

The three-fold search, First in heaven for any redeemed saints to claim the earth's title deed... No one was found.

Second, on Earth:

Who could accomplish in the sinful environment of Earth what no man could achieve even in the sinless environment of Heaven?

Third, Under the Earth (in Hades). If no saints or angels could purify this earth, then certainly no sinner or demon could, even if it were possible. No one was found.

Chapter 6:

Seals of Wrath and Chaos or The Seal Judgments

a. The First Seal........The White Horse

b. The Second Seal....The Red Horse

c. The Third Seal.......The Black Horse

d. The Fourth Seal......The Pale Horse

e. The Fifth Seal.........The Souls of the Martyrs

f. The Sixth Seal.........The Day of Wrath at Hand

Symbols Encountered

The White Horse_____Cold War

The Red Horse_____Hot War

The Black Horse_____Famine

The Pale Horse_____Widespread Death by War, Starvation, and Wild Beasts

Chapter 7:

There is a short interlude between the sixth and seventh seals and it is a parenthetical passage in the book. It comes between the sixth and seventh seals and contains some explanations of events that will transpire after the sixth seal. Things that are not contained in the seals, trumpets, and vials are revealed. We recognized it as parenthetical because it breaks up the natural order of things taking place. The explanation is of two companies of redeemed people, the 144,000 Jewish Evangelists and the Tribulation Saints.

Chapter 8:

Introduction: A cascade of dramatic events pours from the Book of Revelation as the book unfolds. John narrates his vision in a torrent of images such as the seals (Revelation 8:1), many of which may seem confusing to some. However, close observation reveals that the action is not random. John's vision is told in a tightly woven structure that offers important clues to understanding the book.

One way to summarize the material in Revelation is based on the three-times frame that Jesus told John to write about: "Write the things which you have seen, and the things which are, and the things which will take place after this" (Revelation 1:19). This yields the following outline for the book:

"The things you have seen" (1:1-20)

a. Greetings and praise (1:1-8)

b. A vision of the risen Christ (1:9-20)

Chapter 9:

This is the most unusual chapter of the entire Bible and perhaps the most difficult to interpret. It begins with the fifth angel blowing a judgment trumpet. This is the beginning of three "woes" that are pronounced by God upon mankind. (Chapter 8:13)

a. A star falls from heaven to the earth (Revelation 9:1-2)

b. Fallen angels are found in Chapter 3

c. These are not normal locusts

d. Their strange description (Revelation 9:7-10)

e. Their power is in their tail to sting and torment men for five months (Chapter 9:5)

f. The King's spirit is Abaddon in Hebrew and Apollyon in Greek

g. The location of this abyss seems to be in the area near the Euphrates River

h. The Second Woe is announced (Chapter 9:12)

Chapter 10:

In chapter 5, it was a Sealed Book. Here in chapter 10, it is an Open Book. The Open Book is one of the messages of the Sealed Book, for it appears under the Sixth Trumpet, which came out of the Seventh Seal.

It seems to be an announcement in a setting of awful majesty that the end is near (10:7); but that before the end comes, there is yet another prophetic period to cover (10:8-11), as told in the next chapter.

"Time no longer" (10:6) may mean that in eternity, our earthly concept of time will have been abolished; and like Jesus, we can say, "Before Abraham was I am," But "Delay" is thought to be a more accurate translation than "Time," in which case the meaning would be, The Great Day of God is Come; the Hour of Doom is about to strike.

The particular message of the Open Book seems to be the prophecy about the Temple being Measured and the Two Witnesses (chapter 11), a prophecy that made John sick at Heart (10:10).

The Little Book   Chapter 10:1-11

Chapter 11:

This parenthetical passage (Chapters 10:1-11:13) continues with the measuring of the temple and is followed by the revelation of the two witnesses.

The reed referred to here is also mentioned in Rev. 21:15-16. It is like a rod or scepter and is about twelve-and-a-half feet long. The measuring done in this scene is not for building, but destruction. Passages such as 2 Sam. 7:14; Psalm. 2:9; Psalm 89:32; Isaiah. 11:4; Lam. 2:8; Ezekiel. 20:37 and 1 Cor. 4:21 bring out the thought of a rod of chastisement.

This is not Herod's temple. That temple was destroyed some twenty-five years before John had this vision, during the destruction of Jerusalem, 70 A.D.

The Seventh Trumpet   Chapter 11:15-19

Then the seventh angel sounded: And there were loud voices in Heaven saying, "The kingdoms

411

of this world have become the kingdoms of our Lord and His Christ, and He shall reign forever and ever."

Chapter 12:

Up to this point in the Seven Seals and Seven Trumpets, the story has been carried forward to the day of Final Judgment (11:15, 18), dealing largely with the fate of the world.

Here in chapter 12, the writer returns to the starting place and, in another series of visions, begins portrayal of things previously omitted, relating largely to the fate of the CHURCH.

The dragon is identified as the Devil, Satan, the Old Serpent (12:9). He had already been mentioned as persecuting the churches in Smyrna and Pergamum (2:10, 13); and he, or one of his angels, from the abyss, as king of the army of Demon Locusts (9:11), and murderer of the Two Witnesses (11:7). "Red" (12:3) may symbolize his murderous nature.

"Seven Crowned Heads and Ten Horns" (12:3) symbolizes his dominion as Prince of this World, permitted in the wisdom of God, for some reason beyond human understanding, to make trouble for a while. But he is not God. There are not two Gods. Satan is not all-powerful. He is not everywhere, nor does he know everything. He fears the name of Christ. And his doom is inevitable.

"Stars of Heaven" (12:4), which he cast to the earth, may symbolize his power to gather hosts of the unseen world against saints or to influence church leaders to apostasy or both.

A Woman Gives Birth   Chapter 12:1-6

The woman about to give birth to a child represents Israel. The Great Beast from The Sea is the antichrist.

The Leopard-Beast (Chapter 13:1-10) seems to be the beast who killed the two witnesses (Chapter 11:7); and which is more fully described in Chapter 17. The dragon is the devil, having failed to destroy the church by persecution, now installs himself in this Beast to continue the war against the Saints (Chapter 12:13 & Chapter 13:1).

The Beast had an appearance of a Leopard, a Bear and a Lion (13:2); symbols Daniel had used for world power (Daniel 7: 3-6).

The Lamb-Beast (Chapter 13:11-18). This beast looked like a lamb (Chapter 13:11). The first beast looked like a Leopard. But they are allies. The Leopard-Beast had been killed (Chapter

13: 3). The Lamb-Beast brought him to life (Chapter 13:15), the dragon working in them both (Chapter 13: 2,4,11).

The Lamb-Beast was the revived Leopard-Beast. While looking like a lamb, he spoke like a Dragon (Chapter 13:11). He had the power to kill whoever would not wear his mark (Chapter 13:15). He blasphemed the name of God and made war on the Saints (Chapter 13:13:6, 7).

His identification card was the number 666 (Chapter 13:18). This Lamb-Beast is hereafter called the "False Prophet" (Chapter 16:13; Chapter 19:20, Chapter 20:10), that is, the Pretender-Lamb. The Dragon, having failed in the attack on the Church from without, now attacks from within, while pretending to be the Lamb.

"666" the number of the Beast (13:18) called a man. It could possibly be a set of men or an institution headed by a man, or a set of men. It seems to mean a name, the letters of which when regarded as numerals total 666. Irenaeus, a pupil of Polycarp, who was a pupil of John, understood the 666 to be the Greek word "Lateinos": L=30; A= 1; T=300; E=5; I=10, N=50; O=70; S=200. These total 666. "Lateinos means "Latin Kingdom." Papal Rome made Latin its official language. And it still is. Rome's canon, missals, prayers, decrees, bulls blessings, and cursings are in Latin.

The coalition of Leopard-Beast and Lamb-Beast continued as the world government for 42 months (Chapter 13:5). It seems to be another symbol of the Holy City being exploited by the world for 42 months (Chapter 11:2). A Beast looking like a Lamb and ruling in the name of the Lamb, and the Holy City being trodden underfoot by the Nations—these two symbols seem to mean a world government operating in the name and by the aid of an apostate church.

SYMBOLISM

Leopard-Beast represents Secular Power. Lamb-Beast represents Pretended Christian Power. The dragon uniting them into One World Power. This coalition is later called "Babylon," and is more fully described in Chapters 17 & 18.

The Lamb-Beast will have personal characteristics as follows:

a. He will be an intellectual genius (Daniel 8:23).

b. He will be an oratorical genius (Daniel 11:36).

c. He will be a political genius (Revelation 17:11).

d. He will be a commercial genius (Revelation 13:16, 17, Daniel 11:43).

e. He will be a military genius (Revelation 6:2, 13:2).

f. He will be a religious genius (Revelation 13:8, 2 Thessalonians 2:4).

The Seven Heads and Ten Horns: The dragon had them (Revelation 12:3). The Leopard-Beast had them (Revelation 13:1). The Scarlet-Colored Beast of Babylon had them (Revelation 17:3). Seven as a symbol of completeness, and Ten as a symbol for World Power. The Seven Heads and Ten Horns seem to represent World Power as a whole.

Chapter 13:

The Beast Out of the Sea	Chapter 13:1-10
The Beast Out of the Earth	Chapter 13:11-18

The presence of pain, suffering, and evil in the world causes some people to wonder whether a good God exists, and if He does, why He doesn't put an end to it if He can. John's vision of a beast rising out of the sea (Revelation 13:1) and causing great havoc in the world does not explain why there is evil, but it sounds an important note of encouragement: the evils of this world happen by "permission," and those that do occur have precise limits imposed on them by God. Notice that the beast "was given authority to continue for forty-two months" (Revelation 13:5).

II Chronicles 7:14

If my people who are called by my name will humble themselves and pray, and seek my face, and turn from their wicked ways, then I will hear from heaven and will forgive their sin and heal their land.

Psalm 122:6

Pray for the peace of Jerusalem; they shall prosper who love thee.

Lesson Plan 132

The Book of Revelation

Chapters 14 & 15

Objective: To learn and gain insight concerning future events which God has in store for both the Faithful and the Unfaithful; e. g. the Rapture of the Church, the Great Tribulation, the Antichrist, the Millennium, and other related events.

Objective Breakdown:

1. Review

2. The Lamb Calls His Own   Revelation 14:1-5

3. Angels with Announcements   Revelation 14:6-13

4. Reaping the Earths Harvest   Revelation 14:14-20

5. A Vision of Seven Plagues   Revelation 15:1-8

Review: There is Hell on Earth in chapter 11. God raises up two witnesses who are called to preach the Word of God and call the Jewish people to faith in Christ. The antichrist will be upset, and the two witnesses will be slain. They are left for dead in the streets of Jerusalem for 3½ days. After that, they are resurrected and caught up into heaven (11:7-12).

In chapter 12, God says "Enough of all this." The accuser of the brethren will be cast down to the earth. His time is short and he will pour out his wrath upon planet Earth. Chapter 12 begins with a look at the seven symbolic players in the great end-times drama.

These seven symbolic players are (1) Woman=Israel, (2) Dragon= Satan, (3) Male Child=Christ, (4) Michael=Archangel, (5) Seed of the Woman=Believing Jews, (6) Beast of the Sea= Antichrist, and (7) Beast of Earth=False Prophet.

In chapter 14, we see the bowls of wrath that are the final bowls of judgment. There is a parallel of events between the trumpet judgments and the bowl judgments, in which one-third of everything is affected. They land on the same objects. The trumpet judgments affected the earth, the oceans, the rivers, the sun, the sky, and the atmosphere–just like the bowl judgments do. As we look at the list of judgments, the bowls involve the earth burning up, the oceans polluted, the rivers polluted, the scorching sun, and the great army from the east.

But before John introduces the seven bowls of judgment beginning in the fourteenth chapter, we have the message of three angels. These angels fly across the horizon of the earth, announcing one last time the opportunity of grace and salvation from God Himself.

In chapter 15, we see the "seven last plagues," and "in them is filled up the wrath of God."

The Lamb calls His Own: Chapter 14:1-5

John had just seen a vision of a Beast pretending to be the Lamb (13:11). Here we see the True Lamb Himself (14:1). The 144,000 Lamb's faithful followers were marked with the Lamb's Name (14:1). These are Jews who followed the ministry of the two witnesses. They have no guile in their mouth and were without fault before God.

God is married to Israel and the 144,000 are His. Christ is married to the church and the church is His first fruits.

These are to God and to the Lamb the first Jewish fruits of the Tribulation!

Angels with Announcements   Chapter 14:6-13

The three messages of the three angels give warnings and announce the doom of the beast worshipers.

In chapter 14:6-11, there are messages from the three angels. The angels are proclaiming the warnings to the earth. Why? Because the church, the two witnesses, and the 144,000 are now in Heaven and there is no more human ministry on the earth because now the beast is in control!

Reaping the Earth's Harvest   Chapter 14:14-20

The Harvest of the human race had been spoken of long centuries before, in Joel 3:13-16: "Multitudes, multitudes in the valley of decision. Put in the sickle the Harvest is ripe" "Earth Harvest Ripe" (14:15). Waiting for this may be one of the reasons why the Lord delays His Coming. The "Harvest" seems to be of the saved. The Vintage of the Lost. The winepress is of the wrath of God on the wicked.

A Vision of Seven Plagues   Chapter 15:1-8

This chapter reveals the seven final plagues that will be unleashed during the last 42 months of the Tribulation.

II Chronicles 7:14

If my people who are called by my name will humble themselves and pray, and seek my face, and turn from their wicked ways, then I will hear from heaven and will forgive their sin and heal their land.

Psalm 122:6

Pray for the peace of Jerusalem; they shall prosper who love thee.

God's Blessing on Israel (Numbers 6:24-27)

Lesson Plan 133

The Book of Revelation

Chapters 16, 17, & 18

Objective: To learn and gain insight concerning future events which God has in store for both the Faithful and the Unfaithful; e.g. the Rapture of the Church, the Great Tribulation, the Antichrist, the Millennium and other related events..

Objective Breakdown:

1. Introduction

2. Seven Bowls Pour Out   Chapter 16:1-21

3. The Harlot Babylon   Chapter 17:1-18

4. Babylon's Corruption   Chapter 18:1-10

5. Collapse of The Global Economy   Chapter 18:11-24

Introduction: Chapter 15 was an introduction to the vials or bowls of God's Wrath, which represents the final, awesome judgments of God upon the earth. Another great sign was seen in Heaven, its contents containing the seven last plagues filled with wrath of God. The seven angels having these plagues will not be regular angels, but seven redeemed men who are in Heaven with glorified bodies at the time of the fulfillment of this book.

As previously noted in the earlier part of the book of Revelation, angels sometimes refer to men. The literal translation is "messenger." As we will see in Revelation 17, when John was shown the judgment of the great whore and the beast that carried her; John fell down at the angels foot to worship him. The angel responded, "See thou do it not; for I am thy fellow servant, and of thy brethren the prophets and of them which keep the sayings of this book: worship God." Let's look quickly at Revelation 19:9-10; 22:8-9. The angel clearly declares that he is a redeemed man (Revelation 21:17).

Seven Bowls Pour Out   Chapter 16

The Vial Judgments

"and I heard a great voice out of the temple saying to the seven angels, Go your ways and pour our the vials of wrath of God upon the earth" Revelation 16:1.

a. The first vial is a judgement against the Religious System.

   A sore broke out on the men who had the mark of the beast (Revelation16:2)

b. The second vial is a Judgment against the Marine Life System.

   The sea became as blood and every living thing died (Revelation 16:3)

c. The third vial is against the Ecological System.

   The rivers and fountains became as blood (Revelation 16:4)

d. The fourth vial is against the Cosmic System

   Power is given to the sun to scorch men with fire (Revelation 16:8)

e. The fifth vial is against the Political System.

   Darkness fell upon the kingdom of the beast (Revelation 16:10)

f. The sixth vial is against the Military system.

   The Euphrates river dries up for the kings of the East (Revelation 16:12)

g. The seventh vial causes hail weighing over 100 pounds to fall!.

Note: When the U.S. detonated two nuclear bombs underwater in the Pacific, it shot ten million tons of water seven miles high in the atmosphere. The water turned to ice and produced hail stones weighing 100 pounds that sunk two ships. Blasphemers were to die by stoning. Men will be "stoned with ice from heaven!"

In Revelation 16:16 we see the warning concerning the Battle of Armageddon.

In Chapter 16 we also see: (KJV)

a. The Great Voice (verse 1)   d. The Great Earthquake (verse 18)

b. The Great Heat (verse 9)   e. The Great City (verse 19)

c. The Great River (verse 12)   f. The Great Babylon (verse 19)

g. The Great Day (verse 14)   i. The Great Hail (verse 21)

h. The Great voice (verse 17)   j. The Great Plague (verse 21)

At the seventh trump the "mystery is finished" and at the seventh vial the judgements are finished.

The Babylon, the Great Harlot   Chapter 17

Chapter seventeen deals with the description of mystery Babylon, while chapter eighteen reveals the destruction of mystery Babylon

"The Great Harlot" (17:1), in Illegitimate Relation with Kings (17:2), sitting upon a Scarlet-colored Beast, full of names of Blasphemy, having Seven Heads and Ten Horns (17:3), the Harlot arrayed in Purple and Scarlet, Reveling in her Luxury and Filth (17:4), her Name, Babylon the Great (17:5), Drunk with the blood of Martyrs (17:6).

The Woman is a City. The Harlot Woman, in alliance with the Beast, called Babylon on a Throne of World Government, reigning over the earth. The True Church, the Bride of Christ, Wife of the Lamb, is also called a City, The New Jerusalem, the Holy City (19:7; 21:2,9). Two Women: the Harlot and the True Bride of Christ. Two Cities: Babylon and the New Jerusalem. The Harlot Church and the other. The One seated in Power on a Throne of Worldly Splendor, driving the Other Underground by Persecution. This all seems to identify Babylon the Harlot of this chapter, with the Leopard-Lamb-Beast of chapter 13. "Babylon is stated to be the great city reigning over the kings of the earth (17:18) which at the time was Rome." Rome is further identified in the expression, "The Seven Heads are Seven Mountains of which the Woman sits" (17:9) for Rome, literally was built on Seven Mountains and was known as the "Seven-Hilled City."

1. Introduction to the visions:

a. The introduction of the vision (17:1-2)

b. The introduction of the woman on the beast (17:3-6)

c. The interpretation of the vision (17:7-18)

2. A key to the interpretation may be a coin minted in A. D. 71.

During the reign of Vespasian (A.D. 69-79) a coin was minted called the Dea Roma Coin. The coin shows the emperor on the front with the words, "EMPEROR CAESAR VESPASIANVS

AGUSTUS PONTIFIX MAXIMUS." The reverse is the goddess Roma in military dress, sitting on seven hills with a small sword in her hand. The "S" and "C" stand for "a resolution of the senate." She is sitting beside an animal representing the Tiber River!

a. This Greek goddess was worshiped in Smyrna and Hadrian.

b. The symbolism of the woman on the beast was known as Roma.

c. The name of Rome came from a legend of the infants Romulus and Remus being nursed by a she-wolf.

d. The Latin term "she-wolf," had the connotation "prostitute" and may have contributed to the idea that Roma was the "prostitute of Rome."

3. More Information on the vision of the woman:

"And here is the mind which hath wisdom. The seven heads are seven mountains, on which the woman sitteth .... And he said to me, the waters which thou sawest, where the whore sitteth, are peoples, and multitudes, and nations, and tongues" Revelation 17:9,15.

The angel interprets the vision for John.

The woman is a city.

Old Testament prophets often referred to cities in the feminine form (she or her). "And the woman which thou sawest is that great city, which reigneth over the kings of the earth" Revelation 17:18.

1. Rome was the city and the empire ruling over the earth in John's day.

2. In 303 A.D., Eusebius said this passage was a reference to Rome.

The woman is sitting on seven mountains.

1. One of two interpretations given by the angel of the seven mountains.

2. The phrase "seven hills" as a symbol for Rome occurs frequently in writers following the mid first century B. C.

3. The historian Varro (116-127 B. C.), listed the seven hills as:

a. Capitol,

b. Aventine

c. Caellan

d. Esquiline

e. Quirina

f. Vimnal

g. Patiline

The historian Strabo (63 - 21 B.C.) also lists the seven hills.

"It is the city of Rome, called the city of seven hills, that the entire area of Vatican State proper is now confined. "

The woman is "seated by many waters" (17:1).

1. "Many waters" is a metaphor alluding to peoples or armies (Psalms 144:7,Isaiah 8:6-7; Jeremiah 47:2).

2. Rome is on the Tiber River. The meaning of "many waters" alludes to the many nations where the woman's influence is controlling the kings of the earth.

The woman (city) is called a "harlot" (17:1).

In the Old Testament the image of prostitution is applied to godless cities. (Isaiah 1:21; Isaiah 23:16-17; Jeremiah 3:6-10; Hosea 4:12-13, 5:3). This city was a city of religious prostitution, or false doctrine and wickedness.

The city was drunk with the blood of the martyrs and the blood of Jesus (17:6)

The Roman empire was guilty of the crucifixion of Jesus and the thousands of martyrs from the year 30 through the third century. Paul was beheaded in Rome and many tortures were invented against the early Christians!

1. The woman is dressed in purple and scarlet and decked with wealth (17:4).

2. Purple garments represent royalty (Judges 8:26, Lamentations 4:5, Daniel 5:7).

3. Polycarp associated the color purple with carnality.

The harlot is riding upon a scarlet colored beast (17:3).

This ten-horned beast is the same beast referred to in Daniel 7:7,19-20. It is Daniel's fourth kingdom, which alludes to Rome. The woman is the city of Rome and can represent the Holy Roman Empire, which has controlled the kingdoms of Europe since the 5th century.

1. There is a great red dragon (Revelation 12), who is Satan.

2. There is a scarlet colored beast (Revelation 17) the harlot is riding.

3. The beast has seven heads, which are seven mountains and empires.

4. The beast has ten horns, which are the ten kings of Bible prophecy.

Here is the strange paradox: the ten kings destroy the woman (the city).

"And the ten horns which thou sawest upon the beast, these shall hate the whore, and shall make her desolate and naked, and shall eat her flesh, and burn her with fire. For God hath put in their hearts to fulfill his will, and to agree, and give their kingdom unto the beast, until the words of God shall be fulfilled" Revelation 17:16-17.

Without a doubt, the woman represents the city of Rome. While the Roman empire ceased in the fifth century, the Holy Roman Empire carried on through the ages. The most powerful religion in Europe and the Middle East has been Roman Catholic.

WE MUST UNDERSTAND WHY ROME IS CALLED "MYSTERY BABYLON."

1. The reasons for calling Rome "Babylon"

a. The religious system did not fully exist at the time of John's writing.

b. John could have been killed had he written of the destruction of Rome.

c. John veiled the writing as "mystery Babylon."

2. Rome was known in Jewish s Writings as "Babylon"

a. According to the Apocalypse of Ezra (4 Ezra 2 and 2 Ezra 3:14)

b. According to the Syriac Apocalypse of Baruch

c. According to the Sibylline Oracles (Greek prophetic literature)

Babylon's Corruption   Chapter 18:1-10

Collapse of The Global Economy   Chapter 18:11-24

2 Chronicles 7:14

If my people, which are called by my name, shall humble themselves, and pray, and seek my face, and turn from their wicked ways; then will I hear from heaven, and will forgive their sin, and will heal their land.

Psalm 122:6

Pray for the peace of Jerusalem: may they prosper who love thee.

Lesson Plan 134

The Book of Revelation

Chapters 19 & 20

Objective: To learn and gain insight concerning future events which God has in store for both the Faithful and the Unfaithful; e.g., the Rapture of the Church, the Great Tribulation, the Antichrist, the Millennium, and other related events.

Objective Breakdown:

1. Introduction

2. Rejoicing in Heaven   Chapter 19:1-16

3. King of Kings & Lord of Lords   Chapter 19:17:21

4. Judgments on Satan   Chapter 20:1-10

5. The Great White Throne Judgment   Chapter 20:11-15

Introduction: Will evil ever get its reward? Anyone who pays attention to today's headlines is likely to wonder what happened to ethics and justice. Sometimes it seems like fairness never happens in matters of business, government, the law, and world affairs. But for those who long to see justice reign, the Book of Revelation offers powerful hope.

God will not turn his back on injustice. His scripture promises that He will deal with evil in absolute and final ways. John's vision foresees this triumphant accomplishment:

Chapter 17 deals with religious Babylon, the Harlot. Chapter eighteen reveals the wealth of this same city, and how she will be destroyed! This chapter is similar to Jeremiah 51 and 52. Babylon's Corruption, Chapter 18:1-10; Collapse of The Global Economy, Chapter 18:11-24. Rejoicing in Heaven, Chapter 19: 1-16.

Three events are happening at one time in chapter nineteen. The scene changes from Babylon's destruction to heaven where the saints are singing. Chapter 19 records the four "alleluias."

The Four Alleluias

The first is all the Saints praising God. (19:1-2)

The second is praising God for the destruction of mystery Babylon. (19:3)

The third alleluia is sounded by the 24 elders and four beasts (19:4).

The fourth alleluia is an eruption from all of heaven like thunder (19:6).

Note In Revelation chapter 11:15, 17, the words "to reign" are in future tense. Now the Greek tense has changed to the "Lord has begun to reign" (Revelation 19:6).

Events in Heaven

"Let us be glad and rejoice, and give honor to him for the marriage of the lamb is come, and his wife hath made herself ready" Revelation 19:7.

God will not turn his back on injustice. His scripture promises that He will deal with evil in absolute and final ways. John's vision foresees this triumphant accomplishment:

God will bind evil and cast it into a bottomless pit (Revelation 20:2-3).

He will place a seal on the source of evil (Revelation 20:3).

He will administer judgment and restore believers who have been killed unjustly (Revelation 20:4).

He will deal finally with Satan after allowing him one last attempt to deceive (Revelation 20:7-9); the devil's punishment will include eternal torment (Revelation 20:10,14).

The dead will stand before God and be judged (Revelation 20:11-15).

Great White Throne Judgment Opening of the Books

There are at least five sets of books available to be opened:

1. The Book of Conscience   (Romans 2:15)

2. The Book of Words   (Matthew 12:36-37)

3. The Book of Secret Words   (Romans 2:1, Ecclesiastes 12:14)

4. The Book of Public Works   (2 Corinthians 11:15)

426

5. The Book of Life   (Exodus 32:32-33, Psalm 69:28,
                                                    Daniel 12:1, Philippians 4:3,
                                                    Revelation 3:5, 13:8, 17:8, 20:12,15,
                                                    21:27, 22:19.)

II Chronicles 7:14

If my people who are called by my name will humble themselves and pray, and seek my face, and turn from their wicked ways, then I will hear from heaven and will forgive their sin and heal their land.

Psalm 122:6

Pray for the peace of Jerusalem; they shall prosper who love thee.

Lesson Plan 135

The Book of Revelation

Chapters 21 & 22

Objective: To learn and gain insight concerning future events which God has in store for both the Faithful and the Unfaithful; e.g., the Rapture of the Church, the Great Tribulation, the Antichrist, the Millennium, and other related events.

Objective Breakdown:

1. Introduction

2. A New Heaven and a New Earth   Chapter 21:1-8

3. The New Jerusalem   Chapter 21:9-27

4. Eden Is Restored   Chapter 22:1-5

5. I Am Coming Quickly   Chapter 22:6-17

6. A Final Warning   Chapter 22:18-21

Introduction: In the last chapter, we looked at the White Throne Judgment, but I did not mention the five sets of books. I feel it important to say a word about each and then proceed to the beautiful end of the Book of Revelation. At the White throne Judgment, the jury will have five sets of Books.

The First is the Book of Conscience (Romans 2:15). Although man's conscience is not an infallible guide, he will nevertheless be condemned by those occasions when he deliberately violates it.

The Second is the Book of Words (Matthew 12:36,37). "But I say unto you every idle word that men speak, they shall give account thereof in the day of judgment. For by thy words thou shalt be justified, and by thy words thou shalt be condemned."

The Third is the Book of Secret Words. "God shall judge the secrets of men by Jesus Christ" (Romans 2:16). "For God shall bring every work into judgment, with every secret thing, whether it be good, or whether it be evil" (Ecclesiastes 12:14).

The Fourth Book is the Book of Public Works. "Whose end shall be according to their works" (2 Corinthians 11:15). For the Son of man shall come in the glory of His Father with his Angels; and then He shall reward every man according to his works" (Matthew 16:27).

The Fifth Book is the Book of Life (Exodus 32:32,33, Psalm 69:28, Daniel 12:1, Philippians 4:3, Revelation 3:5, 13:8, 17:8, 20:12,15, 21:27, 22:19). Only unsaved people will stand before this throne.

Now for Chapters 21 and 22. The Wife of the Lamb is introduced. "And there came unto me one of the Seven Angels saying Come hither, I will show thee the bride, the Lamb's Wife" (Revelation 21:9).

A New Heaven and a New Earth	Read Chapter 21:1-8
The New Jerusalem	Read Chapter 21:9-27
Eden is Restored	Read Chapter 22:1-5
I Am Coming Quickly	Read Chapter 22:6-17
A Final Warning	Read Chapter 22:18-21

II Chronicles 7:14

If my people who are called by my name will humble themselves and pray, and seek my face, and turn from their wicked ways, then I will hear from heaven and will forgive their sin and heal their land.

Psalm 122:6

Pray for the peace of Jerusalem; they shall prosper who love thee.

Summary of The Book of Revelation

Jesus Christ is the Central Figure of Revelation 1:1-8. He is:

1. The Source of revelation (1:1)

2. The Channel of the Word and the testimony of God (1:2)

3. The Faithful Witness, the Firstborn of the dead, and the Ruler of earth's kings (1:5)

4. The God of grace who loves us, has cleansed our sins, and has made us a kingdom and a priesthood (1:5-6)

5. The coming King whose return will be powerful and glorious (1:7)

Earth	Revelation 1-3
Heaven	Revelation 4-5
Earth	Revelation 6:1-8
Heaven	Revelation 6:9-11
Earth	Revelation 6:12-16
Heaven	Revelation 7:1-8:6
Earth	Revelation 8:7-11:14
Heaven	Revelation 11:15-12:4
Earth	Revelation12:5-14:20
Heaven	Revelation 15:1-8
Earth	Revelation 16-18
Heaven	Revelation 19:1-10
Earth	Revelation 19:11-20:10
Heaven	Revelation 20:11-22:21

Four Ages in Revelation

Chapters	Age	Years
Chapter 1 – 3	Church Age	? Years
Chapter 4 – 19	Tribulation Age	7 Years
Chapter 20	Kingdom Age	1,000 Years
Chapter 21 – 22	Eternal Age	Endless

Parallels Between Matthew 24 and Revelation 6 – 7

Matthew 24	Revelation 6 – 7
False Christs (24:4–5)	The rider on the white horse (6:1-2)
Wars and rumors of wars (24:6-7a)	The rider on the red horse (6:3-4)
Famine (24:7b)	The rider on the black horse (6:5-6)
Famines and plagues (24:7b; Luke 21:11)	The rider on the pale horse (6:7-8)
Persecution and martyrdom (24:9-10)	Martyrs (6:9-11)
Terrors and great cosmic signs (24:29; Luke 21:11)	Terror (6:12-17)
Worldwide preaching of the gospel (24:14)	Ministry of the 144,000 (7:1-8)

The Seven Churches

1. Ephesus – the Orthodox, but Lost-love Church

2. Smyrna – the Suffering Church

3. Pergamum – the Compromising Church

4. Thyatira – the Tolerant, Permissive Church

5. Sardis – the Dead Church

6. Philadelphia – the Faithful Church

7. Laodicea – the Lukewarm, Useless Church

Structure of Letters to the Seven Churches

The Commission

The Character

The Commendation (letters to Sardis and Laodicea lack this)

The Condemnation (letters to Smyrna and Philadelphia lack this)

The Correction

The Call

The Challenge

Gentile Empires of the Earth

Revelation 17:9-11

1. Egypt

2. Assyria

3. Babylon

4. Medo-Persia

5. Greece

6. Historical Roman Empire

7. Revived Roman Empire (Revelation)

8. The Eighth Kingdom: Antichrist

The Seven Seal Judgments

First Seal (6:1-2)	White Horse: Antichrist
Second Seal (6:3-4)	Red Horse: War
Third Seal (6:5-6)	Black Horse: Famine
Fourth Seal (6:7-8)	Pale Horse: Death and Hell
Fifth Seal (6:9-11)	Martyrs in Heaven
Sixth Seal (6:12-17)	Universal Upheaval and Devastation

Seventh Seal (8:1-2)	The Seven Trumpets

Titles of the Coming World Ruler

The little horn (Daniel 7:8)

The coming prince (Daniel 9:26)

The willful king (Daniel 11:36)

The man of lawlessness (2 Thessalonians 2:3)

The son of destruction (2 Thessalonians 2:3)

The Antichrist (1 John 2:18, 22)

The rider on the white horse (Revelation 6:2)

The beast (Revelation 13:1-10)

The Seven Trumpet Judgments

First Trumpet (8:7)	Bloody Hail and Fire: One-third of Vegetarian Destroyed
Second Trumpet (8:8-9)	Fiery Mountain from Heaven: One-third of Oceans Polluted
Third Trumpet (8:10-11)	Falling Star: One-Third of Fresh Water Polluted
Fourth Trumpet (8:12)	Darkness: One-Third of Sun, Moon, and Stars Darkened
Fifth Trumpet (9:1-12)	Demonic Invasion: Torment
Sixth Trumpet (9:13-21)	Army of 200 Million: One-Third of Mankind Killed
Seventh Trumpet (11:15-19)	The Announcement of Christ's Reign: The Kingdom

The Two Babylons of Revelation 17-18

	Revelation 17	Revelation 18
	Religious Babylon	Political/Commercial Babylon
Focus:	Babylon as a System	Babylon as a City

Timing:	Falls at the Beginning of the Great Tribulation	Falls at the End of the of Great Tribulation
Destroyer:	The Beast and the Ten Kings	Jesus Christ at His Second Coming
Result:	No Mourning	Great Mourning

Seven Bowl Judgments

Revelation 16:1-21

1. First Bowl (16:2) upon the Earth: Sores on the Worshipers of the Antichrist

2. Second Bowl (16:3) upon the Seas: Turned To Blood

3. Third Bowl (16:4-7) upon the Fresh Water: Turned to Blood

4. Fourth Bowl (16:8-9) upon the Sun: Intense, Scorching Heat

5. Fifth Bowl (16:10-11) upon the Antichrist's Kingdom: Darkness and Pain

6. Sixth Bowl (16:12-16) upon the River Euphrates: Armageddon

7. Seventh Bowl (16:17-21) upon the Air: Earthquakes and Hail

Symbol	Meaning
The seven stars (1:16)	seven angels (1:20)
The seven lampstands (1:13)	seven churches (1:20)
The hidden manna (2:17)	Christ in glory (Exodus 16:33-34; Hebrews 9:4)
The morning star (2:28)	Christ returning before the dawn, suggesting the church's rapture before the establishment of the kingdom (Revelation 22:16; 2 Peter 1:19)
The key of David (3:7)	the power to open and close doors (Isaiah 22:22)
The seven lamps of fire	the sevenfold Spirit of God (4:5)
The living creatures (4:7)	the attributes of God
The seven eyes	the sevenfold Spirit of God (5:6)

The odors of the golden bowls	the prayers of the saints (5:8)
The four horses and their riders (6:1)	successive events in the developing tribulation
The fallen start (9:1)	the angel of the abyss, probably Sata (9:11)
The great city (11:8), Sodom and Egypt (11:8)	Jerusalem (in contrast to the new Jerusalem, the heavenly city)
The stars of the sky (12:4)	fallen angels (12:9)
The woman and the child (12:1-2)	Israel and Christ (12:5-6) Satan the great dragon, the old serpent, and the devil (12:9; 20:2)
The time, times, and half a time	1,260 days (12:6) (12:14)
The beast out of the sea (13:1-10)	the future world ruler and his empire
The beast out of the earth (13:11-17)	the false prophet (19:20)
The prostitute (17:1)	the great city (17:18), as Babylon the great (17:5), as the one who sits on seven hills (17:9), is usually interpreted as apostate Christendom
The waters (17:1) on which the woman sits	the peoples of the world (17:15)
The ten horns (17:12)	ten kings associated with the beast (13:1; 17:3, 7-8, 11-13, 16-17)
Fine linen	the righteous deeds of the saints (19:8)
The rider of the white horse	Christ, the King of kings (19:11-16, 19)

Paradise Lost	Paradise Regained
Eden	*New Heavens and New Earth*
1. River (Genesis 2:10)	River of Life (Revelation 22:1)
2. Tree of Life (Genesis 2:9)	Tree of Life (Revelation 22:2)
3. Human Innocence (Genesis 2:25)	Redeemed Humanity (Revelation 22:4)
4. Spoiled by Sin (Genesis 3:6)	No Sin Allowed to Enter (Revelation 22:3)

435

5. Sun and Moon (Genesis 1:16)   No Need of Sun (Revelation 22:5)

6. Redemption Promised (Genesis 3:15)   Redemption Realized (Revelation 22:4)

7. Banishment (Genesis 3:23)   Eternal Residence (Revelation 22:5)

Revelation Made Simple

Chapter 1	Chapter 2	Chapter 3	Chapter 4	Chapter 5
Letters to the 7 Churches				
John on Patmos Vision of Christ in Glory	Ephesus Smyrna Pergamos Thyatira	Sardis Philadelphia Laodicea	Vision of God's Throne	Seven Seal Book opened by the Slain Lamb

Chapter 6	Chapter 7	Chapter 8	Chapter 9	Chapter 10
Tribulation Trumpets 7th Seal opened				
6 Seals Opened 6 Seals 4 Horsemen White, Red, Black, Pale Souls under the altar Wrath of God (preview)	Sealing of the 144,000 Great multitude of Tribulation Saints	4 Trumpets 1/3 Judgments Grass Sea Waters (Wormwood) Sun Moon Stars	2 Trumpets (2 Woes) Locusts 200 million man army 1/3 mankind killed	The Mighty Angel with the Little Book 7 Thunders

Chapter 11	Chapter 12	Chapter 13	Chapter 14	Chapter 15
7 Heavenly Signs (Visions)				
2 Tribulation Witnesses 42 Months 1260 Days (3rd Woe) 7th Trumpet	Woman with man child Red Dragon Woman in Wilderness Time, Times and half a Time	7 Headed Beast anti-Christ govt 42 months Lamb/Dragon False Prophet	Jesus & 144,000 3 Angels Christ reaps the harvest	Vials Given to 7 Angels Victorious Saints Moses' Song

Chapter 16	Chapter 17	Chapter 18	Chapter 19	Chapter 20
7 Vials (Bowls)	Mystery Babylon	Babylon is Fallen!	Marriage Supper	Millennium
7 Final Full	The Great		of the Lamb	Satan bound 1,000
Judgments			War with Beast	years
Sores			Armageddon	Battle of Gog &
Seas				Magog
Rivers				Lake of Fire
Sun				White Throne
Darkness				Judgment
Armageddon				
Earthquake &				
Hail				

Chapter 21	Chapter 22

New Jerusalem

New Heaven	New Jerusalem
New Earth	Eternity with
	Christ

Supplemental Resources

Vocabulary of Salvation

There are a number of terms associated with salvation. These terms are: Conversion, Substitution, Reconciliation, Propitiation, Remission, Redemption, Regeneration, Imputation, Adoption, Supplication (prayer), Justification, Sanctification, Glorification, Preservation, Origination, Election, and Predestination. We will now look at each term's definition:

The term Adoption is the act of taking a child of one parent into the family of another parent. Scripturally, it is the act of God's grace by which sinful people are brought into the redeemed family of God. Thus, adoption gives believers status as sons in God's family.

Apostasy

Apostasy is the falling away from the faith and is defined as the determined and willful rejection of Christ and His teachings by a Christian believer (Hebrews 10:26-29; John 15:22). The nation of Israel fell into repeated backsliding (Jeremiah 5:6, RSV). Some of the noted apostates in the Bible are King Saul, who turned back from following the Lord (1 Samuel 15:11); Hymenaeus and Alexander, who "suffered shipwreck" of their faith (1 Timothy 1:19-20); and Demas, who forsook the apostle Paul because he loved the present world (2 Timothy 4:10).

In Acts 21:21 the Apostle Paul was described falsely as one who taught the Jews living among the Gentiles to commit apostasy (forsake NKJV). Second Thessalonians 2:3 declares that the Day of Christ "will not come unless the apostasy comes first" NASB). This great apostasy will be the time of "the final rebellion against God, when wickedness will be revealed in human form" (2 Thessalonians 2:3 (NEB). Apostasy is different from false belief, or error, which is the result of ignorance. Some Christians groups teach that apostasy is impossible for those persons who have truly accepted Jesus as savior and Lord. This is why it is so important for the Christian who has been "born again" to stay in the Word of God and thrive on His Spiritual food. A Christian who has totally committed himself to God, and "walks the talk" and has given his Heart, Soul, Mind, and Spirit to the Lord Jesus Christ irrevocable, will never have to fear falling into apostasy.

Atonement is the act by which God restores a relationship of harmony and unity between Himself and human beings. The word can be broken into three parts that express this great

438

truth in simple and profound terms: "at-one-ment." Through God's atoning grace and forgivingness, we are reinstated to a relationship of at-one-ment with God, despite our sin.

The term Conversion has reference to a twofold turning on the part of an individual. One has to do with repentance and turning away from evil deeds and false worship, and the other with faith or a turning to God.

The term Election in reference to salvation takes place "in Christ" as part of God's purpose for the human race. Ephesians 1 verse 4 states "According as he hath chosen us in him before the foundation of the world, that we should be holy and without blame before him in love."

Thus, we are his workmanship, created in Christ Jesus unto good works, which God hath before ordained that we should walk in them. (Ephesians 2:10) As part of God's eternal plan, He allows man, to use his freedom of will rebel against Him but is gracious to those who find salvation through His Son Jesus Christ. Election is gracious, unconditional, and unmerited and is an expression of the sovereign will of God. The elect believe, but they do not believe against their will. Election is a necessary condition for our salvation along with faith and trust in Jesus Christ.

The term Glorification is the ultimate and absolute physical, mental, and spiritual perfection of all believers. This will occur when we are raptured and can be similar to the glorification and manifestation of Jesus in transfiguration. It will be a body where the Spirit predominates.

The term Grace is favor or kindness shown without regard to the worth or merit of the one who receives it and in spite of what the same person deserves. Grace is almost always associated with love, mercy, compassion, and patience as a source of help with deliverance from distress. Grace is one of the key attributes of God and the Lord God is "merciful and gracious, long-suffering and abounding in goodness and truth" (Exodus 34:6). The Grace of God revealed in Jesus Christ is applied to human beings for their salvation by the Holy Spirit, which is called "the Spirit of Grace" (Hebrews 10:29). The Spirit is the One who binds Christ to His people so that they receive forgiveness, adoption to sonship, and newness of life, as well as every spiritual gift of grace (Ephesians 4:7).

The term *Imputation* means the act of adding something good or bad to another person's account. In scripture, we see where we had the imputation of Adam's sin to us, his descendants. Also, we have the imputation of the Believers sin to Christ's account (2 Corinthians 5:21); and finally, we have the imputations of Christ's Righteousness to the Believer, and we will appear before God faultless (Jude 24).

The term *Justification* is thus the legal act whereby man's status before God has been changed for good by His grace. Being justified by his grace through the redemption that is in Christ Jesus (Romans 3:24). That being justified by His grace, we should be made heirs according to the hope of eternal life (Titus 3:7).

The term *Origination* as stated in Webster's New Collegiate Dictionary is to give rise, to begin, to originate, to create. Scripturally it is defined by the Westminster Shorter Catechism as follows: "The decree of God which is his eternal purpose according to the counsel of His will, whereby for His own glory, He hath foreordained whatsoever comes to pass."

The term *Predestination* is biblical teaching (doctrine) that declares the sovereignty of God over man in such a way that the freedom of the human will is also preserved. There are two major concepts involved in the biblical meaning of predestination. First, God, who is all powerful in the universe, has foreknown and predestined the course of human history and the lives of individuals. If He were not in complete control of human events, He would not be sovereign and thus would not be God. Second, God's predestination of human events does not eliminate human freedom of choice. A thorough understanding of how God can maintain His sovereignty and still allow human freedom seems to be reserved for His infinite mind alone.

Although, the word predestination is not in the bible the Apostle Paul alludes to it in Ephesians 1:11 which states: "In whom also we have obtained an inheritance, being predestinated according to the purpose of Him who worketh all things after the counsel of His own will."

The term *Preservation* as stated in the Webster's New Collegiate Dictionary that preservation means to keep safe from injury, harm, or destruction, to protect, keep alive and from decay. Scriptures say that the very God of peace will sanctify you wholly; and that your whole spirit and body and soul will be preserved blameless unto the coming of the Lord Jesus Christ. Faithful is He that calleth you, who also will do it (1 Thessalonians 5:23-24).

The term *Propitiation* means to render favorable, to satisfy, to appease. And Jesus is the propitiation for our sins; and not for ours only, but the sins of the whole world (1 John 2:2).

The term *Reconciliation* to change from that of enmity to that of friendship. Scripturally Christ having made peace through the blood of His cross, by Him to reconcile all things unto Himself. By Him, I say, whether they be things in earth or things in heaven. And you, that were sometime alienated and enemies in your wicked works, yet now hath He reconciled, in the body of His flesh through death, to present you holy and unblameable and unreproveable in His sight. (Colossians 1:20-22).

The term *Redemption* means deliverance by payment of a price. In Holy Scripture the word redemption refers to salvation from sin, death, and wrath of God by Christ's sacrifice.

The term *Regeneration* means a spiritual change brought about in a person's life by an act of God. In regeneration, an individual's sinful life is changed, and he is able to respond in faith to God.

The term *Remission* basically means forgiveness. It refers to sending back or putting away. For this is my blood of the New Testament which is shed for many for the remission of sins (Matthew 26:28).

The term *Sanctification* is to set apart and it is the process of God's grace by which the believer is separated or set apart from sin and becomes dedicated to God's Righteousness. In Roman's Chapter 6, the Apostle Paul lays out a lifelong process where the believer can grow in grace and spiritual maturity. This is known as sanctification.

The term *Substitution* according to Webster's New Collegiate Dictionary is the substituting of one person for another and according to scripture, Christ once suffered for our sins, the Just (Jesus) for the unjust (us),that he might bring us to God....(1 Peter 3:28). In the Old Testament prior to Calvary, the sheep died for the shepherd. In the New Testament, the Shepherd (Jesus) died for the sheep (us).

The term *Supplication* or prayer is to humbly ask in earnest of God. Be careful for nothing; but everything in prayer and supplication with thanksgiving let your requests be made known to God (Philippians 4:6).

James 2:10 Whoever keeps the whole law and yet stumbles at one point has broken the whole law.

Matthew 27:52 And the graves were opened; and many bodies of the saints who had fallen asleep were raised; and coming out of the graves after His resurrection, they went into the holy city and appeared to many.

1 Corinthians 15:6 After that He was seen by over five hundred brethren at once, of whom the greater part remain to present, but some have fallen asleep.

God's Blessing on Israel   (Numbers 6:24-27)

Words for Comfort of the Soul

Ephesians 4:29 Let no corrupt word proceed out of your mouth, but what is good for necessary edification, that it may impart grace to the hearers.

Ephesians 4:30 Do not grieve the Holy Spirit of God, by whom you were sealed for the day of redemption.

Ephesians 4:31 Let all bitterness, wrath, anger, clamor, and evil speaking be put away from you, with all malice.

Ephesians 4:32 Be kind to another, tenderhearted, forgiving one another, even as God in Christ forgave you.

How Each Apostle Died

All of the apostles were insulted by the enemies of the Master. They were called to seal their doctrines with their blood and nobly did they bear the trial.

Peter was crucified at Rome with his head downward.

Andrew was bound to a cross, whence he preached to his persecutors until he died.

James, the Greater, was beheaded at Jerusalem.

John was put in a cauldron of boiling oil, but escaped death in a miraculous manner, and was afterward banished to Pathos.

Philip According to tradition preached in Phrygia and died at Hierapolis.

Bartholomew was flayed alive.

Thomas was run through the body with a lance at Coromandel in the East Indies.

Matthew suffered martyrdom by being slain with a sword in a distant city of Ethiopia.

James, the Less, was thrown from a lofty pinnacle of the temple, and then beaten to death with a fuller's club.

Leblaeus Thaddaeus is unknown by information either in the Bible or by tradition.

Simon the Canaanite is unknown by information either in the Bible or by tradition.

Judas Iscariot committed suicide by hanging himself.

Matthias was selected to replace Judas Iscariot by the Apostles, was first stoned and then beheaded.

Paul formerly known as Saul was selected by Jesus Christ to replace Judas Iscariot. After various tortures and persecutions, was at length beheaded at Rome by Emperor Nero.

Disciples

Mark expired at Alexandria, after being cruelly dragged through the streets of that city.

Luke was hanged upon an olive tree in the classic land of Greece.

Jude was shot to death with arrows.

Barnabas of the Gentiles was stoned to death at Salonica.

Forgiveness

Luke 17:3. Take heed to yourselves: If thy brother trespass against thee, rebuke him; and if he repent, forgive him.

Mark 11:25-26. 25. And when ye stand praying, forgive, if ye have ought against any: that your Father also which is in heaven may forgive you your trespasses.

26. But if ye do not forgive, neither will your Father which is in heaven forgive your trespasses.

Matthew 5:43-45. 43. Ye have heard that it hath been said, Thou shalt love thy neighbour, and hate thine enemy. 44. But I say unto you, Love your enemies, bless them that curse you, do good to them that hate you, and pray for them which despitefully use you, and persecute you;

45. That ye may be the children of your Father which is in heaven: for he maketh his sun to rise on the evil and on the good, and sendeth rain on the just and on the unjust.

Matthew 6:14-15. 14. For if ye forgive men their trespasses, your heavenly Father will also forgive you: 15. But if ye forgive not men their trespasses, neither will your Father forgive your trespasses.

Matthew 6:12. And forgive us our debts, as we forgive our debtors.

Matthew 18:35. So likewise shall my heavenly Father do also unto you, if ye from your hearts forgive not every one his brother their trespasses.

Romans 12:19. Dearly beloved, avenge not yourselves, but rather give place unto wrath: for it is written, Vengeance is mine; I will repay, saith the Lord.

Luke 23:33-34. 33. And when they were come to the place, which is called Calvary, there they crucified him, and the malefactors, one on the right hand, and the other on the left.

34. Then said Jesus, Father, forgive them; for they know not what they do. And they parted his raiment, and cast lots.

Acts 7:59-60. 59. And they stoned Stephen, calling upon God, and saying, Lord Jesus, receive my spirit. 60. And he kneeled down, and cried with a loud voice, Lord, lay not this sin to their charge. And when he had said this, he fell asleep.

Ephesians 4:31-32. 31. Let all bitterness, and wrath, and anger, and clamour, and evil speaking, be put away from you, with all malice: 32. And be ye kind one to another, tenderhearted, forgiving one another, even as God for Christ's sake hath forgiven you.

Colossians 3:13-14. 13. Forbearing one another, and forgiving one another, if any man have a quarrel against any: even as Christ forgave you, so also do ye. 14. And above all these things put on charity, which is the bond of perfectness.

Warnings & Guidance

Psalm 66:18. If I regard iniquity in my heart, the Lord will not hear me:

Job 11:14. If iniquity be in thine hand, put it far away, and let not wickedness dwell in thy tabernacles.

Proverbs 15:29. The Lord is far from the wicked: but he heareth the prayer of the righteous.

Isaiah 1:15. And when ye spread forth your hands, I will hide mine eyes from you: yea, when ye make many prayers, I will not hear: your hands are full of blood.

Definitions:

Forgive: To cease to feel resentment against an offender; pardon; pardon one's enemy; to grant forgiveness; excuse.

Trespass: A violation of moral or social ethics; an unlawful act committed on the person, property or rights of another.

The Reason for the Christmas Season of Celebration

Old & New Testaments

Objective: To give each of us insight concerning the greatest gift that we have received from our Creator Jesus Christ...our eternal Salvation.

Objective Breakdown:

1. God Creates People Male and Female	Genesis 1:26-31
2. God Places the Man in Eden	Genesis 2:10-17
3. Woman is Created and Marriage Is Established	Genesis 2:18-25
4. Adam and Eve Disobey	Genesis 3:1-7
5. Adam and Eve Hide from God	Genesis 3:8-13
6. Curses from God	Genesis 3:14-19
7. A Sign: A Virgin Shall Conceive	Isaiah 7:10-14
8. A Prince of Peace Will Be Born	Isaiah 9:6-7
9. A Shepherd Will Come from Bethlehem	Micah 5:2
10. The Birth of Jesus	Matthew 1:18-25
11. Luke's Preface	Luke 1:1-4
12. An Angel Promises Zacharias a Son	Luke 1:5-25
13. Mary Learns That She Will Bear the Messiah	Luke 1:26-38
14. Elizabeth and Mary Praise God	Luke 1:39-56
15. John the Baptist Is Born	Luke 1:57-80
16. The Birth of Jesus	Luke 2:1-15
17. The Crucifixion	Luke 23:26-49
18. The Resurrection	Luke 24:1-12

II Chronicles 7:14

If my people, which are called by my name, shall humble themselves, and pray, and seek my face, and turn from their wicked ways; then will I hear from heaven, and will forgive their sin, and will heal their land.

Psalm 122:6

Pray for the peace of Jerusalem; they will prosper that love thee.

Who Is This Jesus?

<u>I Want to Talk to You About Jesus...</u>

He is The Sinner's Savior

He is The Centerpiece of Civilization

He Stands Alone in Himself

He is Unique

He is Unparalleled

He is Unprecedented

He is Supreme

He is Preeminent

He is The Loftiest Person in Literature

He is The Highest Concept in Philosophy

The Fundamental Truth in Theology

The Cardinal Necessity in Religion

He is The King

He is The Miracle of The Ages

He Supplies Strength for The Weak

He is Available for The Tempted and The Tired

He Sympathizes and He Saves

He Guards and He Guides

He Heals The Sick

He Cleanses Lepers

He Forgives Sinners

He Discharges Debtors

He Delivers Captives

He Defends The Feeble

He Blesses The Young

He Serves The Unfortunate

He Guards The Ages

He Rewards The Diligent

He Beautifies The Lakes

Do You Know Him?

He is The King of Knowledge

He is The Well Spring of Wisdom

He is The Doorway of Deliverance

He is The Pathway of Peace

He is The Roadway of Righteousness

He is The Highway of Holiness

He is The Gateway of Glory

He is The Master of The Mighty

He is The Captain of The Conqueror

He is The Head of The Hero

He is The Leader of The Legislators

He is The Overseer of The Over Comer

He is The Governor of The Governors

He is The Prince of Princes

He is The King of Kings

He is Lord of Lords

His Life is Matchless

His Goodness is Limitless

His Mercy is Everlasting

His Love Never Changes

His Word is Enough

His Grace is Sufficient

His Reign is Righteous

His Yoke is Easy

His Burden is Light

I am Trying to Describe Him to You.

The Problem is That He is Indescribable

He is Irresistible

He is The One Who is Incomprehensible

He is Invincible

Pharisees Hate Him

Jews Rejected Him

Pilate Condemned Him

Romans Crucified Him

Our Sins Killed Him

The Rich Man Buried Him

But Death Could Not Handle Him

He Arose Triumphant on the Third Day

Jesus is the Theme of The Bible

It is All About Him—Hallelujah

It is All About Him—Hallelujah

The Savior Did For Us What We Could Not Do For Ourselves

He Took Our Sin Upon Himself

He Suffered and Died in Our Place

He Shed His Blood For Us

If He is Really Who He Said He Was

The Only Question is ---- Is He Yours? Are you His?

Source: Minister Shadrach Meshach Lockridge (1913-2000 A.D.) of Calvary Baptist Church, San Deigo, CA

Doctrine of Baptisms

Hebrews Chapter 6:2-6 Written 64-68 A.D.

In Hebrews chapter 6:2, it refers to the doctrine of Baptisms, of Laying on of hands, of the resurrection of the dead, and eternal judgment.

Objective: To discern the issues in Hebrews 6:2: Baptisms, Laying on of Hands, the Resurrection of the Dead, and Eternal Judgment.

Objective Breakdown:

1. Introduction

2. Doctrines of Baptisms

3. Laying on of Hands

4. Resurrection of the dead

5. Eternal Judgment

Introduction: The verses of Hebrew Chapter 6:2-6 discuss apostasy and its results. Like the fallen angels which followed Lucifer (Satan), there will be no redemption. These verses let us know that at the White Throne judgment, they (Fallen Angels and those guilty of Apostasy) will not have the ability to be pardoned nor will any other of God's creatures (mankind) who have fallen away and followed the same steps as these fallen angels.

In Paul's day, the people did not have the scriptures available to them (as we have today) and most teaching was a result of word of mouth. These people were going through a transition from the Old Testament teaching to the New Testament teaching. Since there were many false teachers and Judaizers much incorrect information and syncretism (a blending of religions) existed. This is the situation Paul had to deal with.

What is Baptism: Baptism is basically the first step in the spiritual and public identification of a commitment and covenant to surrender our spirit to the ordinances of God. It also symbolically reflects both the death of sin, the death and the resurrection of Jesus Christ, and the adoption of those who follow Him.

Doctrines of Baptism

The Bible lists 7 Baptisms in the Bible:

1. Baptism of Moses   (1 Corinthians 10:1-3 & Exodus 13:21)

2. Baptism of John   (Mark 1:4)

3. Baptism of Jesus   (Matthew 3:13-17)

4. Baptism of Fire   (Matthew 3:11-12)

5. Baptism of Holy Spirit   (Ephesians 1:13-14, 1 Corinthians 12:13, Acts 2:38, 8:17-19)

6. Baptism of the Cross   (Mark 10:35-39)

7. Baptism of the Believer   (Matthew 28:19, Romans 6:3-4)

1. Baptism of Moses (1 Corinthians 10:1-3 & Exodus 13:21)

1 Corinthians 10:1-3 Moreover, brethren, I would not that ye should be ignorant, how that all our fathers were under the cloud, and all passed through the sea;

1 Corinthians 10:2 And were all baptized unto Moses in the cloud and in the sea;

1 Corinthians 10:3 And did all eat the same spiritual meat;"

Exodus 13:21 And the Lord went before them by day in a pillar of a cloud, to lead them the way; and by night in a pillar of fire, to give them light; to go by day and night:

Exodus 13:22 He took not away the pillar of the cloud by day, nor the pillar of fire by night, *from* before the people.

2. Baptism of John (Mark 1:4)

Mark 1:4 John did baptize in the wilderness, and preach the baptism of repentance for the remission of sins.

Mark 1:5 And there went out unto him all the land of Judaea, and they of Jerusalem, and were all baptized of him in the river of Jordan, confessing their sins.

3. Baptism of Jesus (Matthew 3:13-17)

Matthew 3:13 Then cometh Jesus from Galilee to Jordan unto John, to be baptized of him.

Matthew 3:14 But John forbad him, saying, I have need to be baptized of thee, and comest thou to me?

Matthew 3:15 And Jesus answering said unto him, Suffer it to be so now: for thus it becometh us to fulfil all righteousness. Then he suffered him.

Matthew 3:16 And Jesus, when he was baptized, went up straightway out of the water: and, lo, the heavens were opened unto Him, and He saw the Spirit of God descending like a dove, and lighting upon Him:

Matthew 3:17 And lo a voice from heaven, saying, This is my beloved Son, in whom I am well pleased.

4. Baptism of Fire (Matthew 3:11-12)

Matthew 3:11 I indeed baptize you with water unto repentance: but he that cometh after me is mightier than I, whose shoes I am not worthy to bear: he shall baptize you with the Holy Ghost, and *with* fire:

Matthew 3:12 Whose fan *is* in his hand, and he will thoroughly purge his floor, and gather his wheat into the garner; but he will burn up the chaff with unquenchable fire.

5. Baptism of Holy Spirit (Ephesians1:13-14; 1 Corinthians 12:13) Acts 238; Acts 8:17-19

Ephesians 1:13 In whom ye also *trusted,* after that ye heard the word of truth, the gospel of your salvation: in whom also after that ye believed, ye were sealed with that holy Spirit of promise,

Ephesians 1:14 Which is the earnest of our inheritance until the redemption of the purchased possession, unto the praise of his glory.

1 Corinthians 12:13 For by one Spirit are we all baptized into one body, whether *we be* Jews or Gentiles, whether *we be* bond or free; and have been all made to drink into one Spirit.

Acts 2:38 Then Peter said unto them, repent, and be baptized every one of you in the name of Jesus Christ for the remission of sins, and ye shall receive the gift of the Holy Ghost.

Acts 8:12 But when they believed Philip preaching the things concerning the kingdom of God, and the name of Jesus Christ, they were baptized, both men and women.

Acts 8:13 Then Simon himself believed also: and when he was baptized, he continued with

Philip, and wondered, beholding the miracles and signs which were done.

Acts 8:14 Now when the apostles which were at Jerusalem heard that Samaria had received the word of God, they sent unto them Peter and John:

Acts 8:15 Who, when they were come down, prayed for them, that they might receive the Holy Ghost:

Acts 8:16 (For as yet he was fallen upon none of them: only they were baptized in the name of the Lord Jesus.)

Acts 8:17 Then laid they *their* hands on them, and they received the Holy Ghost.

Acts 8:18 And when Simon saw that through laying on of the apostles' hands the Holy Ghost was given, he offered them money,

Acts 8:19 Saying, Give me also this power, that on whomsoever I lay hands, he may receive the Holy Ghost.

6. Baptism of the Cross (Mark 10:35-39)

Mark 10:35 And James and John, the sons of Zebedee, come unto him, saying, Master, we would that thou shouldest do for us whatsoever we shall desire.

Mark 10:36 And he said unto them, What would ye that I should do for you?

Mark 10:37 They said unto him, Grant unto us that we may sit, one on thy right hand, and the other on thy left hand, in thy glory.

Mark 10:38 But Jesus said unto them, Ye know not what ye ask: can ye drink of the cup that I drink of? and be baptized with the baptism that I am baptized with?

Mark 10:39 And they said unto him, We can. And Jesus said unto them, Ye shall indeed drink of the cup that I drink of; and with the baptism that I am baptized withal shall ye be baptized.

7. Baptism of the Believer (Matthew 28:19; Romans 6: 3-4)

Matthew 28:19 Go ye therefore, and teach all nations, baptizing them in the name of the Father, and of the Son, and of the Holy Ghost:

Matthew 28:20 Teaching them to observe all things whatsoever I have commanded you: and, lo, I am with you always *even* unto the end of the world. Amen.

Romans 6:3 Know ye not, that so many of us as were baptized into Jesus Christ were baptized into his death?

Romans 6:4 Therefore we are buried with him by baptism into death: that like as Christ was raised up from the dead by the glory of the Father, even so we also should walk in newness of life.

Romans 6:5 For if we have been planted together in the likeness of his death, we shall be also *in the likeness* of *his* resurrection:

Romans 6:6 Knowing this, that our old man is crucified with *him,* that the body of sin might be destroyed, that henceforth we should not serve sin.

Note: In 1 Corinthians 15:29 Paul refers to those who baptize for the dead. If you don't believe in the resurrection, why do you baptize for the dead? (Paul was challenging their understanding and reasoning). It is believed that the false teaching of being baptized for the dead may have originated from a pagan belief in an ancient mystery religion that was centered in Eleusis. Eleusis is a region on the coastline of Greece Northwest of Athens about 100 miles as the crow flies.

This practice (baptizing for the dead) is continued today in Mormonism. About 15 months ago, an individual in the Mormon denomination was recognized for his completion of being baptized 1,000,000 times for the dead. He apparently is still being baptized for those who are dead. One can verify Mormon baptism for the dead by Googling it.

****<u>The bottom line is that baptism must be done while we are here on earth and during our lifetime.</u> Those who may not have had the opportunity or knowledge of the need for Baptism will be judged by the Creator. <u>Baptism for the dead is too late; it must be done during your lifetime here on earth.</u>

For those who never heard the Word, the following scriptures <u>may</u> apply (Romans 4:15) "Because the law worketh wrath: for where no law is, *there is* no transgression."

<u>Romans 5:13 For until the law sin was in the world: but sin is not imputed when there is no law.</u>

Finally, we have to deal with eternal judgment. This is basically the White Throne Judgment. This is covered in Revelation 20:11-15 and states as follows:

Judgment Before the Great White Throne

Revelation 20:11 And I saw a great white throne, and Him that sat on it, from whose face the earth and the heaven fled away; and there was found no place for them.

Revelation 20:12 And I saw the dead, small and great, stand before God; and the books were opened: and another book was opened, which is *the book* of life: and the dead were judged out of those things which were written in the books, according to their works.

Revelation 20:13 And the sea gave up the dead which were in it; and death and hell delivered up the dead which were in them: and they were judged every man according to their works.

Revelation 20:14 And death and hell were cast into the lake of fire. This is the second death.

Revelation 20:15 And whosoever was not found written in the book of life was cast into the lake of fire.

Note: Then a New Heaven and a New Earth is created for all the good guys (Revelation 21:1-27) Amen!

The Crucifixion and Resurrection of Jesus Christ

by

John, Mark, Luke and Matthew

The Final Events of Jesus Prior to His Crucifixion

Objective: To Review the Final Events Leading up to Jesus' Crucifixion

Objective Breakdown:

1. Background/Introduction	John	Chapter 12:1-11
2. Jesus and the Twelve Eat the Passover	Luke	Chapter 22:7-38
3. Leaders Plot to Destroy Jesus	John	Chapter 11:45-57
4. Jesus Washes the Disciples' Feet	John	Chapter 13:1-20
5. Judas Leaves to Betray Jesus	John	Chapter 13:21-30
6. Jesus Predicts Peter's Denial	John	Chapter 13:36-38
7. Jesus Prays in the Garden of Gethsemane	Mark	Chapter14:32-42
8. Jesus Prays in the Garden of Gethsemane	Luke	Chapter 22:42-44
9. Jesus is Arrested	John	Chapter 18:1-14
10. Jesus is Arrested	Luke	Chapter 22:49-51
11. Peter Denies Knowing Jesus	John	Chapter 18:15-27
12. Jesus is Taken to Pilate	John	Chapter 18:28-40
13. Pilate Sends Jesus to be Crucified	John	Chapter 19:1-16
14. The Crucifixion	John	Chapter 19:17-37
15. Jesus' Body is Laid in the Tomb	John	Chapter 19:38-42
16. The Resurrection	John	Chapter 20:1-10
17. The Guards are Bribed	Matthew	Chapter 28:11-15

Background/Introduction: Six days before the Passover, Jesus went to Lazarus' home in Bethany. Lazarus was whom Jesus had raised from the dead. There they made Jesus a supper; and Martha served: and Lazarus was one of them that sat at the table with Jesus.

Then took Mary a pound of ointment of spikenard, very costly, and anointed the feet of Jesus, and wiped his feet with her hair: and the house was filled with the odour of the ointment.

Then saith one of his disciples, Judas Iscariot, Simon's son, which should betray him,

Why was not this ointment sold for three hundred pence, and given to the poor?

This he said, not that he cared for the poor; but because he was a thief, and had the bag, and bare what was put therein.

Then said Jesus, Let her alone; against the day of my burial hath she kept this. For the poor always ye have with you; but me ye have not always. Much people of the Jews therefore knew that he was there: and they came not for Jesus' sake only, but that they might see Lazarus also, whom he had raised from the dead. But the chief priests consulted that they might put Lazarus also to death because by reason of him many of the Jews went away, and believed on Jesus.

The oil that Mary used on Jesus (John Chapter 12:3) was probably nard a perfume used by women. Imported from India. It was extremely costly and was known for its strong fragrance.

It was the same perfume used by the women that Solomon praised in his Song of Solomon (1:12;4:13).

<u>Jesus and the Twelve Eat the Passover</u>   Luke   Chapter 22:7-38

7. Then came the day of unleavened bread, when the Passover must be killed.

8. And he sent Peter and John, saying, Go and prepare us the Passover, that we may eat.

9. And they said unto him, Where wilt thou that we prepare?

10. And he said unto them, Behold, when ye are entered into the city, there shall a man meet you, bearing a pitcher of water; follow him into the house where he entereth in.

11. And ye shall say unto the goodman of the house, The Master saith unto thee, Where is the

guest chamber, where I shall eat the Passover with my disciples?

12. And he shall shew you a large upper room furnished: there make ready.

13. And they went, and found as he had said unto them: and they made ready the Passover.

14. And when the hour was come, he sat down, and the twelve apostles with him.

15. And he said unto them, With desire I have desired to eat this passover with you before I suffer:

16. For I say unto you, I will not any more eat thereof, until it be fulfilled in the kingdom of God.

17. And he took the cup, and gave thanks, and said, Take this, and divide it among yourselves:

18. For I say unto you, I will not drink of the fruit of the vine, until the kingdom of God shall come.

19. And he took bread, and gave thanks, and brake it, and gave unto them, saying, This is my body which is given for you: this do in remembrance of me.

20. Likewise also the cup after supper, saying, This cup is the new testament in my blood, which is shed for you.

21. But, behold, the hand of him that betrayeth me is with me on the table.

22. And truly the Son of man goeth, as it was determined: but woe unto that man by whom he is betrayed!

23. And they began to inquire among themselves, which of them it was that should do this thing.

24. And there was also a strife among them, which of them should be accounted the greatest.

25. And he said unto them, The kings of the Gentiles exercise lordship over them; and they that exercise authority upon them are called benefactors.

26. But ye shall not be so: but he that is greatest among you, let him be as the younger; and he that is chief, as he that doth serve.

27. For whether is greater, he that sitteth at meat, or he that serveth? is not he that sitteth at meat? but I am among you as he that serveth.

28. Ye are they which have continued with me in my temptations.

29. And I appoint unto you a kingdom, as my Father hath appointed unto me;

30. That ye may eat and drink at my table in my kingdom, and sit on thrones judging the twelve tribes of Israel.

31. And the Lord said, Simon, Simon, behold, Satan hath desired to have you, that he may sift you as wheat:

32. But I have prayed for thee, that thy faith fail not: and when thou art converted, strengthen thy brethren.

33. And he said unto him, Lord, I am ready to go with thee, both into prison, and to death.

34. And he said, I tell thee, Peter, the cock shall not crow this day, before that thou shalt thrice deny that thou knowest me.

35. And he said unto them, When I sent you without purse, and scrip, and shoes, lacked ye any thing? And they said, Nothing.

36. Then said he unto them, But now, he that hath a purse, let him take it, and likewise his scrip: and he that hath no sword, let him sell his garment, and buy one.

37. For I say unto you, that this that is written must yet be accomplished in me, And he was reckoned among the transgressors: for the things concerning me have an end.

38. And they said, Lord, behold, here are two swords. And he said unto them, It is enough.

Leaders Plot to Destroy Jesus   John   Chapter 11:43-57

43. And when he thus had spoken, he cried with a loud voice, Lazarus, come forth.

44. And he that was dead came forth, bound hand and foot with graveclothes: and his face was bound about with a napkin. Jesus saith unto them, Loose him, and let him go.

45. Then many of the Jews which came to Mary, and had seen the things which Jesus did,believed on him.

46. But some of them went their ways to the Pharisees, and told them what things Jesus had done.

47. Then gathered the chief priests and the Pharisees a council, and said, What do we? for this

man doeth many miracles.

48. If we let him thus alone, all men will believe on him: and the Romans shall come and take away both our place and nation.

49. And one of them, named Caiaphas, being the high priest that same year, said unto them, Ye know nothing at all,

50. Nor consider that it is expedient for us, that one man should die for the people, and that the whole nation perish not.

51. And this spake he not of himself: but being high priest that year, he prophesied that Jesus should die for that nation;

52. And not for that nation only, but that also he should gather together in one the children of God that were scattered abroad.

53. Then from that day forth they took counsel together for to put him to death.

54. Jesus therefore walked no more openly among the Jews; but went thence unto a country near to the wilderness, into a city called Ephraim, and there continued with his disciples.

55. And the Jews' Passover was nigh at hand: and many went out of the country up to Jerusalem before the Passover, to purify themselves.

56. Then sought they for Jesus, and spake among themselves, as they stood in the temple, What think ye, that he will not come to the feast?

57. Now both the chief priests and the Pharisees had given a commandment, that, if any man knew where he were, he should shew it, that they might take him.

Jesus Washes the Disciples' Feet   John   Chapter 13:1-20

1. Now before the feast of the Passover, when Jesus knew that his hour was come that he should depart out of this world unto the Father, having loved his own which were in the world, he loved them unto the end.

2. And supper being ended, the devil having now put into the heart of Judas Iscariot, Simon's son, to betray him;

3. Jesus knowing that the Father had given all things into his hands, and that he was come from God, and went to God;

4. He riseth from supper, and laid aside his garments; and took a towel, and girded himself.

5. After that he poureth water into a basin, and began to wash the disciples' feet, and to wipe them with the towel wherewith he was girded.

6. Then cometh he to Simon Peter: and Peter saith unto him, Lord, dost thou wash my feet?

7. Jesus answered and said unto him, What I do thou knowest not now; but thou shalt know hereafter.

8. Peter saith unto him, Thou shalt never wash my feet. Jesus answered him, If I wash thee not, thou hast no part with me.

9. Simon Peter saith unto him, Lord, not my feet only, but also my hands and my head.

10. Jesus saith to him, He that is washed needeth not save to wash his feet, but is clean every whit: and ye are clean, but not all.

11. For he knew who should betray him; therefore said he, Ye are not all clean.

12. So after he had washed their feet, and had taken his garments, and was set down again, he said unto them, Know ye what I have done to you?

13. Ye call me Master and Lord: and ye say well; for so I am.

14. If I then, your Lord and Master, have washed your feet; ye also ought to wash one another's feet.

15. For I have given you an example, that ye should do as I have done to you.

16. Verily, verily, I say unto you, The servant is not greater than his lord; neither he that is sent greater than he that sent him.

17. If ye know these things, happy are ye if ye do them.

18. I speak not of you all: I know whom I have chosen: but that the scripture may be fulfilled, He that eateth bread with me hath lifted up his heel against me.

19. Now I tell you before it come, that, when it is come to pass, ye may believe that I am He.

20. Verily, verily, I say unto you, He that receiveth whomsoever I send receiveth me; and he that receiveth me receiveth him that sent me.

21. When Jesus had thus said, he was troubled in spirit, and testified, and said, Verily, verily,

22. I say unto you, that one of you shall betray me.

23. Then the disciples looked one on another, doubting of whom he spake.

24. Now there was leaning on Jesus' bosom one of his disciples, whom Jesus loved.

25. Simon Peter therefore beckoned to him, that he should ask who it should be of whom he spake.

26. He then lying on Jesus' breast saith unto him, Lord, who is it?

27. Jesus answered, he it is, to whom I shall give a sop, when I have dipped it. And when he had dipped the sop, he gave it to Judas Iscariot, the son of Simon.

28. And after the sop Satan entered into him. Then said Jesus unto him, That thou doest, do quickly.

29. Now no man at the table knew for what intent he spake this unto him.

30. For some of them thought, because Judas had the bag, that Jesus had said unto him,

31. Buy those things that we have need of against the feast; or, that he should give something to the poor.

32. He then having received the sop went immediately out, and it was night.

Jesus Predicts Peter's Denial   John   Chapter 13:36-38

36. Simon Peter said unto him, Lord, whither goest thou? Jesus answered him, Whither I go, thou canst not follow me now; but thou shalt follow me afterwards.

37. Peter said unto him, Lord, why cannot I follow thee now? I will lay down my life for thy sake.

38. Jesus answered him, Wilt thou lay down thy life for my sake? Verily, verily, I say unto thee, The cock shall not crow, till thou hast denied me thrice.

Jesus Prays in the Garden of Gethsemane   Mark   Chapter 14:32-42

32. And they came to a place which was named Gethsemane: and he saith to his disciples, Sit

ye here, while I shall pray.

33. And he taketh with him Peter and James and John, and began to be sore amazed, and to be very heavy;

34. And saith unto them, My soul is exceeding sorrowful unto death: tarry ye here, and watch.

35. And he went forward a little, and fell on the ground, and prayed that, if it were possible, the hour might pass from him.

36. And he said, Abba, Father, all things are possible unto thee; take away this cup from me: nevertheless not what I will, but what thou wilt.

37. And he cometh, and findeth them sleeping, and saith unto Peter, Simon, sleepest thou? couldest not thou watch one hour?

38. Watch ye and pray, lest ye enter into temptation. The spirit truly is ready, but the flesh is weak.

39. And again he went away, and prayed, and spake the same words.

40. And when he returned, he found them asleep again, (for their eyes were heavy,) neither wist they what to answer him.

41. And he cometh the third time, and saith unto them, Sleep on now, and take your rest: it enough, the hour is come; behold, the Son of man is betrayed into the hands of sinners.

42. Rise up, let us go; lo, he that betrayeth me is at hand.

Jesus Prays in the Garden of Gethsemane (continued)   Luke 22:42-44

42. Saying, Father, if thou be willing, remove this cup from me: nevertheless not my will, but thine, be done.

43. And there appeared an angel unto him from heaven, strengthening him.

44. And being in an agony he prayed more earnestly: and his sweat was as it were great drops of blood falling down to the ground.

Jesus is Arrested   John   Chapter 18:1-14

1. When Jesus had spoken these words, he went forth with his disciples over the brook Cedron, where was a garden, into the which he entered, and his disciples.

2. And Judas also, which betrayed him, knew the place: for Jesus ofttimes resorted thither with his disciples.

3. Judas then, having received a band of men and officers from the chief priests and Pharisees, cometh thither with lanterns and torches and weapons.

4. Jesus therefore, knowing all things that should come upon him, went forth, and said unto them, Whom seek ye?

5. They answered him, Jesus of Nazareth. Jesus saith unto them, I am he. And Judas also, which betrayed him, stood with them.

6. As soon then as he had said unto them, I am he, they went backward, and fell to the ground.

7. Then asked he them again, Whom seek ye? And they said, Jesus of Nazareth.

8. Jesus answered, I have told you that I am he: if therefore ye seek me, let these go their way:

9. That the saying might be fulfilled, which he spake, Of them which thou gavest me have I lost none.

10. Then Simon Peter having a sword drew it, and smote the high priest's servant, and cut off his right ear. The servant's name was Malchus.

11. Then said Jesus unto Peter, Put up thy sword into the sheath: the cup which my Father hath given me, shall I not drink it?

12. Then the band and the captain and officers of the Jews took Jesus, and bound him,

13. And led him away to Annas first; for he was father in law to Caiaphas, which was the high priest that same year.

14. Now Caiaphas was he, which gave counsel to the Jews, that it was expedient that one man should die for the people.

Jesus is Arrested (continued)   Luke 22:49-51

49. When those around Him saw what was going to happen, they said to Him, "Lord, shall we strike with the sword?"

50. And one of them struck the servant of the high priest and cut off his right ear.

51. But Jesus answered and said, "Permit even this." And He touched his ear and healed him.

Peter Denies Knowing Jesus   John   Chapter 18:15-27

15. And Simon Peter followed Jesus, and so did another disciple: that disciple was known unto the high priest, and went in with Jesus into the palace of the high priest.

16. But Peter stood at the door without. Then went out that other disciple, which was known unto the high priest, and spake unto her that kept the door, and brought in Peter.

17. Then saith the damsel that kept the door unto Peter, Art not thou also one of this man's disciples? He saith, I am not.

18. And the servants and officers stood there, who had made a fire of coals; for it was cold: and they warmed themselves: and Peter stood with them, and warmed himself.

19. The high priest then asked Jesus of his disciples, and of his doctrine.

20. Jesus answered him, I spake openly to the world; I ever taught in the synagogue, and in the temple, whither the Jews always resort; and in secret have I said nothing.

21. Why askest thou me? ask them which heard me, what I have said unto them: behold, they know what I said.

22. And when he had thus spoken, one of the officers which stood by struck Jesus with the palm of his hand, saying, Answerest thou the high priest so?

23. Jesus answered him, If I have spoken evil, bear witness of the evil: but if well, why smites thou me?

24. Now Annas had sent him bound unto Caiaphas the high priest.

25. And Simon Peter stood and warmed himself. They said therefore unto him, Art not thou also one of his disciples? He denied it, and said, I am not.

26. One of the servants of the high priest, being his kinsman whose ear Peter cut off, saith, Did not I see thee in the garden with him?

27. Peter then denied again: and immediately the cock crew.

Jesus is Taken to Pilate   John   Chapter 18:28-40

28. Then led they Jesus from Caiaphas unto the hall of judgment: and it was early; and they

themselves went not into the judgment hall, lest they should be defiled; but that they might eat the Passover.

29. Pilate then went out unto them, and said, What accusation bring ye against this man?

30. They answered and said unto him, If he were not a malefactor, we would not have delivered him up unto thee.

31. Then said Pilate unto them, Take ye him, and judge him according to your law. The Jews therefore said unto him, It is not lawful for us to put any man to death:

32. That the saying of Jesus might be fulfilled, which he spake, signifying what death he should die.

33. Then Pilate entered into the judgment hall again, and called Jesus, and said unto him, Art thou the King of the Jews?

34. Jesus answered him, Sayest thou this thing of thyself, or did others tell it thee of me?

35. Pilate answered, Am I a Jew? Thine own nation and the chief priests have delivered thee unto me: what hast thou done?

36. Jesus answered, My kingdom is not of this world: if my kingdom were of this world, then would my servants fight, that I should not be delivered to the Jews: but now is my kingdom not from hence.

37. Pilate therefore said unto him, Art thou a king then? Jesus answered, Thou sayest that I am a king. To this end was I born, and for this cause came I into the world, that I should bear witness unto the truth. Every one that is of the truth heareth my voice.

38. Pilate saith unto him, What is truth? And when he had said this, he went out again unto the Jews, and saith unto them, I find in him no fault at all.

39. But ye have a custom, that I should release unto you one at the Passover: will ye therefore that I release unto you the King of the Jews?

40. Then cried they all again, saying, Not this man, but Barabbas. Now Barabbas was a robber.

Pilate Sends Jesus to be Crucified   John   Chapter 19:1-16

1. Then Pilate therefore took Jesus, and scourged him.

2. And the soldiers platted a crown of thorns, and put it on his head, and they put on him a purple robe,

3. And said, Hail, King of the Jews! and they smote him with their hands. Pilate therefore went forth again, and saith unto them, Behold, I bring him forth to you, that ye may know that I find no fault in him.

4. Then came Jesus forth, wearing the crown of thorns, and the purple robe. And Pilate saith unto them, Behold the man!

5. When the chief priests therefore and officers saw him, they cried out, saying, Crucify him, crucify him. Pilate saith unto them, Take ye him, and crucify him: for I find no fault in him.

6. The Jews answered him, We have a law, and by our law he ought to die, because he made himself the Son of God.

7. When Pilate therefore heard that saying, he was the more afraid;

8. And went again into the judgment hall, and saith unto Jesus, Whence art thou? But Jesus gave him no answer.

9. Then saith Pilate unto him, Speakest thou not unto me? knowest thou not that I have power to crucify thee, and have power to release thee?

10. Jesus answered, Thou couldest have no power at all against me, except it were given thee from above: therefore he that delivered me unto thee hath the greater sin.

11. And from thenceforth Pilate sought to release him: but the Jews cried out, saying, If thou let this man go, thou art not Caesar's friend: whosoever maketh himself a king speaketh against Caesar.

12. When Pilate therefore heard that saying, he brought Jesus forth, and sat down in the judgment seat in a place that is called the Pavement, but in the Hebrew, Gabbatha.

13. And it was the preparation of the Passover, and about the sixth hour: and he saith unto the Jews, Behold your King!

14. But they cried out, Away with him, away with him, crucify him. Pilate saith unto them,

15. Shall I crucify your King? The chief priests answered, We have no king but Caesar.

16. Then delivered he him therefore unto them to be crucified. And they took Jesus, and led him away.

The Crucifixion   John   Chapter 19:17-37

17. And he bearing his cross went forth into a place called the place of a skull, which is called in the Hebrew Golgotha:

18. Where they crucified him, and two other with him, on either side one, and Jesus in the midst.

19. And Pilate wrote a title, and put it on the cross. And the writing was "JESUS OF NAZARETH THE KING OF THE JEWS."

20. This title then read many of the Jews: for the place where Jesus was crucified was nigh to the city: and it was written in Hebrew, and Greek, and Latin.

21. Then said the chief priests of the Jews to Pilate, Write not, The King of the Jews; but that he said, I am King of the Jews.

22. Pilate answered, What I have written I have written.

23. Then the soldiers, when they had crucified Jesus, took his garments, and made four parts, to every soldier a part; and also his coat: now the coat was without seam, woven from the top throughout.

24. They said therefore among themselves, Let us not rend it, but cast lots for it, whose it shall be: that the scripture might be fulfilled, which saith, They parted my raiment among them, and for my vesture they did cast lots. These things therefore the soldiers did.

25. Now there stood by the cross of Jesus, his mother, and his mother's sister, Mary the wife of Cleophas, and Mary Magdalene.

26. When Jesus therefore saw his mother, and the disciple standing by, whom he loved, he saith unto his mother, Woman, behold thy son!

27. Then saith he to the disciple, Behold thy mother! And from that hour that disciple took her unto his own home.

28. After this, Jesus knowing that all things were now accomplished, that the scripture might be fulfilled, saith, I thirst.

29. Now there was set a vessel full of vinegar: and they filled a spunge with vinegar, and put it upon hyssop, and put it to his mouth.

30. When Jesus therefore had received the vinegar, he said, It is finished: and he bowed his head, and gave up the ghost.

31. The Jews therefore, because it was the Preparation Day, that the bodies should not remain upon the cross on the Sabbath day, (for that Sabbath day was an high day,) the Jews besought Pilate that their legs might be broken, and that they might be taken away.

32. Then came the soldiers, and brake the legs of the first, and of the other which was crucified with him.

33. But when they came to Jesus, and saw that he was dead already, they brake not his legs:

34. But one of the soldiers with a spear pierced his side, and forthwith came there out blood and water.

35. And he that saw it bare record, and his record is true: and he knoweth that he saith true, that ye might believe.

36. For these things were done, that the scripture should be fulfilled, a bone of him shall not be broken.

37. And again another scripture saith, They shall look on him whom they pierced.

Jesus' Body is Laid in the Tomb   John   Chapter 19:38-42

38. And after this Joseph of Arimathea, being a disciple of Jesus, but secretly for fear of theJews, besought Pilate that he might take away the body of Jesus: and Pilate gave him leave. He came therefore, and took the body of Jesus.

39. And there came also Nicodemus, which at the first came to Jesus by night, and brought a mixture of myrrh and aloes, about an hundred pound weight.

40. Then took they the body of Jesus, and wound it in linen clothes with the spices, as the manner of the Jews is to bury.

41. Now in the place where he was crucified there was a garden; and in the garden a new sepulchre, wherein was never man yet laid.

42. There laid they Jesus therefore because of the Jews' Preparation Day; for the sepulchre

was nigh at hand.

The Resurrection   John   Chapter 20:1-10

1. The first day of the week cometh Mary Magdalene early, when it was yet dark, unto the sepulchre, and seeth the stone taken away from the sepulchre.

2. Then she runneth, and cometh to Simon Peter, and to the other disciple, whom Jesus loved, and saith unto them, They have taken away the Lord out of the sepulchre, and we know not where they have laid him.

3. Peter therefore went forth, and that other disciple, and came to the sepulchre.

4. So they ran both together: and the other disciple did outrun Peter, and came first to the sepulchre.

5. And he stooping down, and looking in, saw the linen clothes lying; yet went he not in.

6. Then cometh Simon Peter following him, and went into the sepulchre, and seeth the linen clothes lie,

7. And the napkin, that was about his head, not lying with the linen clothes, but wrapped together in a place by itself.

8. Then went in also that other disciple, which came first to the sepulchre, and he saw, and believed.

9. For as yet they knew not the scripture, that he must rise again from the dead.

10. Then the disciples went away again unto their own home.

The Guards Are Bribed   Matthew 28:11-15

11. Now when they were going, behold, some of the watch came into the city, and shewed unto the chief priests all the things that were done.

12. And when they were assembled with the elders, and had taken counsel, they gave large money unto the soldiers,

13. Saying, Say ye, His disciples came by night, and stole him away while we slept.

14. And if this come to the governor's ears, we will persuade him, and secure you.

15. So they took the money, and did as they were taught: and this saying is commonly reported

among the Jews until this day.

Jesus Appears to Mary and Disciples   John   Chapter 20:11-29

11. But Mary stood without at the sepulchre weeping: and as she wept, she stooped down, and looked into the sepulchre,

12. And seeth two angels in white sitting, the one at the head, and the other at the feet, where the body of Jesus had lain.

13. And they say unto her, Woman, why weepest thou? She saith unto them, Because they have taken away my Lord, and I know not where they have laid him.

14. And when she had thus said, she turned herself back, and saw Jesus standing, and knew not that it was Jesus.

15. Jesus saith unto her, Woman, why weepest thou? whom seekest thou? She, supposing him to be the gardener, saith unto him, Sir, if thou have borne him hence, tell me where thou hast laid him, and I will take him away.

16. Jesus saith unto her, Mary. She turned herself, and saith unto him, Rabboni; which is to say, Master.

17. Jesus saith unto her, Touch me not; for I am not yet ascended to my Father: but go to my brethren, and say unto them, I ascend unto my Father, and your Father; and to my God, and your God.

18. Mary Magdalene came and told the disciples that she had seen the Lord, and that he had spoken these things unto her.

19. Then the same day at evening, being the first day of the week, when the doors were shut where the disciples were assembled for fear of the Jews, came Jesus and stood in the midst, and saith unto them, Peace be unto you.

20. And when he had so said, he shewed unto them his hands and his side. Then were the disciples glad, when they saw the Lord.

21. Then said Jesus to them again, Peace be unto you: as my Father hath sent me, even so send I you.

22. And when he had said this, he breathed on them, and saith unto them, Receive ye the Holy

Ghost:

23. Whose soever sins ye remit, they are remitted unto them; and whose soever sins ye retain, they are retained.

24. But Thomas, one of the twelve, called Didymus, was not with them when Jesus came.

25. The other disciples therefore said unto him, We have seen the Lord. But he said unto them, Except I shall see in his hands the print of the nails, and put my finger into the print of the nails, and thrust my hand into his side, I will not believe.

26. And after eight days again his disciples were within, and Thomas with them: then came Jesus, the doors being shut, and stood in the midst, and said, Peace be unto you.

27. Then saith he to Thomas, reach hither thy finger, and behold my hands; and reach hither thy hand, and thrust it into my side: and be not faithless, but believing.

28. And Thomas answered and said unto him, My Lord and my God.

29. Jesus saith unto him, Thomas, because thou hast seen me, thou hast believed: blessed are they that have not seen, and yet have believed.

The Purpose of John's Gospel   John   Chapter 20:30-31

30. And many other signs truly did Jesus in the presence of his disciples, which are not written in this book:

31. But these are written, that ye might believe that Jesus is the Christ, the Son of God; and that believing ye might have life through his name.

How to Make Sure Heaven Is My Home

Understand That:

1. Heaven is a (Free Gift)

It is not deserved

For the wages of sin is death, but the free gift of God is eternal life in Christ Jesus our Lord. Romans 6:23

It cannot be earned

For by grace you have been saved through faith; and that not of yourselves, is the gift of God; not as a result of works, that no one should boast. Ephesians 2:8-9

Why?

2. Man is a sinner

Is separated from God

For all have sinned and fall short of the glory of God. Romans 3:23

Cannot save himself

There is a way which seems right to a man, but its end is the way of death. Proverbs 14:12

And

3. God is (Holy and Merciful)

Holy – He MUST punish sin

He will by no means clear the guilty. Exodus 34:7a

Merciful – He does not want to punish us

God is love. 1 John 4:8b

4. Jesus Christ

Who is He? – God's Son

Thomas answered and said to Him, "My Lord and my God!" John 20:28

What did He do? Died and Rose Again to pay for my sins and offer eternal life. He made Him who knew no sin to be sin on our behalf, so that we might become the righteousness of God in Him. 2 Corinthians 5:21

Is That All? No.

What Must I Do?

5. Receive God's Living Son

By repenting of sin

The time is fulfilled, and the kingdom of God is at hand; repent and believe in the gospel. Mark 1:15

By receiving Christ

If you confess with your mouth, "Jesus is Lord, "and believe in your heart that God raised him from the dead, you will be saved. For it is with your heart that you believe and are justified, and it is with your mouth that you confess and are saved. As the scripture says, "anyone who trusts in him will never be put to shame." Romans 10:9-11

Not Just:

6. Head Belief

Thou believest that there is one God; thou doest well; the devils also believe and tremble. James 2:19

7. So: Call upon Him in prayer to save you from your sin and the penalty of your sin and be baptized in the name of the Father, the Son, and the Holy Ghost. Amen!

A Suggested Prayer:

Jesus Christ, I know that I am a sinner and do not deserve eternal life. I believe you died for my sins and rose from the grave to purchase a place for me in heaven. Lord, come into my heart and influence my life. Forgive me of my sins. I confess them now and place my trust in you for salvation. I accept your free gift of eternal life, and thank you for it. In Jesus Name, Amen!

God's Promise:

For whoever will call upon the name of the Lord (Jesus) shall be saved. Romans 10:13

For God so loved the world that He gave His one and only Son, that whoever believes in Him shall not perish but have eternal life. John 3:16

Yet to all who received Him, to those who believed in His name, He gave the right to become children of God. John 1:12